# Dancing Gods

## Mexico, Old and New

◆

THESE ARE BORZOI BOOKS, PUBLISHED BY
*Alfred A. Knopf*

*Photograph by the Museum of New Mexico*

DIEGUITO　　　　　　　　　　　　　　[ROBERT HENRI]

# Dancing Gods

### Indian Ceremonials of New Mexico and Arizona

## BY ERNA FERGUSSON

*New York*

## ALFRED · A · KNOPF

### 1934

Southwestern Indians have no better friends than artists, who recognize that the Indian is essentially an artist. They value his art in all its forms, they help him without condescension, and they respect his integrity too much to try to make him over into something foreign. I am grateful to these distinguished artists who permit me to enhance my descriptions of Indians and their dances with their own vigorous, sympathetic, and humorous interpretations of them. E. F.

# Contents

# The Illustrations

are reproduced from paintings by the artists named

# Introduction

ONE DAY AS I WALKED ACROSS THE PUEBLO OF ZUÑI, I fell in with a young Indian who had been away to school. His hair was cut short, he wore American clothes, and his English was as good as mine. Yet we spoke of the Rain-dance I had come to see, he said seriously: " We need rain so much. You see, the clouds are beginning to come up already, even before the dancers are out. Yesterday there were no clouds." His ancestral faith in the power of prayer had not been affected by years of American education. He still believed.

Soon the dancers came out of the kiva, brilliant in masks and jewelry, fox furs and fine white buckskin; and for hours we watched them move through the stately figures of their ancient prayer, accompanied by the insistent beat of the tomtoms, calling on the gods for rain. Later as we drove away across the Zuñi mountains, we looked back and saw the long slanting purple lines of rain falling on the pueblo. Indians say: " White men laugh at our dances, but they are glad, too, when the rain comes."

As a prayer the dance is a very intimate and pervasive factor in Indian life. For the Indian is a truly religious being. No act of daily life is too ordinary to be dignified by ritual, no magnificence of God or nature too awe-inspiring to be explained by myth and influenced by prayer. There are prayers for birth and death, appeal and thanksgiving, prayers connected with the planting and harvesting of crops, the hunt, the journey, grinding the corn, the storm, the sun, and the rain — especially the rain.

The southwestern Indians are, and always have been, farmers and stockmen, and they live in an arid land. In New Mexico and Arizona few crops grow without irrigation, and irrigation depends upon rainfall. Centuries ago Indians learned to conserve their water in tiny reservoirs, to direct its flow in well-plotted ditches, and to make the most of every drop that fell. In the desert, where there are no streams, they learned to plant deep, to locate their fields where they could catch any underground flow of water, and to retain moisture by tireless cultivation. They were the original dry farmers. Both in the river valleys and on the desert uplands, prolonged drought has always been their greatest danger. If it does not rain, the people perish. So in one way or another nearly every prayer is a prayer for rain, for renewal and for growth. Symbols of rain are everywhere. The plumed serpent, which is the lightning, and symbols of clouds and rain and rainbows appear on blankets and pots and baskets for everyday use as well as on shrines and ceremonial garments. Linked closely with the rain as the life-giving principle is, of course, the sun. Prayers for rain ofter include appeals for all life, animal and human as well as plant, and on this is based the occasional complaint that Indian dances are obscene. It all

depends upon the point of view. To an Indian, human generation is no more obscene than is the fertilization and
development of a plant.

This book attempts to give a description of the principal
southwestern Indian dances, based upon observation, and
an account of their significance, based upon all available
sources of information. It is not an exhaustive study, for
several reasons, the most important of which is that the material available is not exhaustive. A few scientists have made
detailed studies of a few of the southwestern Indian dances.
I have consulted those authorities, I have seen most of the
dances which are open to the outsider, I have talked with
many people, both whites and Indians, and I have concluded that nobody knows all about Indian dances, not even
Indians.

Ask an Indian the significance of certain movements
used in the dance or of certain symbols which appear in
costumes or decoration and he will answer you evasively.
This is often because he does not wish to tell, but often it is
true that he does not know. The cacique or medicine-man
knows the mythology which lies behind the ceremonies and
he understands the significance of the various forms, but
his knowledge is sacred to him and he will not divulge it
lightly. The Indian layman, like the Christian layman,
knows merely that certain things must be done in a certain
way because they have always been done so. " Unless we
do it this way, our prayer will not be answered. This is the
way of the ancients."

An Indian dance is not a dance in the sense in which we
use that term. It is a ceremonial, a symbolic representation,

a prayer. It is, in fact, what all dances were in the early days of the race before the dance as a social and dramatic expression grew apart from the ceremonial which gradually developed into the church service. In a sense the mass is still a stately dance, the theatrical production is descended from a prayer. The ancestor of both was the ritual presenting a symbolic act in dramatic form before the altar. David danced before the Lord. The first Greek drama was a ritualistic dance preceding the sacrifice. During the Middle Ages Christian priests gave mystery plays before the high altar, and a modern English prelate has recently recognized the religious value of such drama by permitting the presentation of a medieval miracle play in front of a cathedral. Survivals of these religious dramas are to be found among peasant peoples in various European countries and even in the United States, for the Mexicans of both New Mexico and Arizona have certain ancient religious plays which they give annually at Christmas or Easter time.

Of all these survivals of primitive ritual the Indian dance is probably the most interesting to be found anywhere in the world, for it is not merely a quaint custom largely divorced from its original significance. It is the genuine religious expression of a primitive people which has survived without serious interruption for thousands of years. It belongs to the period of human culture before the religious ritual and the drama had become separate things. The Indian dance is a prayer, performed with the greatest reverence, and it is also a dramatic representation, as finished and as beautiful as a modern ballet. Sometimes it has pantomime, sometimes humor, sometimes only the solemnity

of a religious service. Unhappily it is probably true that as young Indians are trained away from their ancient faiths, the Indian dance will lose its meaning as a religious form. As an art form it should certainly be encouraged and preserved as purely as possible. Fortunately we are still far from the time when the dance has lost its religious significance even for the young Indian. Even those of the younger generation who have been trained in Indian schools and have gone away from home to live, return to their people for the important ceremonies and show a deep belief in their efficacy.

While centuries of Christian training have apparently not affected the deeps of the Indian mind, and Indian ceremonials go on much as from time immemorial, there are superficial modifications which are interesting. Certain Christian symbols appear here and there and, especially among the Pueblo people, Christian feast-days are celebrated. In some pueblos the Indians dance on Christmas, on Twelfth-night, and at Easter, and in all pueblos ancient pagan dances are given on certain saints' days. In a few of the pueblos the Catholic priests permit dancing in the churches at Christmas, probably because they are tolerant enough to realize that any man's prayer, in any man's mode, is acceptable to God. Apparently these Christmas dances were originally a recognition of the winter solstice, a prayer for the return of the sun after his annual withdrawal. Now the Catholic faith seems to have modified at least the layman's conception of the meaning of the ceremony. I once asked an Isleta Indian what dance they would give in his pueblo on Christmas Eve, and he said: " We dance in honor of the Christ-child." He said it with the completest reverence.

This mingling of faiths seems to be due to a quality of mind which makes it possible for the Indian not only to be tolerant of the beliefs of others, but to adopt them into his own practice. He seems to feel that every form of worship is good. Indians have always respected the religion of other Indians, and when the first white men came, they welcomed their religion as merely a different expression of fundamental truth. They readily accepted the new faith, but they continued with the old. Evidence of this dualism is still found in the use of prayer-meal in the Indian's home, and holy water in his church, prayer-sticks before the ancient shrines, and rosaries before the saints, and in the age-old serpent symbol of the sinuous course of streams painted on the holy-water vessels in some churches.

Most of the Indian ceremonials are extremely elaborate, lasting for days and ending on the last day or night with the dance. Outsiders are usually permitted to see only the dance. The secret ceremonies take place in the kiva or medicine lodge and are open only to clan members or to the dancers. Sometimes they are historical or legendary in character, presenting the life of the whole people or of a certain hero. Often elaborate altars are erected and painted with symbolic decorations, sand paintings are made and destroyed at specified hours and with meticulous care for detail, costumes are prepared for the dance, masks are painted and decorated with feathers, prayer-sticks are made. The dancers must be purified by means of fasting and medication, bathing the body, and washing the hair.

Everything is done under the direction of the cacique or medicine-man, whose duty it is to see that nothing goes wrong, as the slightest slip may ruin the effect of the entire ceremony.

From the chronicles of the early Spanish explorers and from the reports of American Army officers and Indian agents it appears that white men were long welcomed to all dances, even the ceremonies now held most secret. As time went on, white missionaries showed a disposition to impose their beliefs on the Indians to the exclusion of their old faiths and they naturally grew more and more secretive until now they shut white men out of the most sacred parts of all their ceremonies and exclude them altogether from certain more important and probably more beautiful dances.

In addition to prayers for rain and for fructification generally, there is an almost unlimited variety of dances, ranging all the way from ceremonials of the utmost solemnity, in which the gods themselves are personified, to dances of a purely social and humorous character. In the masked dances the masked figures symbolize the actual presence of the god. Ceremonies for the initiation of children at puberty introduce the candidate to the man behind the mask, much as our children are permitted to see the man behind the whiskers of Santa Claus. The masked figure is not the god, he merely personifies the god, and all adults understand that. The masked figure may also be the messenger of the gods, as is the great Shalako at Zuñi. After the dance he returns to a secret shrine on a neighboring mountain, taking the message of the people to the god. This is also the significance of the snakes in the Hopi Snake-dance. The snakes are brothers of the members of the Snake Clan and they carry back to the gods the people's prayer for rain. The Yei who appear masked in the medicine ceremonies of the Navajos are representations of the gods and are treated with suitable reverence during the entire nine days' ceremony.

A similar idea is to be found in the animal dances which are among the winter ceremonies of the Pueblos. Dancers are dressed to represent deer, buffalo, antelope, or mountain sheep, and superficially the dance is a pantomime of the hunt, but its esoteric significance is deeper than that. It goes back to the time when men and animals still lived together in the underworld; for to all southwestern Indians the original happy home was underground or below a lake where the gods still live waiting to welcome the people back after death. Thus to the Indian both the Garden of Eden and heaven lie underground. It is generally believed that before they emerged on this earth, men and animals all lived together and spoke the same language. So in the hunting-dances the performers propitiate the game by reconstructing the time when animals understood men and were willingly sacrificed for the good of their human brothers.

As is true of all primitive peoples, southwestern Indians have dances for the cure of disease, notably the great " medicine sings " of the Navajos. These are elaborate nine-day ceremonials, which include prayers and the making of sand paintings in secret, sweat baths and medications for the patient, and finally the all-night dance, which is open to visitors. Through it all moves the stately dignified presence of the medicine-man. His ability to conduct one of the greater ceremonials is the result of years of study and training, as he must know every least detail of the ritual, every song, every sand painting, every word, and every movement. He is supposed to be a man of great spirituality, for he is priest as well as physician.

The intense seriousness of the Navajo nature is reflected in all their ceremonies, which are much less lightened by humor than are those of the Pueblos. Life has always been precarious to the Navajo. First as nomads dependent upon hunting and upon occasional raids against the peaceable Pueblos and later when their marauding days were forcibly ended and they were confined to an arid reservation, they seem to have felt the importance of propitiating the gods. Their songs and dances all contain a note of insistent urgency which reflects a deep ancestral fear. Most of their dances are prayers for the cure of a particular person's illness. The patient's relatives arrange everything, and both patient and sponsors are important figures in the ceremonial. Such a dance seems to include also an invocation of the great powers for all the people, a presentation of ancient symbolism, and incidentally an opportunity for a gathering of the whole tribe. Often thousands of Navajos attend. They come to assist the prayers for a sick friend and they are most serious about it. In addition they enjoy coming; they meet their friends, they feast largely, and they see much magic, for medicine-men can make feathers dance in baskets and run up and down sticks.

Dances as drama and for fun are found among the

Pueblos rather than among the Navajos. Many pueblos have pantomimic representations of the coming of the first white men — "men with pale skins who came across the great water in boats with wings." They prance about on sticks with such dramatic power that one clearly sees the *conquistadores* in their coats of mail, and they stage most realistic sham battles between wild Indians and blue-coated Americans. The Pueblos still remember that it was the United States troops who first gave them protection from the marauding Navajos and Apaches, and in these dramas their sympathy is with the soldiers. The modern American seems to fill them with less respect and more amusement. Usually he is the comic figure in the hunt, the man who trails his gun until he falls over it, who blunders on the game and scares it away, who loses his way and wanders bewildered for hours around one tiny spruce-tree. Clowns are endlessly fertile in ideas for burlesquing Americans, and often they are as funny as our best comedians. Practically every pueblo dance includes a clown who has absolute license to do or say what he pleases. In fact, there are in all the pueblos clans of clowns who serve as public censors by making fun of the foibles of the people.

War-dances are still given here and there. They come closer than any of the other southwestern dances to approximating the traditional notion of an Indian dance as a succession of war-whoops and mad gyrations. In a war-dance one may see real scalps, fine old painted shields of buffalo hide, beaded quivers full of arrows, ancient flint-locks, and powder-horns dating from the days of the first American occupation. Among the war-dances is the Comanche dance, which was borrowed from the now almost extinct enemy by all the Pueblos and which they love to give for inquisitive whites. This is only one of many borrowings. Indians are inveterate travelers and they love to learn each other's songs and dances. Sometimes they give them seriously, as the Jemez give a series of Hopi dances in the fall; sometimes they burlesque them, as the Zuñi mimic the Navajo Yebetchai.

In the war-dances as now given we have an excellent example of what is probably doomed to happen to all Indian dances. There being no more wars among these savages, the war-dances, once most earnest prayers for strength to fight and win, are now preserved by the Indians themselves as interesting survivals of a bygone day. In time, as Indians are weaned from their ancient faiths, it is likely that all their ceremonies will lose meaning in the same way, and it is important that interested white people should help them to preserve their dances as an art form when they no longer serve as a religious form.

As an art, Indian dances command the respect of artists. Dancers, singers, actors, and painters all recognize the southwestern Indian as a real artist. Ted Shawn, a great dancer and a deep student of the dance in many lands, says that the Indians truly understand the spirit of the dance, a fact which they demonstrate in many ways. They dance in the open air, instead of in crowded over-heated halls. The dance is an affair of the whole community, for everyone is obliged to take part some time during the year, either as singer or as dancer, and always those who are not dancing or singing are understanding and interested spectators.

Most important of all, the Indian dance has significance. There is meaning in every item of costume and decoration, in every step and movement. Mr. Shawn and all who know dancing, agree that the Indian is a fine performer technically. His foot-work is exquisite, the control of body and breath masterly, and the careful precision of the whole performance truly artistic. The steps vary widely, as will appear to anyone who knows dance steps and will watch them carefully or, better still, try to copy them. Every dance is full of tricky changes of tempo and rhythm, of the graceful turnings of long rows of dancers like wheat ruffling in the wind, of that deceptive appearance of ease which is based on years of training for each dancer and days of intensive practice for each performance.

The intricacies of tempo and rhythm are based on the music, which commands as much respect in high circles as does the dancing. Efrem Zimbalist, who has studied primitive music in all parts of the world, says that the American Indian's music is the most difficult he knows. Lacking harmony, the Indian achieves his effects entirely by rhythm, often combining several rhythms in one song and always using short intervals and very baffling pauses. It is notable that most musicians trying to play Indian music fail to catch the correct rhythm unless they hear it first. Often in the dances one can distinguish as many as four rhythms used at once, one maintained by the tomtoms, one by the singers, one by the dancers, and a fourth by the clowns, whose apparent indifference to the affair gives it the final touch of unity and charm. Indians often sing alone — love-songs, cradle-songs, grinding-songs, songs just for fun —

but usually, and especially in connection with the dances, Indians sing in chorus. In the pueblos a chorus of old men accompanied by tomtoms provides the music for the dance. The Navajos, wonderfully trained and controlled, tighten the muscles of the torso and sing while they dance, keeping it up for hours with no appearance of weariness. There is no part-singing among either. The voices blend with each other and with the accompanying instruments and are emphasized by the click of shells on costumes and the steady beat of gourd rattles. The Navajos use a queer falsetto voice, whose whining insistent appeal going on all night has a hypnotic effect even on the listener who does not understand a word of the prayer.

Lately, with the increasing interest in Indian affairs, white people are showing a disposition to assist the Indian to preserve his dances in their purity. Various shows in New Mexico are featuring Indian dances. At first the old men of all the tribes were opposed to having their ceremonials presented away from the pueblos or off the reservations. They quite naturally dread to see the commercializing of their religious rituals, they hate the effect of applause on their young men, and they resent all change. Through their influence many dances are not given at all in the white man's towns; most of them are given only in part. This resistance is slowly breaking down, however, and it may be that giving the dances for white audiences will prove the means of perpetuating them as an art form when their significance as a religious form has unhappily passed away.

It is still true that the only way to see the best dances in their entirety and done with real reverence is to go to the pueblos or the reservations where they are danced in the " way of the ancients." There you get a sense of the magnificent antiquity behind them, a feeling of the marvelous strength and cohesion of a people who through four centuries of foreign domination have maintained their ancestral worship. We have here, held in modern civilization as in a matrix, a complete and extraordinarily beautiful survival of primitive life — a survival which should certainly be treated respectfully and preserved as an art if it must pass as a living belief.

# Dancing Gods

# I: The Pueblo People

Sᴜɴ-ᴅʀᴇɴᴄʜᴇᴅ ᴀɴᴅ ǫᴜɪᴇᴛ sᴛᴀɴᴅ ᴛʜᴇ ᴘᴜᴇʙʟᴏs ᴏғ ɴᴇᴡ ᴍᴇxɪᴄᴏ ᴀɴᴅ ᴀʀɪᴢᴏɴᴀ, queerly withdrawn from the modern life about them. Usually built of the soil on which they stand, they appear to have grown out of it, and their color is the same. There are few trees in the villages, but they are surrounded by cultivated fields, and cottonwoods and willows grow along the watercourses. The houses huddle in solid blocks of adobe like slightly battered apartment houses. Irregular ladder-poles rise sharply here and there and protruding beams drop deep black shadows against the walls. Always there is a mission church, carrying the cross aloft on weather-worn adobe towers, and a government building whose machine-made angularities are an insult to the softly molded contours of the adobe. Drifting in and out are the people, brown-skinned and enigmatic, with sloe-black eyes, sliding walk, and flashes of vivid color in blanket, sash, or head-band.

Who are they? Where do they come from? There are two ways of arriving at the answer to these questions. One is to ask the Indians themselves. The other is to consult the archæologist or the ethnologist. It is interesting how often

3

Indian tradition agrees in essentials with the finds of scientific investigators. Isleta, for instance, has a tradition that its people came from the north, that they crossed the sea " where it is so narrow that a ten-year-old boy could throw a stone across it," and then, finding very little sun, that they came farther and farther south until they finally settled at Isleta. More than one archæologist is satisfied that the Pueblo people did come from the north, crossing Bering Strait and drifting south. Taos, according to their tradition, came north, following a bird and making many villages, until they finally found the right location at the foot of their sacred Pueblo Peak and on both sides of their ever-running stream. This movement northward also has its scientific supporters, who think that these Indians came from Mexico, offshoots perhaps of the Aztec stock.

All the Indians who now live in villages in New Mexico and Arizona are Pueblo people, which simply means town people. They were so called by the Spanish explorers who found them in the middle of the sixteenth century and were naturally struck by their towns and town organization. There are now about nine thousand Indians living in pueblos in New Mexico and Arizona. They form self-governing communities who support themselves by farming the lands they own communally, and who live a life of astonishing independence of thought, organization, and religious belief in the center of a modern American state. Today they speak five Indian languages in the New Mexico pueblos, and another in Arizona, where the Hopis cling to their rocky heights. They also speak Spanish, which is preached to them in their Catholic churches, and the young ones all

*Photograph by the Museum of New Mexico*
(Owned by W. H. Klauer)

LAGUNA OVENS                    [WALTER UFER]

speak English, which they learn in the government Indian schools and in which they trade with store-keepers and make interesting and inaccurate statements to tourists.

### THE CLIFF DWELLERS

BEHIND THE PUEBLO LIFE AS WE SEE IT WAS THE LIFE OF the cliff dwellings and of the great communal villages. These habitations are being studied with meticulous care by archæologists, who examine literally every foot-mark and finger-print for clues as to who these mysterious folk were and how they lived. Here, too, Indian tradition is a check and stimulus to scientific investigation. The Hopis have a legend, for instance, that their ancestors undertook to build a great temple, that they were struck with a confusion of tongues and had to leave it unfinished, and that they then moved south and established the present Hopi villages. Archæologists, excavating at the Mesa Verde, uncovered there what they chose to call the Sun Temple. It was obviously a very important effort, probably for ceremonial purposes only, and it was left unfinished for obscure reasons. A Hopi Indian, visiting the place soon after the discovery of the Sun Temple, identified it absolutely and with great excitement as the very place of the legend.

Archæologists learn a great deal about prehistoric life from the Pueblos, all of whom have traditions connecting them with the inhabitants of the ruins which are found all over the southwest. The Santa Clara people, for instance, claim descent from the inhabitants of Puye, and all the Keres of the Rio Grande valley consider the Rito de los

Frijoles as their ancestral home. In these cases and in many others the medicine-men of the modern villages make ceremonial visits to the ancient home sites; and ancient shrines, such as that of the stone lions of Cochiti, are visited by all Indians. Ceremonial objects from the ruins always fill a modern Indian with reverent interest. Aniceto Suaso, working with Jeançon at Po-Shu, recognized and arranged in order certain bases for prayer-plumes and readily told the uses of a prehistoric spear-head, which he said would bring prowess in the hunt to anyone who had it. Also at Po-Shu, an Indian woman in child-birth tied into her girdle an ancient fetish found there, and reported that it helped her very much. This obstetrical fetish was in the shape of a large-stomached woman. Hunting-charms are usually in the form of animals, preferably lions or bears. In Zuñi we may still see the fetishes in ceremonial use. In other pueblos they are used only in secret ceremonies, though every modern Indian carries his medicine-bag, containing his personal fetish, bits of various metals, and the corn-pollen which is always the sacred symbol of life.

Much of the fascination of modern Indian ceremonial is due to the antiquity of its rites and forms. Religious form is always the last human habit to yield to change; and in the altars, sacred symbols, and customs of the modern Indian we can trace the history of his ancestors. The most ancient of whom we have any record were wandering tribes who made no permanent homes, contenting themselves with slight brush shelters — the prototype of the *kisi* in which the modern Hopis keep the snakes during their annual Snake-dance. Later, as agriculture developed and the people needed more stable homes, they dug into the ground and made a circular room, roofed with mud-daubed logs and entered from above by means of a ladder. These people are called the " small house " or " pre-pueblo " people, according to the degree of their development, and their house is still a prominent feature of every pueblo, for it is the kiva, the ceremonial lodge. As the people drew together into villages, they probably maintained their blood-relationships through certain ceremonies conducted in the kivas, thus establishing the clans which are the unit of pueblo organization today. The modern kiva is still the center of clan and religious life, and until very recently all young men were required to sleep in the clan kiva until marriage. The whole history of kiva architecture may be traced in the modern pueblos, from those entirely underground as at Taos and in the Hopi villages, to those entirely above ground as in most of the Rio Grande pueblos. At Zuñi and at Acoma the kivas are square and are built into the block of houses, probably to conceal them from Christian priests who would abolish them.

The modern kiva has retained many features of the original home — the ladder entrance from above through a hole which is also the smoke-vent, the ventilator and smoke-screen, the fire in the center, the absence of windows, and even the hole in the floor, which typifies *sipapu,* the entrance to the underworld. Today the preliminary services for every dance are performed in the kiva, the men meet there for all clan and pueblo business, and some form of the old custom of youths' living in the clan kiva is found almost everywhere.

The pre-pueblo people left little except the type of their home and bits of crude pottery and weaving. Their descendants of the cliff dwellings and of the communal villages are easily studied and their life has been reconstructed in considerable detail. These two types of building were probably contemporaneous, as Bandelier makes clear in his novel *The Delight Makers,* in which he pictures prehistoric life in the Rito de los Frijoles. Bandelier thinks that at Puye the cave houses, built along the south face of the cliff, were the winter homes of the people who in summer occupied the communal dwelling on top of the breezy mesa. At both Puye and the Rito de los Frijoles the homes are very simple rooms built in terraces against the friable tufa cliffs, in which were artificial or natural caves used for storage rooms. The communal village was architecturally a development of this type. The cliff idea was retained in the outer wall, built solid as a defense, and the terraced houses stepped down from that to the central plaza. The Chaco Canyon villages and the pueblo of Pecos are both excellent examples of this type.

The finest cliff dwellings are at the Mesa Verde. The first sight of the Cliff Palace or the Balcony House is had on stepping out to the brink of a narrow canyon, fringed with tall pines and dropping hundreds of feet into the leafy stream bed below. Just under the canyon's brim stand those marvelous dwellings, still in the sunlight, just as they have stood for more than a thousand years. The walls of stone, finely worked and fitted, are solid, rising as high as five stories and giving the general effect of an enchanted castle held under a spell of silence and distance. Nowadays one can approach by graded government trails adapted to the tenderest of feet, but once the active brown dwellers climbed up and down by toe and hand holes which only a very skillful or daring modern will attempt. Remember, also, that the cliff man not only got himself over those trails, but also his game after the hunt, and the crops which he raised either on the valley floor below or on the plateau above his home. It must have been hard living, but worth it in the security from marauding bands of nomadic Indians, once one was snugly there.

Wherever the prehistoric Indian built, he always chose sites well defended by nature, as were the cliff dwellings, or easily defended by man, as were the Chaco Canyon villages, which stand in a plain over which no enemy larger than a coyote could approach unseen. Besides security he needed water and arable land, game, and timber suitable for building, but not too large to be cleared away with stone implements. In some places the water-supply which served the prehistoric Indian has disappeared, either by dropping into the sand, as at the Gran Quivira, or because grazing animals have destroyed the grass roots and allowed great arroyos to wash away the soil, as at Chaco Canyon.

How many of these places were inhabited at one time and why they were abandoned cannot yet be determined with any accuracy. Recently, however, A. E. Douglass of the University of Arizona has perfected his discovery of the determination of prehistoric dates by tree-rings. In the southwest rainfall varies so much from year to year that annual tree-rings differ greatly and accordingly, wider rings indicating heavier rainfall. By comparing series of rings in living trees with identical series in beams and supports found in ruins, Professor Douglass has finally worked out a chronology continuous from the tenth century to the twentieth. So it is now definitely established that the southwestern Indians were building their finest houses when William the Conqueror was conquering the tribes of Britain.

Between that time and the Spanish conquest the Indian had developed his religion, his government, his art, and his architecture to its height. Take away from the modern Pueblo what the white man has brought him, and you will see what he used and how he lived before the white man came. His rooms, then as now, were built of stone or adobe, roofed with piñon or cedar beams over which were laid saplings or brush and earth. The rooms were small because the only trees manageable with primitive tools were small trees. Floors were of hard-packed earth finished with adobe mixed with blood. A fire-place, built in the corner, gave light and heat and smoke. In many ruins are found alternate layers of smoke and fresh plaster, indicating an effort at good housekeeping against very heavy odds. A niche in the wall held the sacred meal, poles hung on thongs held garments or drying meat, and metates or grinding-stones were set in the floor. Then as now meal was ground by a kneeling woman who swung her body back and forth, bearing down on the *mano* which crushed the kernels into finer and finer meal. No doubt the prehistoric woman sang the very songs which still celebrate the wonder of the corn, for then as now the corn was the sacred mother, typical of all good, on whose bounty life depended.

Decorations were scanty, though sometimes simple fres-
coes are found in ruins, especially in kivas or on cliffs outside the houses. These pictographs may have been messages, drawings for ceremonial purposes, or effusions of
bad boys done for fun. They have not been fully deci-
phered, though various symbols of sun, moon, stars, rainbow, rain, clouds, animals, and various clan symbols used
today are found among them.

Among the furnishings of the prehistoric homes were the
looms on which the men wove cotton garments. Men were
weavers then and women potters, a distinction still found in
Hopiland, where the men weave ceremonial garments.
These Hopi mantles, kirtles, and sashes were probably the
customary dress of the cliff dweller when he did not wrap
himself in skin skirts as the snake-dancer does now. Moccasins were the same as now with the exception that the ancient Indian did not make cow-hide soles. He made blankets
of sinew wound with rabbit-skin for warmth, or feathers
for beauty. Feathers were very important, especially the
plumes of the eagle and the turkey, which have always
been used ceremonially. Personal adornment included jewelry of colored stones, of bones, of shells traded with sea-
side tribes, and of turquoise polished and strung as beads
or inlaid in stone or bone. All of these ornaments are made
today, but the work was finer in the Great Age than any
which is done now.

The women made baskets, an art which has almost disappeared from modern pueblo life, except in the Hopi villages and in some of the Rio Grande pueblos. None of the
present-day work is as fine as that of the prehistoric women.

They also made pottery, developing it from the crudest uncolored coiled ware to the height of the beautifully decorated glazed ware of the Great Age. The art of glazing declined rapidly after the arrival of the white man, until it was altogether lost. Painted pottery is still a fine art in most of the pueblos. Through pottery most of the prehistoric chronicle has been read, for pottery is at once the most perishable and the most enduring of household goods. A broken pot is of no value. Nobody making a move would think of taking it, but, left on the rubbish-heap, the pieces last forever and archæologists coming along a thousand years later can learn much from the broken bits. Besides pottery, excavations yield a vast number of bone and stone tools and implements, everything that was needed for working stone, skins, cotton, and clay. Thrilling things are occasionally found, like flutes on which a few notes may still be blown or head-dresses such as are worn in the dances of today.

Kidder places the Great Age of pueblo development at about the year 1000, a time when the population had drawn together, because of the pressure of outside tribes, and " when they had reached that vital moment in their history when opportunity and necessity were evenly balanced." The inhabited area had shrunk steadily from the time when roving small bands spread over a territory reaching from southern Utah to the border of Mexico. It was to shrink still further, for the peaceful pueblo people were constantly subject to raids of wandering tribes of Apaches, of Comanches, and later of the Navajos, who became the traditional enemy. There was a period between 1000 and 1540, however, when the pueblo people had attained a height of development in government, in religion, and in art which gave promise of even finer things to come.

## THE WHITE MAN; POPÉ OF SAN JUAN

THEN CAME THE WHITE MAN. KIDDER, IN WRITING OF THE Great Age, says: " There can be little doubt that had they been allowed to work out their own salvation, they would eventually have overcome their difficulties and might well have built up a civilization of a sort not yet attempted by any group of men. It is the tragedy of native American history that so much human effort has come to nought, and that so many hopeful experiments in life and living were cut short by the devastating blight of the white man's arrival."

What the white man did especially, with the devastating blight of his arrival, was to check the growth of a truly democratic state. The prehistoric Indian was completely democratic, as is the Indian of today in so far as we allow him to be. Everybody lived in the same sort of house on the same sort of food, everybody worked, and the only honors and distinctions were those won by personal merit. As there was no personal accumulation of wealth, there was no inheritance of dignity or position. When the Spaniards came, they found the Indians governed by their old men in council, with the cacique, or religious leader, as final arbiter. The cacique was the only man exempted from labor, and that was because his time was given to prayer and meditation for the benefit of all. That is still true today.

The cacique's fields are tilled for him, communal hunts provide his meat, wood is chopped and hauled to his door. In return he is expected to be a spiritual man as well as a wise one, trained by years of self-abnegation to understand the ways of " those above " and to be the spiritual guide of his people.

The Spaniards found the Indian friendly, but disappointingly lacking in the gold and jewels they sought. Fray Marcos de Nizza, a Franciscan monk, headed the first expedition which came up from Mexico, in 1539. It was his reports of great wealth that aroused all the Spaniards in Mexico with a desire to explore, to enrich themselves, and incidentally to save souls. Fray Marcos got no farther than a sight of Habikuh, the first Zuñi village on his line of march. The friar, having been ordered to take care of himself and return with facts about the fabled cities of wealth, prudently looked upon Habikuh from a neighboring hill and retired, satisfied that he had seen a great city, probably paved with gold, undoubtedly studded with turquoise, and unquestionably hiding untold wealth in its cellars. If he happened to see Habikuh at sunset and if it glowed in the changing light as modern Zuñi does now, he was certainly justified in thinking of any amount of gold. But Habikuh was an adobe town whose only stores were those of garnered crops. Fray Marcos went no farther, because the leader of his advance guard, the Negro Estevan, had been killed at Habikuh, and his band frightened out of their wits. It was reported that Estevan had made too free with the Indian women, and that he was killed in consequence. At Santo Domingo they still occasionally enact the coming of the Spaniards, with a swaggering Negro for comedy relief. He leers and makes ribald remarks to women, and he is properly scorned by the *conquistadores*, who grandly ride steeds which would be merely hobby-horses were it not for the histrionic gift of the actors.

Marcos de Nizza undoubtedly reported in Mexico what he thought he had seen, and his tales brought further expeditions seeking gold. In 1540 Francisco Vásquez de Coronado followed Fray Marcos's route. He visited all the Zuñi villages, saw Acoma, struck the Rio Grande a few miles south of where Albuquerque now stands, and followed that stream northward as far as Taos. Unfortunately Coronado sent out two young lieutenants who precipitated warfare. Tovar, visiting the Hopi villages, fired on the peaceful people who came out to meet him; and Alvarado, demanding gold bracelets at Pecos, imprisoned and flogged two Indian leaders who had never seen or heard of gold. It was the beginning of the Indian's deep-seated distrust of the white man, who was henceforth considered never to keep his word.

While Coronado was frankly in search of wealth, he was accompanied by monks to convert the heathen, and he left two of them when he returned to Mexico, Juan de Padilla and Luis de Escalona, both of whom were killed by the people they had come to save, thus attaining the distinction of being the first of a long line of martyrs. In general, the monks seem to have stood out against the grasping cruelty of the military, though it was a monk who encouraged Tovar to attack the Hopis; and much of the history of the province of New Mexico deals with the conflict between the

Church, which sought the souls of the Indians, and the civil government, which sought their wealth and their bodies in slavery.

Time moved slowly in those days, and a whole generation grew up between Coronado's expedition and the next one, when Antonio de Espejo made a brief tour in 1581. Espejo was as notable for kindliness and fair dealing as Coronado had been for ruthless inhumanity, with the result that not a single life was lost on his expedition. He was hospitably received even where Coronado had been most barbarous. Later leaders were not always like Espejo, and the Spaniard soon forgot the original kindly welcome of a people who might easily have exterminated the first expeditions. So began the long course of the white man's encroachment on the Indian's land, breaking treaties and agreements until finally it came about that any Indian, claiming his own, was looked upon as a treacherous savage.

The Spaniards filtered slowly into the country, spreading their gospel, their agriculture, their domestic animals, and their government. They sought gold always, but with less and less hope of finding it, until their zeal for converts supplanted their zeal for wealth. They planted a cross on every village, as it proved to have more spiritual than material value, and they wrote long memorials to the viceroy in Mexico, proudly claiming so many converts for the true faith and so many new subjects for His Most Catholic Majesty. By the end of the century Spain had decided that the country north of the Rio Grande was worth holding, even if it was not full of gold nuggets to be had for the picking up. So expeditions were organized for permanent occupation, never forgetting the need for recurrent baptism and conversion. Thousands of Indians were reported baptized, but thousands apparently needed to be baptized again and again.

In 1598 Juan de Oñate arrived with a train that must have been a spectacle. He brought cattle and sheep, wagonloads of household goods, artisans and priests, women and children. His wagons were of the type we know as " *carretas* " — inadequate-looking baskets of saplings mounted on groaning, screeching wheels of solid wood, and loaded, no doubt, with furniture, tools, food, and seeds, and surmounted with frightened women holding babies. Months they struggled over deserts and climbed mountains, the wagons lurching crazily over grassy hummocks and lava beds, while the leaders tried to renew treaties of peace and establish confidence among the Indians.

Oñate visited all the pueblos and received submission from all except Acoma, which had to be separately " reduced " from time to time. When he got as far north as the pueblo of San Juan, he was so courteously received that he gave it the honorable title " de los Caballeros " (of the gentlemen) and made his capital in its neighborhood. The first capital of New Mexico was San Gabriel, and the name New Mexico was then established, though it had probably first been used by Ibarra in 1565. By 1607 the capital had been moved to Santa Fe, but during his stay at San Gabriel, Oñate had solidified his position as governor. He called a conference of Pueblo leaders at Santo Domingo and formally received their united allegiance to the Spanish crown. He also got the caciques to agree to adopt the Christian religion if, after suitable instruction, they decided that they liked it. Their acceptance of the new faith, even conditionally, was probably made easier by the fact that nearly all Indians had a belief that a white god would come to save them. This god was so readily identified with the Christ whom the monks preached that as late as 1900 an old Indian interpreting a sermon in the pueblo of Jemez used the name of the ancient god as a translation of " Christ." That they never allowed the new faith to supplant the old is obvious everywhere today. For four hundred years the Indian has pursued his ancient ways, while making reverent, but rather distant, obeisance before the Christian altars.

Most of the records of the seventeenth century were destroyed in 1680, and so what went on is known only in general. Civil and ecclesiastical governments were established along the lines laid down for all Spanish colonies. In 1630 Fray Alonzo de Benavides, then " custodio " for New Mexico, reported that there were fifty friars, serving over sixty thousand Christian Indians, living in ninety pueblos, each with its own church. He asked for the establishment of a bishopric, which he said could be easily supported from the tithes. The friar probably greatly exaggerated both the number of converts and the number of churches, but no doubt there were enough missions to bring all the Pueblos under the domination of the Church. During the century they suffered increasing exactions from both lay and clerical Spaniards. Occasional uprisings were attempted and sternly put down by the governors, who imprisoned, flogged, enslaved, and hanged with a ruthless hand. From being a free people eagerly working out their own salvation, the Indians had become a slave population, owing so much labor to the crown and the Church, and so bewildered, undoubtedly, by a superimposed civilization that their own development came to a complete standstill, and deterioration set in. Their arts declined, their democratic government was overlaid by royal governors and tax- and tithe-gatherers, and as the subject and despised race they faced that death of the spirit which is the worst of all. In time all of this became too heavy to be borne, and in 1680 they made their great effort to throw off the yoke of a people fated, by the ownership of the heavier artillery, to dominate them.

Popé, a medicine-man of San Juan, organized the revolt. Working from Taos as his headquarters, he went quietly from pueblo to pueblo, arousing the people to a sense of their wrongs, choosing leaders, making plans, and managing to keep the secret through months of organizing. The plan was a general uprising on August 11 in which every Spaniard — every man, woman, and child — should be killed. The secret was so well kept that it was only a few days before the time that an Indian convert told his priest. Governor Otermín was at once notified and plans were made to check the revolt. But it was too late, or Popé was too quick for them. He moved his date a day, and on August 10 the Indians rose so unitedly and so vigorously that every Spaniard was either killed or forced to flee. Many stories are told of priests who tried to hold their converts by standing bravely before the altars with sacred vessels in their hands, only to be struck down. Otermín made a brave stand at Sante Fe, but when he was informed that all the villages south of San Felipe had been abandoned, he finally withdrew, unmolested by the Indians. He gathered up his people as he retreated, and finally reached El Paso, where he made the best of a bad situation, sent to Mexico for help, and began to organize for a return. However cruel and intolerant the Spaniards were, they never lacked courage, and Otermín made a determined effort to regain his lost province, but unsuccessfully.

The Indians, free at last, celebrated by destroying church and government records, by dancing around a great fire in the Santa Fe plaza, by solemnly forswearing allegiance to the new religion, and by washing off the taint of baptism in amole suds. Popé, swollen with pride and full of Spanish ideas, then tried to make himself a king and so brought about the final downfall of his people. He rode from pueblo to pueblo accoutered and attended as he had seen Spanish governors do, and he made enemies everywhere. The twelve years during which the Spaniards were away were years of increasing internal dissension, until finally pueblo was warring against pueblo, and the stage was set for an easy reconquest by Don Diego de Vargas, who entered the province in 1692.

De Vargas tried kindly measures. He promised forgiveness to all who would submit to Spanish rule, he appointed Indian leaders to positions of authority, he tried in every way to efface the impression of Spanish cruelty and to bind to him as many pueblos as possible. He succeeded fairly well with the Keres people, and he finally conquered the

Tewas who held Santa Fe. The old palace was again purified of a false faith, and de Vargas set out from there to
complete the reconquest of his province. It was not easy to
do, for the Tewas had retreated to the Black Mesa at San
Ildefonso, where they could hold him off indefinitely.
Jemez Indians allied themselves with the Navajos, Taos
called in the Utes to help, and a natural distrust of Spanish
promises caused many a " reduced " pueblo to backslide
into the arms of its intractable neighbors. In a few brisk
battles, however, and with some clever diplomacy, the
Spaniards finally succeeded in overcoming the Indians, and
New Mexico was " restored." Acoma, as usual, required
more than one reduction, and the Hopi villages never did
submit. They remained, in fact, a thorn in the side of the
Spanish during their entire administration of New Mexico.
At this time a handful of Tewas emigrated to join the
Hopis, settling on the First Mesa, where a hamlet still carries their name and where certain Tewa dances are still
given.

During the years of reconquest and for the century following there was much shifting of Pueblo population. So
many villages moved that very few of them today occupy
exactly the same sites on which the Spaniards first found
them. In some places, as at Jemez, several pueblos drew
together to form one. During the years that Acoma was unconquered, friendly Acomas joined people from Zuñi and
formed the new Laguna villages. Clans migrated from
place to place, taking their ceremonies with them. A mixture of the blood of plains Indians must have occurred,
especially in places like Jemez and Taos. The entire

population shrank considerably, and certain linguistic groups, like the Piros, disappeared entirely, literally harried out of existence by their warring neighbors.

New Mexico remained a Spanish province for a hundred and twenty years. During that time its history was a monotonous succession of squabbles between civil and ecclesiastical powers, petty warfare against outside Indians, repeated " reductions " of Acoma, futile attempts to conquer the Hopis. Meanwhile Church and State between them collected enough tithes and taxes, required enough labor, and inflicted enough punishment to make the Indian's life a hard one. The Indians, very naturally, drew into a hard impenetrable shell of silence and concealment. The old forms of worship were not abandoned; they were performed secretly in the kivas or in hidden places, thus establishing the custom of concealing all important ceremonies from the whites. The priests, in their efforts to suppress these rites, adopted the custom of considering them witchcraft and of treating the Indian caciques as wizards and sorcerers. Many of them were whipped, branded, enslaved, even killed for practicing the old religions. The ceremonies which were conducted openly were combined with the observance of Catholic feast-days in the extraordinary mixture of faiths which still prevails.

## THE PUEBLO INDIAN AND THE AMERICAN

IN 1822 MEXICO DECLARED ITS INDEPENDENCE OF SPAIN and established a republic, weak enough at its center, absolutely impotent on its distant frontier in New Mexico. It was then only a matter of time until the United States, vigorously pushing westward, should take over so desirable a territory as New Mexico, which then extended to the Pacific Ocean. In 1846 General Stephen W. Kearny marched into New Mexico, and the Mexican General fled before him. Kearny made proclamations claiming New Mexico for the United States, granting amnesty, religious freedom, citizenship, and undisturbed ownership of land to everybody; and then passed on to California. He inaugurated the business of chasing Navajos, Apaches, and Comanches, an exercise which was the preoccupation of the American Army in the southwest for about seventy years, until the Indians were finally exterminated or penned on reservations and more or less habituated to staying there. The United States specifically recognized the right of the Pueblos to their pueblos and surrounding lands, which had been granted them by the Spanish crown in the sixteenth century and confirmed by the Mexican government in the nineteenth. Finally, during the presidency of Abraham Lincoln, governors of all pueblos journeyed to Washington and were presented with silver-headed canes, inscribed: "Pueblo of —. A. Lincoln, President. 1863." These canes, with older ones presented by the Spaniards, are today the honored possessions of the pueblo governors and the badge of office.

The Pueblo Indians probably noticed very little change under the new régime, except that the blue-coats gave them better protection from the nomadic enemies. Spain had given them very little help during the last years of its administration; Mexico practically none at all. The United

States relieved them of the menace of their ancient foes and otherwise gave them little attention, except to appoint Indian agents to look after them. These agents were first military men, who looked upon Indians as a conquest, and then political appointees, who considered them a plum. They naturally permitted many abuses, especially in the matter of encroachment on Indian lands and the violation of Indian water-rights. Recent legislation promises to make fair adjustment and restitution in both these matters.

Now the Indian agents are Civil Service employees who consider themselves and are generally considered the guardians and advocates of the Indians under their care. They are assisted by experts in irrigation, agriculture, and stock-raising, by doctors, and recently by nurses. In matters of contract, such as leasing of lands and rights of way, the agent acts for the pueblo, which cannot make a legal agreement without the consent of the Secretary of the Interior.

The Pueblos own their lands communally and assign plots to individual Indians, who are granted as much as they can cultivate. As far as possible the Indians are allowed to govern themselves, and most agents observe that the best-governed pueblos are those in which the influence of the white man is least felt. Pueblo life is so unified that as outside influence breaks down old ways of living and of worshiping, old moralities are forgotten, reverence for old people and the ancient religion is lost, even self-respect declines.

The breaking-down of the old ways is accomplished in the schools. For years after the American occupation of New Mexico the government made no provision for Indian education, and the Catholic missions, already established, were permitted to continue their religious instruction. In time Protestants realized that they were overlooking a fertile field, Protestant missions were established, and the government allowed various religious sects, both Catholic and Protestant, to conduct Indian schools under contract. Abuses developed and finally government schools were established on a non-sectarian basis. They are operated as military schools and they take the children from the fourth grade to or through the high school. The first four grades are usually covered in day-schools in the pueblos. The training follows the usual course of the American public schools with the addition that Indian girls are given training in housekeeping, and the boys in farming and in trades. The avowed purpose is to prepare the young Indian for citizenship and for making a living.

Actually very little attention is paid to his special needs or aptitudes or to the revival or maintenance of his arts and crafts. The result is to unfit him for life among his own people. In pueblo life the adolescent years are very important for learning the clan and tribal traditions, the songs and dances. The Indian school-child misses all this, and when he returns to the pueblo, he is a misfit, almost a stranger, with his American clothes and his short hair. Until recently short hair was considered a disgrace, and in some places it still bars a man from the dances. Sometimes they allow their hair to grow, pick up the old ways as well as they can, take part in pueblo affairs, and make some sort of adjustment. Sometimes they can only withdraw sullenly from the pueblo and seek work in the white man's towns. In

Winslow, Arizona, there are a hundred and seventy Laguna Indians working on the railroad. Such a group has, of course, lost the advantage of the closely knit pueblo group with its rich social and ceremonial life, which is their heritage. It portends the inevitable end: the dissolution of pueblo life and the abandonment of the pueblos.

Meanwhile everything about pueblo life is in a state of flux, including the government, which is a combination of the old and the new. The governor, elected annually by the heads of families, is the civil officer with whom the white man deals. He has one or two lieutenants, elected with him or appointed by him. All of them are nominated by the cacique, that hidden force who is the final arbiter. The governor and his lieutenants act as judges, the disputants being permitted to choose which man shall hear their case. The governor appoints a sheriff. There is a war captain, probably equal in power with the governor. Wars being rare in these days, the war captain's duties have to do with the dances: setting the dates, calling the dancers, and being the officer in charge on dance days. Sometimes he is in charge of the ditch to see that all landholders secure a fair amount of water. Other officers are appointed as needed. A few modern pueblos, such as Isleta and Laguna, have treasurers and secretaries and own government bonds. Most pueblos have checking-accounts in Albuquerque or Santa Fe banks.

Behind the governor stands the body of men known as the *principales,* or council. They are selected differently in different pueblos; sometimes they are all the men who have served as governors. The *principales* seem to be the turning-point between the open and the hidden government of the pueblo, for they are answerable also to the cacique. The governor, bearing his cane of office, is a dignified person with every appearance of authority, but if he is asked something unusual or something which might run counter to pueblo tradition, he at once becomes the mouthpiece of the *principales;* and sooner or later the persistent inquirer finds that the *principales* are dependent finally upon the decision of the cacique. Naturally one who deals directly with the gods in secret rite and receives mystic guidance through prayer and trance must be heeded. More than one white man has found that his affair must wait until the cacique has retired to his hidden shrine for prayer and fasting and direction as to what to do.

All of this means that the Pueblo Indian is a person of dual nature. The white man's Indian is trained in a government school and turned out as a fairly good carpenter, farmer, and Christian. In so far as the education has been a success, he apes the ways of the white man even to the extent of living in the white man's town rather than in his own. The other face of him, however, is turned away from the white man and everything he typifies. Turning his back on the government school, the Catholic mission, and the Protestant church, he is dominated by his ancient beliefs, guided by his ancestral leaders. His real life centers in the kiva, his real hope is in the gods of the ancients, those potent beings who still bring him water and corn, prowess in the hunt, happiness in his life, and a deep spiritual understanding such as the white man does not know.

*Photograph by the Museum of New Mexico*

SANTA CLARA PUEBLO                    [GRACE RAVLIN]

# II: Dances of the Rio Grande Pueblos

THE RIO GRANDE PUEBLOS ARE THE INDIAN VILLAGES OF New Mexico from Acoma eastward to the Rio Grande and north to Taos. Zuñi and the Hopi villages are of the same type, but they are so different and so distinctive in their ceremonial life that they can best be handled separately.

The Rio Grande Pueblos are divided, linguistically, into four groups. The Keres include the people of Acoma and Laguna, in western New Mexico, and those of the Rio Grande valley: San Felipe, Santo Domingo, Santa Ana, Zia, and Cochiti. The Tewa language is spoken in the villages north of Santa Fe: Tesuque, Santa Clara, San Ildefonso, San Juan, and the dying Nambe. Isleta and Taos, set so far apart, and Picuris belong to the Tanos group and speak the Tiwa tongue. Jemez speaks its own language, its only related pueblo, Pecos, having been abandoned in 1838 when the survivors moved to Jemez. Their descendants still maintain some autonomy, and certain old Pecos ceremonies are celebrated at Jemez in their honor.

In spite of differences of language, these people all show a close similarity of ceremonial form and organization,

29

and their dances may be considered as a group. All these pueblos are divided into clans, groups related through the mother, and intermarriage within the clan is still prohibited. When the extinction of a clan is threatened, as recently happened at Tesuque, a woman of the failing clan may be introduced from another village, so close is the association. Besides the clans there are esoteric societies, into which one is initiated and not born. These are very secret, and most Indians, in casual conversation, will deny knowledge of them. Women belong to certain of the men's societies, and there are societies exclusively for women. Such societies have their leaders, called fathers or chiefs, and they are responsible for certain ceremonies. They vary somewhat in the different pueblos, but every village seems to have its societies in charge of war, of the hunt, of curing, and of the weather. All pueblos also are divided into the Winter and the Summer People, sometimes called the Turquoise and the Squash People. These groups have general supervision of the ceremonies of their respective seasons and often each of them has a cacique.

The dance is only a part of a long ceremony, which may include visits to secret shrines in the mountains, days of secret ritual in the kivas or in the society rooms, and the public finale in the dance. Even the dance may be secret; probably the most important dances always are. In that case they are performed in hidden places or in the plaza, which is then protected from intruders by guards posted along all roads. In a few places, as at Cochiti and at Jemez, white people are permitted to witness certain dances in the kivas. Dancers usually fast for four days before the dance, which means that they omit certain foods, such as salt or meat. During that time they remain continent and purge themselves daily; sometimes a daily emetic is used. During this time the society altar is built, costumes for the dance are made or refreshed, prayers are chanted, and prayer-plumes are made ceremonially. Prayer-plumes are small sticks, painted and decorated with feathers, often laid on with a skill which a milliner might envy.

Each pueblo has a society of fun-makers: Koshare or Kurena among the Keres, Kossa among the Tewa, Chiffo-nete at Taos. The Chiffonete probably come closest to be-ing a purely fun-making group. Among the other peoples the clown societies are able to cure certain diseases; and their membership is increased by those whom they have cured, or by the initiation of anyone they catch crossing a mystic line of corn-meal drawn about their house on certain occasions. They can control waters by making floods recede or rain fall. Also they can increase fertility in man or beast or plant; and therein lies their license to joke as obscenely as they wish. Whenever they appear in a dance, these fun-makers are privileged to do or say anything, and nobody may resent it; the dancers do not even appear to see them. It is said that the jokes usually are censorious; the Koshare use their privilege to correct the foibles of their people by salutary laughter. They often do this in pantomime, bits of drama which might well be the beginnings of an in-digenous theater. These formless scraps are in fact so like the earliest Greek drama as to be startling. No develop-ment along this line can be hoped for, however. The govern-ment grudgingly permits these ceremonies to continue as they are, but Indian school training has so successfully throttled the Indian's native fertility of imagination that he will go no further. But if the heavy hand could be lifted, imagine what a gorgeous contribution he might make to drama — this Indian with his gift for the grotesque, his sly sardonic humor, and his perception of human frailty which is witty without being bitter!

The usual explanation of the Koshare is that they represent the spirit of the dead or of " the ancients "; hence their invisibility and their supernatural powers. Ordinarily their costumes consist only of a gee-string and a coat of white-wash with which faces, bodies, and hair are smeared, an effect weird and dirty in the extreme. Black-ringed eyes add to the ghostly effect, and sprays of dry corn-husks tied to the hair, and strings of rabbit-skins, typify death to the Indian. Bunches of pine on the arms mean life everlasting. The serious powers and purpose of this society never appear during a dance. Then they are fun-makers purely. Often they alter their costume to suit the pantomime or dialogue of the occasion, especially when they make fun of white people, when their costumes are a sad travesty of the American dress.

Whenever these clowns take part in a dance, it is safe to say that the ceremony is a Katchina dance, which means that the spirit they invoke is actually present. Originally, no doubt, all Katchina dances were masked, as they still are at Zuñi and in the Hopi villages, but wherever the Catholic Church has attained any power, they are performed secretly, or without masks. Even in the Rio Grande villages a quiet investigator may sometimes find the little

Katchina images, dolls made in the likeness of the masked figures. They are carved of cottonwood, painted, dressed, and feathered just as the dancers are. Often Katchinas are playthings for children, but they have a sacred significance and they are usually hidden from white people. This use of images probably facilitated the introduction of Catholic saints. In fact, one Indian was heard to refer to a certain Catholic image as " the Jesus Katchina."

Many new-comers and many insensitive people state that all Indian dances are alike; " when you have seen one, you have seen them all." This is a great protection to those who like the dances, for the mob stampedes to certain well-advertised *fiestas* and leaves the others to the few who appreciate the distinctions. As a matter of fact, the similarity ends with certain points of costume and of form. The usual costume consists of Hopi garments for the men: a white hand-woven kirtle embroidered in red, green, and black, a sash of the same material, either embroidered or finished with a heavy knotted fringe. A fox-skin dangles from the waist-line at the back, its full tail almost sweeping the ground. A turtle-shell rattle is tied under the left knee, a string of shells hangs over one shoulder, the moccasins are edged with skunk fur to keep away witches. If the man's hair is long, it hangs loose, having been freshly washed in amole suds and brushed in the sunshine until it shines. He wears all the family wealth of silver, turquoise, wampum, and coral around his neck. In different dances variety is introduced in head-dresses, feathers, shields, and the paint on his upper body.

The typical woman's dance costume is the squaw dress,

a black one-piece garment of hand-woven wool. It covers the right shoulder, leaves the left one bare, hangs straight to the knees, and is tied at the waist by a red squaw belt. Usually women dance barefooted in order that they may receive from the earth the spirit of fertility. Their hair, too, hangs loose and they wear jewelry. Variety comes in the use of over-garments, head-pieces, feathers.

Why certain people dance on certain occasions does not appear; the Indians simply will not tell. It seems, however, that every Indian, man or woman, owes obligation to take part in certain ceremonies each year. This is powerful enough to bring back to the pueblos many Indians who actually live away from them. The dance groups are probably based on the clan and society affiliations, and apparently a man and his wife do not dance at the same time.

The music for the dance is usually a chant, sung by the dancers or by a chorus, sometimes unaccompanied, but usually assisted by the beat of a drum or by the rubbing of notched sticks across a hollow gourd. The chant is presumably the prayer, though often those who sing it do not understand it all. Apparently the words used are archaic; sometimes the Indians say they are not words at all, merely sounds. The effect is vigorous, almost angular, unmelodious, unharmonized, but marvelously rhythmic and varied in its rhythm.

The dances described here are not all, by any means. These have been selected as most interesting or most characteristic of the people who give them. Whenever an explanation can be found, it has been given. So far, even the most painstaking and the most scientific investigators have

failed to get the hidden significance of most of the movements of a dance. In looking at any Indian dance, therefore,
it is well to imitate the Indian: sit back quietly against an
adobe wall, soak into your body and into your soul the
stimulating warmth of the sunshine, smoke or chat, watch
the *viga* shadows move along the walls as the hours pass,
let the beat of the *tombe* and the dancing feet get into your
blood — and feel what it is all about. This method has the
enormous advantage of permitting no contradiction; every
man's guess is then as good as any other man's.

## WINTER DANCES

JANUARY IN NEW MEXICO IS USUALLY BRILLIANT AND COLD.
Purple mountains stand etched in silver snow against the
sky; streams are icy, but running between banks massed
with red willow and white cottonwoods, which will rattle
their copper leaves until spring growth pushes them off.
Blue smoke rises from painted chimney-pots in the pueblos,
and gaunt horses poke about hopelessly, looking for food.
On all the roads, Indians wrapped in vari-colored blankets
ride from pueblo to pueblo on horses, in wagons, and nowadays in cars. Farmers have no winter work, the ceremonial
season is on, and they love to see each other's dances. Almost any night, chanting may be heard in the kivas, and
on many days dancing may be seen in the plazas.

There are many kinds of dances, almost an endless variety, for summer dances are often given during these
months for practice; but usually winter dances are for the
hunt: prayers for abundant game and for successful

hunters, and apologies to the guardian spirits of the game for the necessary sacrifice.

Probably the ancient ceremonial year of the Pueblos began at the spring solstice, which they could determine in primitive ways. Nowadays the Indians recognize the white man's calendar by electing their governor just before the new year and by inaugurating him on Twelfth-night. So we begin there.

## The Deer-dance at Taos

Before sun-up on January sixth I sat in Taos Pueblo, watching the village come awake. A few thin blue lines of smoke rose from the chimney-pots, but there was no other sign of life. The mountain flanks were black with pines, cottonwood and aspens along the streams were white, and Pueblo Creek was coated thinly with ice. All around Taos are cultivated fields, and the two villages, facing each other across the creek, rise in tiers to a height of four or five stories — the tallest of the famous terraced pueblos.

A few dogs appeared scratching, and then men whom I took to be the Chiffonete. In blankets and moccasins they climbed down ladders from the houses, sometimes stopping at the stream to wash, sometimes going directly to the kivas with mysterious bundles of ceremonial things under their blankets. In Taos the kiva entrances are flush with the ground, boldly announced by the tall ladder-poles. Usually one man sat near the ladder, possibly a door-keeper. A little later women began to emerge from the houses, heavy-legged in buckskin boots, with long, full skirts and shawls of soft colors or black. They carried jars, or lard-pails, to

DEER-DANCE AT TAOS          [ERNEST L. BLUMENSCHEIN]

the stream for water, they swept with bundles of grass, they carried from house to house the stiff carcasses of sheep, which would later feed the dancers.

Finally the newly elected governor stepped out on his house-top and called, urging all the dancers to go to church. Three gubernatorial calls, muezzen-like in the clear air, three peals of the mission bell, and the people began to drift toward the church. Moving softly, they made a brilliant pageant against the adobe church, with its white-washed wall. All were wrapped in blankets, plain or striped, and falling in soft loops on the men and stiff cones on the women from their heads to their moccasined feet. The Catholic priest was not present, but his pagan congregation knelt reverently on the adobe floor and murmured responsive prayers to the Christian God before beginning their appeal to the gods of the hunt.

Chiffonete always appear for this dance, bare bodies painted in stripes, and their faces decorated evidently with much individual license in spirals, whorls, and concentric circles, also in black and white. On their heads they wear corn-husks, which make fine golden sprays above the chignon. They whoop and yell, always with the restrained musical call of the Indian; they rush up and down ladders and in and out of houses, bringing laughter wherever they go. In every house they are given presents, usually food. All day the Chiffonete run round, making "wise-cracks," shivering in the cold, and often yielding to the seductions of a shawl around the middle.

Soon after noon the dancers appear. First comes a group of men and women who perform the Corn-dance, which is a summer dance, but always suitable, since it is a prayer for growth. They dance in two facing rows, their feet shifting lightly, their hands moving up and down, all in perfect time to the chanting of a group of blanketed men who stamp solemnly ahead of them as they move across the plaza. The women carry bunches of feathers in one hand, evergreens in the other; the men have gourd rattles with which they emphasize the steady beat of the song. The costumes are brilliant, and Indian in feeling, though they are composed mostly of the silks and silkalines, ribbons and calicoes which can be bought in the stores. They dance several times, finally finishing in front of the church.

Suddenly queer distant calls are heard, and beyond a broken adobe wall appears a long moving line of deer-antlers. At once the corn-dancers leave and the deer enter, fifty or sixty men and boys wrapped full-length in deer-hides. The heads are well preserved and the faces of the men are hardly noticeable as they move bent over sticks in their hands which make the animal's front legs. There is no color; with dun-colored bodies, horned heads, and weird cries they move like bemused creatures, coming among human beings and knowing themselves for the appointed sacrifice. Among the deer may be a few other animals; men stripped and painted black and wearing heavy buffalo heads; small boys wrapped in the skins of bobcats or coyotes; even tiny tots smothered under the feathers of a turkey. Very small boys walk hidden under the bent bodies of the men.

These costumes are probably an example of the most primitive type of mask: the use of the entire skin to transform the man into the animal and so, somehow, to trick the game into the path of the hunter. This dance as given in Taos today is as ancient as the earliest human efforts at sympathetic magic, and it leads, as we shall see later, to more highly symbolic and artistic versions of the same thing in other pueblos.

Two women lead, dignified figures wrapped in white buckskin robes, or sometimes in white sheets, wearing the usual white boots, their hair flowing down the back and feathered atop. At the nape of the neck hangs the breast of a duck. In one hand each woman carries pine twigs, in the other a gourd. At certain points in the dance each woman moves slowly down the line of waiting men, making sharp peremptory motions with the gourd. As she does this, each man drops to his knees. Returning, she makes a reverse gesture and the men rise. This perhaps typifies the call of the universal spirit of fertility, the usual significance of a woman figure in the Indian dances. They are treated with reverence, and during this figure the nonsense and the thieving of the Chiffonete are stopped.

When the men dance, the Chiffonete bound about, making jokes and, when they can, snatching a small child out of the group and carrying him away. Most of the boys like the fun; if a very small one yells, he is dropped at once. Usually the thief is caught readily by some man from the crowd of watchers, though sometimes the race is a thrilling one before the boy is rescued and returned to the dancing group. This pantomime suggests the legend of the dance.

Long ago, according to the legend, men and animals lived together and understood each other. They spoke the same language, and the animals knew that they must be sacrificed that their human brothers might live. This dance is an appeal to that old understanding. The Chiffonete who snatches a dancer away typifies the hunter who tries to kill the game. The man who saves him is the spirit which always protects the game. In the course of the dance a few Chiffonete get away with their captives, as a few deer must be killed in the course of the year. It is said that in hunting, the Taos Indians do not worry if they are seen by the game, for they know that if the dance has been properly performed, they will be permitted to kill what they need.

The dance is performed several times, but it is soon over and the dancers withdraw to their kiva, still making queer animal-like calls.

In the evening children dance, going in groups from house to house. Each group gives a different dance, the whole thing being a matter of practicing for later and more serious ceremonies. Indian children learn to dance in such ways, following the grown-ups in serious ceremonies and giving dances of their own before the critical but kindly eyes of the elders. The end of the evening is likely to bring an adult group which dances vigorously some such dance as the Comanche dance. Everyone loves such a night, and every house which entertains the dancers is filled with eager friends and replete with hospitality and welcome. White visitors are well received.

### The Buffalo- and Deer-dance at San Felipe

The Hunting-dances in the Keres Pueblos are a step beyond the sympathetic magic of the Taos Deer-dance, and a step closer to drama. The costumes are more symbolic, and the pantomime is more dramatic, being sometimes very close indeed to a play. The Koshare perform their customary burlesque in the intervals of the dance, and late in the day the whole troupe of dancers and fun-makers performs a pantomime of the hunt which often calls for real acting and which has a distinct dramatic form.

The play begins at dawn, when the only woman dancer goes out to lure the game into the plaza. She typifies the spirit which attracts the game, and she is attended by young men, who are the hunters. Always young and generally beautiful, this girl is chosen by the dancers, who take great pride in her grace and in her swiftness, for she must be fleet enough to give real zest to the race. In the low hills which surround the village she discovers the game; mysterious creatures whose horned heads seem to take shape from the mist as they move. The girl and the hunters chase them, a thrilling sight as lithe young bodies flash in and out among the sandy hills. Inevitably the beasts are outrun, and the girl, shaking her gourd rattle, leads them into the village, where all disappear into the ceremonial house for secret rites.

Later in the morning the whole group emerges to dance in the plaza, where small pine-trees have been planted to suggest a forest. The dancers appear four times in the morning and four times in the afternoon for the solemn ritualistic dance, which is the prayer. The chorus enters first, chanting; then the leader, wrapped in a blanket and wearing a feathered war-bonnet; then the girl; and finally

the game. The buffalo maiden dances demurely, eyes down.
Her hair hangs softly down her back from under a head-
dress of iridescent black feathers outlined with white
beads like a widow's cap, and topped with the tiny horns
of a buffalo cow. Her white Hopi dress is caught at the
waist with a red sash, leaving one brown shoulder bare.
Her moccasins are white, edged with skunk fur, and
she is loaded with jewelry. Her hands move stiffly up
and down in time to the chanting, a gourd in one hand,
pine in the other. Dancing, turning, softly drifting, she
is a figure of beauty among the grotesques who are the
game.

The buffalo are played by two men whose bodies, naked
above the waist, are painted black, as are their faces under
the heavy shaggy buffalo heads. They move with the lum-
bering pace of huge animals, carrying bow and arrows in
the left hand, pine in the right. The elk follow, stately
creatures with feathered head-dresses and turquoise-blue
antlers above the white kirtle and sash. Deer and antelope
are similarly accoutered, each wearing a head-dress made
of the horns of the real animal, each moving in the measure
of his kind. There is real art in the unison of effect which
these dancers achieve in spite of the varying tempo of their
steps. The elk are lofty, with heads held high; the deer are
startled and quickly graceful; the antelope frisk so that
the feather fans which make their tails bob over yellow
buckskin leggins. Each dancer bends over a stick held to
suggest the forelegs of the animal. In all these costumes the
artist has triumphed over the realist, and the masks are
primarily effective arrangements of color and design,

BUFFALO-DANCE                                    [GERALD CASSIDY]

merely suggesting the animal by use of real antlers or horns.

Between the figures of the dance the Koshare appear, dressed as white men in long-tailed black coats, cowboy hats, O.D. shirts and trousers, whatever seems to suggest the American. They cut all manner of monkey-shines and carry on dialogue which is apparently about the game, as they point and peer in the direction from which it comes. Even during the dance they carry on their burlesque of the inept white hunter. They trip over their own guns, they frighten the game, they interfere with the Indian hunters, they make generally pestiferous nuisances of themselves and uproarious fun for the onlookers. They are unnoticed, as always, by the dancers, who continue their rhythmic advance and retreat, lured on by the spirit of the maiden, breaking away from her, and lured back again.

Finally the whole effect changes, and the ordered dignity of the dance gives way to the dramatic pantomime of a hunt. Buffalo are hunters now, the maiden disappears, and the game take refuge behind the little pine-trees which suddenly, by the magic of their acting, become a great sheltering forest. The chant throbs more wildly, the audience grows tense, and in a few confused moments the animals are killed. A deer, stalked by a hunter as he flees from tree to tree, is finally struck by an arrow from a twanging bow. Hit in mid flight, the animal leaps into the air, falls limp, and expires in the dust with a few convulsive kicks. Men then rush to him, lift his perfectly relaxed body, throw it over somebody's shoulder, and carry it off to the ceremonial chamber. Inevitably all the game yield to the hunters, the last dancers disappear, and the audience disperses assured of successful hunting for the year.

## SPRING DANCES

WHEN SPRING COMES, THE INDIAN FARMER IS AS BUSY AS the farmer everywhere. Old grass is burned off, plowing and planting must be done, and the ditches cleaned. Deep troughs have become filled with silt and overgrown with last year's weeds. Men go out to dig, leaving the pueblos in the morning, long lines of them in bright blankets, with spades over their shoulders. All day they dig, soft talk and laughter and sometimes song rising above their bobbing heads as they shovel and throw the rich brown dirt. At night they march home again with that peculiar sliding movement of the Indian, leaving clean deep ditches ready for the brown flood which will soon leave the river, make a wide circuit through the ditches, and bring life and growth to the fields.

When these things are done, the Indian farmer is not content, as the white farmer is. Nor does he sit back and fear the worst or petition Congress to do something about it. He goes quietly and assuredly to work to make things come right. Knowing that there are great hidden forces which control all life and which he can reach in ways established æons ago, he finishes his job by calling on the infinite powers to help. He prays for water, for rain to fall so the ditches may run full. He also prays for renewal of life everywhere, for many beasts, for many children. In short, he dances. Certain societies also, very secretly, conduct proper rites to drive witches away from the pueblos and to clear them out of the ground that the good spirits may work unhampered.

Among the Pueblos a belief in witchcraft seems to be very general. Father Dumarest, reporting on Cochiti, says that among the Keres, witches are thought to be the off-spring of a man conceived for evil purposes. Witch families are therefore not uncommon, and as their members are not generally known, the Pueblos are very careful to be courteous to everyone in order that they may not offend a witch and cause trouble. Not only blights on the crops, but sickness, drought, and all evils are brought by witches. The curing societies and the caciques have the power to exorcise witches and are often called upon to perform that office, especially when one seems pursued by an unaccount-able evil, or when a particular person is suspected of prac-ticing the black arts.

### The Parrot-dance at Santo Domingo

One day, driving to Jemez, I picked up an Indian. I always pick up an Indian; partly, I think, in an effort to atone for the injustice my race has done to his; partly, of course, because I always profit thereby. I hear tales and songs, I get nice phrases about life and crops and weather. Sometimes I learn things of great value to me, as on this occasion.

The Indian turned out to be a friend of mine from Santo Domingo, and we talked of many things. His child, he told me, was in the government school now, and it was neces-sary to teach him much of Indian lore so he should not forget all the knowledge of the ancients in learning to read and write. He also told me about the condition of the ditches, and he suggested that we should visit Zia on the way home, blandly assuming that he would also be my guest coming home.

Finally I said: "When are they going to dance the Parrot-dance? I have not seen it for several years and I should like to see it."

"I dunno," said my friend, that deep impenetrable veil falling behind his eyes.

So I knew that it was soon and that he would not tell me when. "I often go to Santa Fe," I said, "by way of Santo Domingo. I might go some day soon and then I could come to see you. I have presents for your wife and the boy."

A long silence while we sped along through the aromatic scrub cedars. We crossed an arroyo in silence. We climbed a hill in silence. We rounded two curves and finally caught the long sweep of the view where the buttes suddenly show the rose tone through the purple.

"You maybe come Tuesday," said my friend.

So that was all of that, except that on Tuesday I drove to Santo Domingo. As I approached the pueblo, I saw Indians standing on the house-tops, so I knew a dance was going on. In the village I found all the people out in their gaudy best, men lounging against the walls or standing on the roofs, women sitting in the *portales* or on benches built against the walls. Children tried out dance steps here and there or hung round my car to see if I had brought candy. Not a white person was in sight. Friends greeted me, and nobody made any objection to my entering the plaza. The

March sun was hot, and from where I sat I could see how its slanting rays made the low purple hills look as though they were upholstered in plush.

In the middle of the plaza, framed by houses, kiva, and hills, was a long line of men and women, dancing. I saw the backs of the men, seventy-five of them, their bodies painted rose, a turquoise band holding sprays of evergreen to each arm, a turquoise band across the shining black back hair and ending over each ear in a trumpet-shaped flower and two black and white feathers. In the middle of each man's back was an octagonal shield, turquoise in the center, but edged with many lines of wool in various colors. Below it spread a huge eagle-tail, and above it sailed two stiff yellow feathers. In spite of the various colors of the flowers and the shields, there was a beautiful uniformity of effect. Black and white feathers fluttered above black heads; the bodies were all rosy pink; the spreading tails white and black; the moving moccasined feet rose and fell in perfect time. The dancers sang, accenting the rhythm with the stamping of their feet, the clash of goats' toes against the turtle-shell tied under the right knee, and the gourd rattle in each man's right hand. In his left hand each man carried the pine, which always typifies everlasting life.

Facing this line was a line of women, their black heads topped with puffs of eagle-down, their hair hanging long behind and given a demure touch in front by a band of white dots painted on the bang. The black squaw dress was almost hidden under a white Hopi mantle or under the brilliant silk scarfs: orange edged with purple, black and white edged with yellow, magenta with a figured edge, rich deep blue bordering a flowered stuff. Their legs were wrapped in white buckskin, and in both hands they carried bunches of spruce, which moved up and down before them or were agitated above their heads like young trees tossing in the wind. The measure of the dance was quick, definite, often changing.

The group was directed by the war captain and three assistants, who wore fringed buckskin leggins and striped blankets — except one who had yielded to the charm of a green cardigan jacket. The leader of the dance bore the basket on which sat the parrot, that mysterious bird whose knowledge of Southern suns was to bring warmth to this country, fertility to man and beast and field. The basket was filled with seeds of all kinds. The leader wore a rare Hopi jacket with unsewn sleeves which hung loose from the shoulders and was embroidered all over in red and blue. His long, loose hair was topped with a tuft of blue-green parrot-feathers. The precious bird, carved of wood and painted all colors, was not in the least like a parrot. Its tail was a sweeping arc of all kinds of feathers, and over it arched the rainbow, which unites the sky father and the earth mother.

When the dance began, the leader stood facing west, holding the bird in the basket at the height of his eyes. A man and a woman advanced from the other end of the lines, dancing quickly, the man's left hand resting on the woman's right shoulder. They were followed by other couples, all of them making a brilliant, complicated moving picture, topped by the floating puffs of eagle-down. As each couple reached the leader, he handed the basket to the woman, who, still followed by the man, turned and presented the bird to the north, the east, the south, and the west, thus calling on all the directions to bring increase and plenty. Then she returned it to the leader and dropped back into the moving line of women, while her partner joined the men's row, and the next couple advanced.

A striking variation in this dance was the singing of the women, a rare thing in pueblo dances. At intervals the men ceased their chant, and the women sang, their voices reedy and shrill, but sweet and true.

Koshare appeared, making nonsense all day long. One drew a fat squaw out of her *portal* and led her about affectionately while his stream of conversation kept the audience roaring. One had great fun at the expense of the white visitor. He moved the ladder which was my only connection with the earth and left me sitting on a roof while he cracked jokes that it was probably my great protection not to understand. Later, after he had gone away and forgotten it, other Indians came quietly and lifted my ladder back into position.

At sunset the dance ended. All the dancers marched away from the plaza and entered a ceremonial house. Then the leader, standing on a ladder, threw the seeds from the basket and there was a general scramble for them. Each year the seeds from the parrot's basket are planted reverently in the fields, where they will surely bring fruitfulness to all.

### The Turtle- or Evergreen-dance at Isleta

In Isleta, just before cleaning the ditches, a day is appointed and they dance. One old man said: " Turtle-dance.

You know, turtle comes with water." Perfectly clear. If
you want water, you bring on the turtle. Another informant,
however, called it the Evergreen-dance and said that it
was the last of the winter series.

A sunny day. The roadway into the plaza is blocked with
a wagon bearing a wabbly sign: " No admission to cars."
So has the old spirit of hospitality yielded to modern ways
and the need of protection against intrusion. The plaza is
a riot of color: men in bright red blankets, women in gaudy
Czecho-Slovakian shawls, children in every sort of gay
apparel. Against the whitened walls they move and lean
and a few decorate the house-tops with brilliant splotches
of color. The dancers, all men, appear several times in the
morning.

This dance is important and has been preceded by days
of secret rite in the ceremonial house. Two days before, the
dancers, mostly young men, have gone to the mountains
for Douglas fir boughs. They leave the pueblo about ten
o'clock at night, walk fifteen or twenty miles, chop all the
next morning, and walk back again. They do not enter the
pueblo at night, but camp near it and come in at dawn.
Dancing begins about ten in the morning, and the group
may contain as many as forty men and boys, nicely graded
as to height, the tallest in the center. They are attended by
the war captain and his assistants, oldish men wrapped in
blankets, with fir wreaths on their heads.

The dancers emerge from the ceremonial house on the
south side of the plaza and walk quickly to the east, where
they stand in a long line, shifting a little to get spaced.
Then the leader begins the chant, shaking his gourd rattle

and swaying into the measure of the dance. As wind runs along a wheat-field, so the movement takes the row of dancers until all are moving in unison, down to the tiniest boy on the end. The costumes are the usual Hopi kirtle and sash, but every dancer wears a graceful swishing skirt of fir, a wreath of fir around his neck, and sprays of it tied to his arms. They wear dark moccasins, and under each knee is tied a turtle-shell or sleigh-bells. The dancing is simple, the left foot not leaving the ground at all, the right moving vigorously and in changing rhythm. Occasionally the whole line faces right or left, showing, as they turn, the head-dress. This is a small *tablita*, cut from wood and covered with red wool, studded with beads and coins and even tiny mirrors. Stiff eagle-quills stand horizontally to the left, fluffy eagle-plumes to the right. Some men have yellow feathers also, a few peacock tail-feathers. Altogether the head-dresses are brilliant above the copper-brown bodies, the dull-green skirts, and brown legs and feet.

Around them prank the Koshare, dressed as young Mexican blades were a couple of generations ago, in tight-fitting buckskin trousers, short fringed leather jackets. They wear high boot moccasins, and their heads are lost in badly shaped masks of white, with silly features painted on them. They are sometimes funny, sometimes not, as is the way with Koshare. On one occasion they were funny when they took off a church service. One of them stood solemnly intoning from a mail-order-house catalogue, held upside down, while the others knelt in the dust before him. Then he closed the book and began to thunder in wrath, waving his arms and vociferating in tones that any European audience would have recognized as American. The angrier he got, the more sleepy grew his audience, until they finally fell over, overcome with sleep. As a take-off on a church, it was almost too good for the taste of many whites in the audience. In contrast to this ironic skit, the Koshare were gentle and nice when they brought a group of children out to play with them. Gently they directed them in a dance, very tenderly one man led about a tiny girl of not more than three or four, who appreciated the fun and faithfully did whatever they told her. The grotesque masks frightened her not at all, and she had a fine time.

The dance ended at sunset, when the dancers filed in front of the ceremonial house, passing the war captain in a serpentining march and finally standing quietly while he chanted a long prayer. Then, followed reverently by many people, they went to another house. In this way each group visited four houses, finally disappearing into their own ceremonial lodge.

This dance is repeated two days later with more horseplay. Early in the afternoon the Koshare enter the plaza one by one, each swinging a dead rabbit in his hand. Women, somehow moved, dash out after that rabbit, and the game is on, the Koshare dodging, swinging his rabbit like a flail, threatening the women with his yucca whip, both running and playing for time and position and followed by delighted cries from the crowd. Eventually the woman always gets the rabbit. Another game has to do with children. In this the Koshare comes in with a ball of fluff which turns out to be a live rabbit, a trembling, frightened

*Photograph by the Museum of New Mexico*

EAGLE-DANCE                    [JOHN SLOAN]

little thing. Boys and girls swarm around and are marshaled by other Koshare into two eagerly expectant rows. Then the rabbit is placed on the ground, where it cowers, frozen with fright until it is goaded into frenzied efforts to escape. A few futile efforts and it is caught by the yelling children.

After this, and all appearances of the Koshare, they utter a short prayer which is an apology to God for whatever offense they may have given Him, or anyone.

### The Eagle-dance at Tesuque

Tesuque is a small pueblo in Tesuque Valley, only nine miles from Santa Fe. The name is interpreted as " Creek with Water in It " or " Place of the Red Willows." Both names suit, for there is often water in the creek, which is dry frequently enough to make water worthy of note; and there are red willows. Along the creek and the ditches, there are also wild plums, whose fluffy white blankets of bloom go off in the spring to make way for golden masses of wild yellow roses.

Often when these fragrant Persian roses are in bloom, the Indians dance the Eagle-dance, which may be done at any time. The plaza is dusty and dry and nothing grows there; one merely sees the tops of orchard trees beyond the church, where cedar posts make silvery fences. The little church has been altered a good deal through the years, but it is still quaint enough to show that it dates from Spanish days. In front of it looms a hideous water-tower which proves that Uncle Sam has been there. Otherwise the two-story terraces, the ladders and chimney-pots might have been made before any white man ever saw the little valley.

The Eagle-dance, I was told, is part of a healing ceremony which will heal any disease. This is because "eagles are always strong, so they can cure anything."

The ceremony begins with the four-day fast, and on the third night the sick are treated in the ceremonial chamber, where an altar has been erected. In some pueblos the Eagle-dance used to be performed by boys, but as boys will no longer do all that is required, older men do it now. The dance on the fourth day is open to visitors. Though danced by only two men, it is one of the most effective of all pueblo dances, and one which white dancers always wish to learn. After a few lessons they readily understand why the dancers must be treated with medicine water for strength before they can do it. It requires unusual skill and an amazing control of leg muscles in its stooping, swooping, varied movements.

The two dancers are accompanied by chanters and drummers, blanketed and sometimes with the added flourish of a feathered war-bonnet. The dancers, slim young men as a rule, wear caps of raw cotton running out into a long, yellow beak over the nose. Their faces are painted yellow, with a red daub under each eye. The upper body is bare and the kirtle is a buckskin. All the body, legs, and arms are painted yellow and feathered with eagle-down stuck on here and there. The striking feature of the costume is the wings. Each arm is feathered from shoulder to fingers with the real quills of the eagle's wing. As the man dances, he moves his body from side to side, swooping, crouching, making sweeping gestures with his wings, which sometimes almost touch the ground, at others make large arcs in the air. First the two men dance facing, their knees bent, their arms extended. Then they stand side by side, rising and falling on their toes as the eagle rides the air; finally they circle round each other, hopping, swooping, performing maneuvers of the greatest intricacy with quick steps and inconceivable grace. The dance is highly conventionalized and at the same time very realistic.

## SUMMER AND AUTUMN DANCES

AT THE SPRING EQUINOX THE WINTER PEOPLE TURN OVER the conduct of ceremonial affairs to the Summer People. The time is announced by the cacique, who determines the date variously in different pueblos. At Cochiti he goes to an appointed place in the mountains, where he plants sticks at marked spots, a forked and a straight one. Keeping his mind and heart free from all mundane thoughts, he waits there, for days if necessary, praying incessantly. In time the shadow of the straight stick will fall exactly in the crotch of the other. Then he knows that the sun has come to the point, and he returns to the village. The equinox is thus established and the Summer People take charge. If there are two caciques, the winter man then yields to the summer incumbent. From that time on, all the dances are for growth and fructification, and especially for rainfall.

Many ceremonies precede the Corn- or *Tablita*-dance and are related to it. At San Juan they make balls of buckskin, filled with seeds, and play long games of hockey across the fields until the bags burst, scattering their precious life-giving seeds abroad. At Jemez they hold races on the banks of the streams, kicking a clay ball or a stick along as the rushing water, when it comes, will roll up the clay. In that pueblo the side which wins the race is put in charge of the summer dances.

The outstanding summer dance is known as the Corn-dance, which the Indians say is a misnomer, or the *Tablita*-dance. "*Tablita*" is a Spanish word meaning "little board" and referring to the head-dresses of the women. It is, however, a prayer for growth and fructifying rain. It is given anywhere and at any time. All the Rio Grande Pueblos dance on the day of the saint for whom the Spaniards named their village, and usually this dance is given then. These performances vary from small badly dressed dance groups of eight or ten in such a pitiful pueblo as Sandia, which has less than a hundred people, to the magnificent spectacle at Santo Domingo on August fourth, when there are often as many as two hundred dancers, perfectly costumed and trained like an operatic chorus.

This dance is also given in the fall, when the harvest is brought in, especially if the saint's day comes then, as it does at Jemez, which celebrates in honor of San Diego on November twelfth.

### The Corn-dance at Santo Domingo

Santo Domingo Indians are considered, by missionaries and the Indian Service, as very conservative and intractable. Nevertheless they make, annually, a gracious gesture toward the prejudices of their white masters. On August fourth, the day of Saint Dominic, they go early to mass in the Catholic mission, and all who have contracted matrimony during the past year are married by the rites of Mother Church. Sometimes bride and groom arrive proudly carrying the baby smothered under coarse lace and pink ribbons. The marrying couples stand together in a group while the priest pronounces them man and wife, and then they and the whole village kneel reverently for the Christian sacrament. Then the bell rings, muskets are fired, men pick up the image of the saint, and in solemn procession headed by the priest, they go out into the sunlight, leaving only the twinkling candles in the darkened adobe church. Slowly they make the tour of the village, all the people following, and finally they bring up beside the kiva, where a shrine has been erected to receive Santo Domingo. Built of leafy boughs, lined with fine cloths and skins, and lighted with candles, it is a fitting shrine for any Catholic saint. Indians in their best white shirts, bright headbands, and moccasins guard him all day with long muskets between their knees, and many visitors kneel reverently before him and drop coins into his box. And there, in the sunny plaza and in the venerable presence of the saint, the ancient Keres-dance is performed.

There is not the remotest connection between the mass for the saint and the ancient ceremony. They sit side by side; that is all; they do not touch.

Later in the day, Koshare come boiling out of the kiva, their black and white bodies, their whitened faces, their dry corn-husks, and their rabbit-skins all reminding that they are the spirits of the dead. They first present a pantomime, easy to read if one has the key. It is a rehearsal of history: the going-out and the return of runners bringing news of the coming of the traditional enemies, Navajos, Comanches, or Apaches; for the Pueblo people always had to protect their crops after raising them. The runners cause great excitement among the group, who gesticulate wildly, yell and whoop, run round the pueblo establishing lines of protection on all sides, and finally summon the dancers whose duty is to call on the gods for help in bringing the crop to maturity and in protecting it. All day the Koshare perform many and interesting bits of burlesque, filling in the intervals of the dance and even crossing the lines of solemn dancers. One of their duties is valeting the performers, tying a loosened sash or rattle, picking up a dropped article. Through it all, the dancers very punctiliously pretend not to see them.

The arrival of the first dance group is heralded by the beat of tomtoms and the chanting of the chorus which enters first. Often fifty or sixty men chant, marking time with their hands and feet, and intoning, hour after hour, the deep, rich call for clouds and rain.

As the chant begins, the dancers appear from inside the kiva, making a brilliantly effective entrance as they stream down the wide adobe steps in two long lines of men and women; shells rattling, bells sounding, and all the sun colors streaming from the leader's pole and flashing in the costumes. Casually they form in two lines, men and women facing, and shift for space and position. At the right point in the chant the leader, in the center of the men's line, begins to lift his feet in the stamp of the dance.

Men on each side of him follow until the movement runs the length of the line and all are dancing. All the time the pole, topped with feathers of sun-yellow, dips and sways above the dancers, the emblem of the sun's fertility tempting the rain to fall.

The men, in white kirtles, wear eagle-feathers in their hair, big shells at their throats above strings of beads, turtle rattles under their knees, spruce tied above their elbows. They dance with a quick insistent step, lifting their feet high and bringing them down hard to call the sleeping powers awake. The women, demure, with soft brown shoulders above black dresses, move among them, their bare feet shuffling in the dust, close to earth that they, and all life, may gain from it the principle of fertility. They carry pine in their hands, which move up and down in time to the chant, and on their heads are the *tablitas;* thin board plaques, painted turquoise-blue, the sky color, and cut at the top into shapes of mesa and cloud. Clouds are typified also in little wisps of eagle-down on the *tablitas* and in their hair.

There are two groups of dancers, one from each kiva, who dance alternately all day until sunset. Movements of the dance are simple at first sight, but they are almost impossible to follow because of the many unannounced changes of rhythm. In form it falls into two figures: first men and women dance facing, with occasional turnings of the whole group; then they form in couples, each man prancing ahead, his head high, his feet spurning the ground, and the women following, eyes downcast, movement slow and gentle.

Witter Bynner describes it:

Before a saint in a Christian dress
I saw them dance their holiness,
I saw them reminding him all day long
That death is weak and life is strong
And urging the fertile field to yield
Seed from the loin and seed from the field.

### The Rainbow-dance at Santa Clara

One of those thunderous, threatening summer after-
noons in the Santa Clara valley. Huge cumulus clouds
sitting still in the sky, and a few dark streaks where rain
is falling in the mountains. Santa Clara Pueblo hot and
dusty, with heavy black shade under its few cottonwoods.
The people listlessly gather to see the dance: women dragging chairs to sit on and carrying babies bobbing in blankets
on their backs; small boys rubbing bare toes through deep
sand; and a scattering of white people dressed in their
idea of real Western garb.

Presently the *tombe's* sound, and a chorus of five or six
men appear, pounding along to the beat of their drumming
and chanting. Then the dancers, three men and three
women. The men's bare bodies are painted black, with
white across the shoulders, and their faces all colors. Their
hair hangs long and shining, with a fan of eagle-feathers
at the nape of the neck; they wear hanks of red and green
yarn around their waists and under their knees; and they
carry willow wands, arched over their heads like the rainbow, painted in many colors, and feathered at intervals.

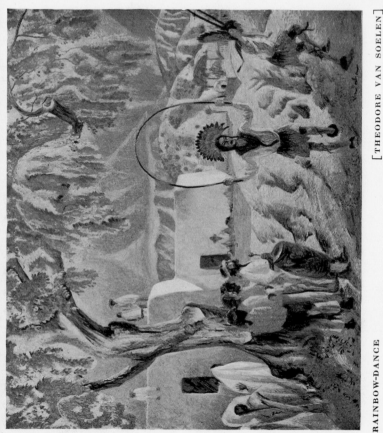

RAINBOW-DANCE

[THEODORE VAN SOELEN]

The women carry bunches of spruce instead of rainbows and they wear in the middle of the back a plaque of many colors, surrounded with eagle-feathers. Each one has a large red spot on each cheek.

The step is not unusual, but the management of the rainbows is. Moving in the ordinary quadrille-like figures, the men, stamping in accurate time, make a jumping-rope of the willow rainbow, flying through its inverted arc like a bird, lighting gently, never missing a step, and raising the arch again above their heads.

Once as I watched this dance, the clouds suddenly drew together, heavy thunder rumbled, and big drops fell. I spoke to an Indian standing near me.

" What a shame that it should rain and spoil the costumes! "

"But no," said he, "this is a Rainbow-dance, and we cannot have a rainbow without rain first."

Quite right he was too, for the shower was brief, just enough to kick up the plaza dust in little puffs and then lay it gently. The dancers kept right on, never missing a beat, and before they ended, the rainbow stood perfectly clear above the Sangre de Cristo range.

### The Pecos Bull at Jemez

Jemez Pueblo on an August afternoon; hot sun and cool breeze. Dark shadows creep along the houses, gradually encroaching on the plaza as the shimmering rays of the setting sun make a golden cloud of dust particles in the air. The little river, clear and cold, rushes between banks heavy with willow bushes, and all the air is sweet with blossoming clematis running riotously along the fences. Vineyards and cornfields are lush green. All is set, incongruously, against sculptured buttes of red and saffron stripes, with castellated white towers outlined on the blue sky.

As the afternoon wears on, women take fragrant bread out of the ovens and sweep in front of their houses with twig besoms or turkey-wings. Children scamper and play, an albino among them. Men move about, in and out of houses and kivas. The real business of the day is in the kivas, where secret rites have been going on for days, this being the fourth.

The feast of Porcingula is celebrated at Jemez on August second in honor of the Pecos people who came to Jemez when they abandoned their own village of Pecos in 1838. The patron saint of the old Pecos mission was Santa Maria de los Angeles, whose original shrine was at Portiuncula, near Assisi in Italy, where Saint Francis once had a vision of the Holy Mary surrounded by angels. In time she came to be known as Porcingula, a name which is sometimes given to women in Jemez, especially to those of Pecos descent.

Great excitement prevails when the call comes: " The bull is out, the bull is out "; and everybody runs to the middle plaza, where the fun is. The bull is covered with flapping black cotton cloth, painted with white rings. The head, long, hanging, and not very realistic, is made of sheepskin and given expression by a pendent red tongue. Underneath is a man in ordinary dance costume. As he prances, the bull, made of ribs of willow, careens precariously from front to back, his sides loosely flapping, his tongue wagging. Men and boys, all of the Pecos Eagle Watchers Society, follow, yelling and jumping, poking the bull with sticks to mimic bullfighters, putting on an endless store of monkey and clown tricks; some really funny, some as pathetically inadequate as most boys' horse-play. All are dressed as white men with long-tailed coats, stiff hats, faces and hands painted white, and often finished with mustache or beard. Occasionally the fun ends in a sprawl of boys in the dust; occasionally it quiets while the bull goes into a house and receives presents of bread or other food, which the boys carry into the house of Porcingula.

Finally six stately priests come out of the kiva, chant a short verse, move slowly the length of the middle plaza, round to the north and back again, chanting at intervals. They are followed by the war captain. All wear white cotton shirts and trousers, with red headband and sash and moccasins, and they form a beautiful frieze as they move against the sunset glow on adobe walls. As they go, the war captain calls the dancers to the kiva, his musical voice mingling with the low chanting of the moving six.

When this solemn interlude is ended, the bull and his tormentors continue their ragging until finally the bull is lassoed and dragged into his house. If the boys still have nonsense in them, they may continue until dark, burlesquing whites in dancing modern dances or singing modern songs. That the white man commands no particular respect grows clearer and clearer. In time the boys subside and the noises of the pueblo run down into quiet, broken only by the hidden beat of tomtoms where the dancers practice, the distant running of the stream, the sounds of animals stirring in the night.

In the morning the bull may appear again, though sometimes he does not emerge until afternoon. When he comes, his attendants come with him and there is more horse-play. Finally the bull is tied to a ladder near the house of Porcingula, and a table is set with food which women bring: women with their gayest silk handkerchiefs hanging down their backs over the black squaw dresses, their hair shining, their legs wrapped hugely in buckskin, and bearing their offerings in bowls or baskets balanced on their heads. Some offer food to the bull, who rests quietly; some touch him with sacred meal. When the feast is ready, the bull-baiters sit and eat, indulging in much profanity, unfortunately a good deal of it in English, as this is also a burlesque of the doings of the whites. The bull may make his presence known by upsetting the table and spilling the food.

Meanwhile preparations for the dance have been going on. Here, as in all the pueblos, the priest sings mass in honor of the patron saint, whose image he afterwards accompanies to the shrine in the plaza. This image is the very one which was brought from Pecos in 1838 and which stands now, equally honored with San Diego, the Jemez patron, in the Jemez church. After the saint is placed, the priest disappears, for he follows the Catholic tradition of being unaware of whatever heathen rites may follow. The rest of the people retire to eat and to await the dancers, who may appear at any time from one to three o'clock. When they do come, they emerge in alternate groups from the Turquoise and Squash kivas, the Turquoise People with

CORN-DANCE

*Photograph by the Museum of New Mexico*

[WILL SHUSTER]

their bodies painted a dull powder-blue, the Squash People saffron-yellow. The dance is the same *Tablita*- or Corn-dance which is given in all the pueblos and which has been described.

The only notable difference is that at Jemez the pole is not carried. It has been suggested that this may be because the dance honors an extinct and not a living people; therefore they do not carry the pole, emblem of life, which lifts its yellow eagle-feather tip to the sun in supplication for increasing life for the tribe. There may even be an ironical note in the whole performance, which does honor to a dying people, certainly, but which seems to contain a note of condescension on the part of a people who have survived and who do increase.

# III: Dances of Zuñi Pueblo

THE FINEST DANCES MAY BE SEEN IN ZUÑI, FOR THERE even the masked dances are open to all visitors, except Mexicans, who are apparently the sole heirs of the ancient resentment against the Spanish conquerors. There is a firm belief that if a Mexican looks upon a mask, he will die; I have seen Mexicans violently driven away from the pueblo during dances. Otherwise whites may see whatever the whole pueblo may see. The attitude toward visitors is one of complete indifference, probably because Zuñi has been much less influenced by missionaries than have the Rio Grande pueblos. Even the Catholic Church withdrew from Zuñi for almost half a century, and today all Christian influence is negligible. The Zuñi religion is so powerful that its rites go on serenely, too haughty to pay the white man even the doubtful compliment of exclusion. Often, thanks to the habit of borrowing dances, one may see at Zuñi dances which he could not witness in their native villages.

Forty miles from the railroad, Zuñi Pueblo has all the charm of remoteness; and its outline, as it sits massed on a hill above the river, is probably little changed since it was settled just after the revolution of 1680. Its terraced houses mount against the sky in a terra-cotta pyramid, with ladder-poles and house-top ovens rising above the empty skull of the abandoned mission. There are too many staring white windows for pure beauty, but even they do not spoil the color tone. The river-bank is the same color as the stone and adobe houses, and where it breaks down to the sluggish stream, it is fringed with silver-gray cedar fences, which sometimes support shelters for stock or ragged green straw stacks. Puffs of gray-blue smoke always drift over Zuñi; and all these colors — terra-cotta and gray, dull green and smoke-blue — are repeated in Corn Mountain, whose sculptured buttes rise a thousand feet above the plain. Corn Mountain not only dominates the scene, but dominates the lives of the people, for there the Zuñis lived for many years, and hidden in its rocks are sacred shrines to which the priests make pilgrimage at appropriate seasons.

The year is divided at Zuñi according to the solstices. Just before the winter solstice the whole village fasts for eight days to the extent of not eating meat or fats. During this time they remain continent, and they do no trading, buying, or selling. No fires are made outside the houses, and all the cone-shaped ovens are cold. Then two masked priests go to a shrine on Corn Mountain, where the Fire-god used to live, and there they ceremonially strike new flame and bring it back to the village. Meanwhile before dawn every housewife has dumped out the last bit of fire, smoldering coal, or ash and swept clean her fire-place, her ovens, even her American stove, that the fire for the new year may be absolutely fresh.

Once every four or eight years there is a ceremonial cleansing of the ovens performed by a masked figure. He is painted black, and from his black cone-shaped mask flames one red plume as the fire flames from the ovens. Attended by members of the two clown societies, he visits every home, climbs into every oven, throws imaginary refuse out of it with yells and hoots, and finally leaves it not only clean, but purified of all evil. On this occasion the clowns must eat everything offered to them, and the Zuñis amuse themselves by offering incredible things like fur and dirt, pieces of metal and so on.

All of this should occur exactly at the winter solstice, and usually the primitive calculations of the priest set it fairly accurately. One year, however, it came very late and I asked a Zuñi about it.

" Oh," he said, " the Sun-priest lost the moon, so everything is late."

That error in calculation was a serious one, and it almost cost the Sun-priest the loss of his honorable position, especially as it was rumored about the village that his reluctance to leave his fascinating spouse for the required eight days had something to do with it.

The bringing of new fires opens Zuñi's great ceremonial season. The personators of the Shalako are appointed for the year, plumes are removed from last year's Shalako houses to those which will entertain the coming season, special dances are announced, and officers are changed if necessary. Annual elections are not held in Zuñi, as in the Rio Grande pueblos, but officers serve an indefinite term.

The outstanding winter ceremonies are the initiation of boys, which occurs only once every four years, and the dance of the sword-swallowers. In addition there is almost continuous dancing, for all the summer dances, as well as all the winter ones, are given, and hardly a week passes without ceremonial. At the spring equinox dancing ends and planting begins. Like farmers everywhere, Zuñis are too busy for anything else in the spring, and there is a recess from dancing until the summer solstice opens the season of dancing for rain. The Rain-dance is given many times, and others may take place; but no dance is given in the summer unless it was given during the preceding winter. The summer dances end when the harvest begins, and the great fall festival, the Shalako, occurs after the crops are in.

In Zuñi the important ceremonial units are the fraternities, groups of people embodying certain features of the creation legend, and potent in curing, or in bringing rain or success in war or the hunt. The Mudheads or Koyemshi and the Galaxy Fraternity or Newewe are the clowns. The Mudheads appear most frequently, wearing mud-daubed masks, like pitifully deformed human faces, for they typify the idiot children of an incestuous union and as such they are a warning against all evil. Their costumes are always the same: ragged kirtle and triangular neck-piece of black wool, and bare bodies daubed with clay the same color as the masks. They appear in most dances during the year, and they are largely supported by contributions. A Koyemshi must never be refused anything he asks, for anyone who denies him any gift will immediately be punished by an apparently accidental fire. In 1929, for instance, a child fell into a fire-place and was so badly burned that she died in spite of the efforts of the government doctor and nurse to save her. All the Zuñis said it was a punishment against the child's mother, who had refused a gift asked by a Mudhead.

The Galaxy, or Newewe, are more purely a fun-making group, and, like the Rio Grande Koshare and Chiffonete, they have absolute license in what they do or say.

There is no cacique, as in the Rio Grande pueblos. The Sun-priest most nearly approximates him, but he can be removed by the other priests for cause. There are six priests, besides the Priests of the Bow, an order which is about to die out, for only those are eligible who have taken a Navajo scalp, and modern prejudice is opposed to that traditional custom. These priests have charge of all ceremonial life, and the Sun-priest must ascertain and announce the dates for all dances. They have no direct part in government, but their indirect influence is great, as they appoint the governor and his assistant and may remove them.

Sacred meal and prayer-sticks are used in Zuñi as in the other pueblos. They make Katchina dolls, and fetishes, quaint animal-like stones of various size or carved wooden birds which swing on cords from the roof above the altar. All fraternity members use the *mili* in ceremonies. It is an ear of corn, perfect to the last kernel, and entirely covered with exquisitely arranged feathers in many colors, laid in spirals and tapering into macaw-feathers at the tip.

The distinctive feature of Zuñi dances is the masks, which are more elaborate, more varied, and in every way more highly developed than any made by other American Indians. People from the other pueblos always say that

Zuñis have the finest masks. Made of leather or sheepskin, they are molded in every size from close skull-fitting hoods to Gargantuan heads, and they are painted with fantastic symbols which only remotely suggest human features. However exquisite the workmanship and strikingly harmonious the color effects, they are always weird, inhuman, and grotesque in effect. These Zuñis show a fertility of imagination probably not exceeded by any of the world's mask-makers; and all the world has made masks, from the most primitive savage to the mask-makers of our modern theater; even the medieval monk masked as the devil in mystery plays, just before he came to America to forbid the converted Indian his masks.

### THE SWORD-SWALLOWERS

WHEN THE ANCESTORS OF THE ZUÑIS WERE WANDERING IN search of the middle of the world, the Wood Fraternity separated from the rest and went northward, carrying two precious fetishes. Once when they made cloud symbols of sacred meal and prayed for rain, snow fell. The people had never seen snow before and they were filled with amazement. They understood its value, however, for making tree and grass roots grow, so these prayers became their special province. This is why the sword-swallowers, who belong to the Wood Fraternity, perform their ceremony only in winter. If they should do it in summer, it would, of course, bring cold rains and kill the corn. The art of sword-swallowing they learned from Achiyalatopa, a curious being with knives for a tail, whose picture may be seen even now on their altars. The Wood people were accompanied on their wanderings by six animals, still sacred to them: the bear, the cougar, the badger, the wolf, the shrew, and the snake. All sword-swallowers originally belonged to one of these clans, but as some of them have died out, this is no longer true.

At Black Rock, where the Indian school now stands, the people stopped and the original director disappeared into the spring, which became a sacred spot to them. They made pilgrimages to it through all the ages until the government made a dam which swallowed up the sacred spring in an artificial lake. They believed that underground roads led from that spring into the fourth, and most sacred, world. In time these wanderings came to an end, and the Wood fraternity found their people at the very middle of the world, where Zuñi now stands. Here possibly we have an example of a legend founded upon the actual wandering of a small group of people who joined a larger group, bringing their ceremonies with them.

The legend continues with much detail of the reception of the Wood Fraternity by Zuñi. The Rain-priest of the North accepted all their sacred objects and assigned to them two more fetishes, one from the Badger and one from the Crane clan. He also appointed maidens to bear the beautiful slender stalks with silver leaves which the corn-maidens brought when they came from the under-world. In time the leaves fell off and were replaced by fluffy white feathers, as we see the corn-maidens carry them today. He also chose two maidens and a youth, all vir-gins, to dance with them. The beast gods who came with them were assigned the task of making music for their dances by rubbing the leg bones of deer over notched sticks.

The medicine of the Wood Fraternity is especially good for sore throat, a wise provision, as they are most active in the season of that affliction. In the treatment, besides prayers, they give the patient a brew of such potency that an outsider breathing the fumes, or even coming into the room, would be overcome. This is also true of the brew used in their ceremonies; so the ceremonial chamber is sealed and nobody, during the rites, must touch a dancer, as the death of one or the other would surely result. A cured patient may request admission to the fraternity, and new members are also solicited. Initiations take place during January and February, when the dances occur.

. .

Several days before the outdoor ceremonies, members of the fraternity gather in the ceremonial chamber to practice songs and to tell tales, especially those relating to the wandering of their people. At this time men and women are appointed to act as directors, the virgins are chosen, the Bow-priests, who dance the circle dance, are invited, prayer-plumes are made. An altar is set up, its central figure the curious bird with knives for a tail. Initiates are ceremonially shampooed and taught the difficult art of swallowing swords. The dangerous medicine, made of a plant which has not been identified, is prepared; but only after every door but one has been plastered over. All the properties are brought from their hiding-places and put in order.

For four days these preliminary rites continue. An important feature is the daily drinking of the sacred medicine to induce vomiting, which is supposed to enlarge the throat. This is not likely, but a doctor whom I asked told me that it might contain a drug which would relax the muscles of the throat and so make the swallowing easier. The swords are continually swallowed during these rites and there is dancing every night and until the morning star appears. Continence is observed, and fasting from whatever the original wanderers could not have had: all food bought in stores, summer fruits, and sweets.

On the fourth night the sword-swallowers dance in the house where the virgins rehearse, and white visitors are admitted. The house shows no preparation for the event. The three young people, wrapped in blankets, sit on the wooden bench against the wall. A group of men chant prayers, smoke, occasionally sing, hawk and spit, laugh and chat; Indians always appear to be on such close terms with the gods that the ordinary affairs of life may be carried on during the most sacred observances. Children spill down the steps from an adjoining room where an iron bed stands unmade, and women move about with bowls of food. Nobody ever seems to put a Zuñi child to bed until it literally falls over with sleep. Those still awake watch their elders with bright black eyes and move their feet in perfect time with the chanting. In the middle of the floor stand two whitewashed boxes, painted with the six beast gods of the fraternity and the curious knife-tailed creature.

On them lie the six notched sticks and the six deer-bones which are to make music, or at least rhythm, for the dancing.

Preparation for the arrival of the dancers consists only in sprinkling the floor. One of the directors dips a gourdful of water from a tin bucket, fills his mouth, and sprinkles widely and accurately until the dirt floor is too moist to raise any dust. Then, about ten o'clock, there is a tightening in the manner of the singers, and a change in the song. Calls are heard outside, and the sword-swallowers enter, following the woman leader. She wears a white ceremonial blanket over the ordinary black wool dress, and a fluffy white eagle-plume in her hair. She carries a pottery basket of sacred meal and the *mili* of the fraternity. The man leader follows her. These two typify the original pair whose wanderings led to the discovery of the art of sword-swallowing and of bringing snow. In his left hand the man carries the original sword, with a turquoise-blue handle, and in his right the regular feathered sword of the fraternity. The swords are made of juniper, as long as from the tip of the middle finger to the elbow, slightly curved, about three quarters of an inch wide, feathered at the top, greased with bear-fat, and colored red. The top, tipped with turkey-plumes, is about twice as long as the blade which is swallowed. The leaders are followed by the warrior of the fraternity, an old man who must belong to the Bear clan. A red feather is tied to his crown and he carries a sword with a zigzag handle, painted blue. His sword ends in an arrow-point, rounded, it is true, but nevertheless very difficult to swallow. His body is bare with the exception of a kirtle and he wears the buckskin baldric and medicine-bag of the Bow-priests.

The size of the group may vary; five women and fifteen men are average. The women wear the black squaw dress, and their faces are covered with the bang, as is true in all dances. The men wear black kirtles and have red or white plumes tied to their heads. One, the headman, wears a kirtle of cougar-skin. Each man carries his sword in his left hand, and in his right a rattle with which he pounds the beat of the chanting. Some of the women carry two eagle-feathers in the right hand, and the sword in the left; most of them carry, and swallow, two swords. If a woman cannot swallow her sword, her " fraternity father," who precedes her in the dance, does it for her — quickly and readily, but with an expression easy to understand if he has been doing this extra service regularly for a week.

The dancing is vigorous, with the men raising their feet higher and stamping harder than the women. They circle the boxes several times, all chanting; then the swallowing begins. Each dancer, as he passes the boxes, waves his sword over them, throws his head back, takes the sword in his right hand, and quickly slides it down his gullet, full length. Some swagger a bit, dancing several steps with the sword within, and pull it out again with the other hand. They pass three times around the boxes, each dancer swallowing the sword every time; then they leave the room.

A few spectators, mostly young men in black blankets and cowboy hats, stand entranced, watching every movement.

Nobody touches a dancer, as to do so would mean death. No attention whatever is paid to white visitors.

After the sword-swallowers leave, the virgins are brought on to the floor. The girls wear the black wool dress and wrapped leggings. The boy has a black kirtle around his slim body, which is otherwise bare. This is obviously a practice affair, as the directors fuss about the dancers a good deal, calling orders. The dancers' figures are slender and pretty; the boy's face shows weariness, but the girls' features are hidden by their long bangs. They have been practicing for four nights and they dance an hour at a time without resting. The girls hold in each hand a bunch of shredded corn-husks, the boy holds one close to his face with both hands.

The first movement is no more than a slight bending of the knees, a strained and difficult gesture, done in time to the chanting. They do this several times, the hands moving up and down; then, on a sudden change of rhythm, they bend at the waist, bringing the corn-husks down in a hard insistent motion. The chanting is varied by one voice wailing the word " *muwaiye*," which is the Zuñi name for the dance. Suddenly the rhythm changes, the wailing voice ceases, and there seems to be hope in the music and a beautiful lightness in the dancing. Now the dancers fling their arms wide as they bend their knees, the right hand coming to the left shoulder as the left arm flies out in a free floating gesture, very graceful and very young. Then the right arm straightens and the left hand comes to the right shoulder. The knees still bend rhythmically, but more easily, and the dancers move slowly the length of the room and back. Then the music changes to the original hopeless note and the figures are repeated. With occasional rests the dancing lasts until the morning star rises.

. .

Wishing to see the very beginning of the big day, we got up before dawn and went to the sacred plaza. Crossing the village was an eerie walk. It was cold, cold, a still and bitter cold. Lights in only a few houses. No sound at all. Occasionally a blanketed figure slipped from a door and melted into the shadows, not seeing us. We made ourselves as comfortable as we could with many blankets in a corner of the deserted little plaza and waited. Finally three men came in, carrying the painted boxes, which they placed ready with the sticks and bones upon them. As they turned to go away, one of them saw the intruders. He approached us, peered, laughed low, and turned back to the others.

"*Belicana*," he said, using the Navajo word for Americans.

They all laughed, and disappeared through the south passage. Then more still and cold, with increasing light, which crawled down the terra-cotta walls and brought out, step by step, the hideous board stairway which defaces one corner of the beautiful old plaza.

Smoke came straight up from a chimney-pot here and there, and when the light was full, the leader of the sword-swallowers appeared from the ceremonial room, carrying the long, slender poles of the Bow-priests, which he left on the house-top. Meanwhile a ceremony was going on inside the house, which visitors are not allowed to see. In fact, nobody sees it except the old warrior of the fraternity, but he reports that when he is there alone, the knife-tailed bird on the altar performs magic and utters oracles.

Finally three musicians entered the plaza and began the grinding of bones on the notched sticks. Two directors entered and prayed and then four girls appeared, carrying the fetishes of four clans; heavy stones, wrapped in buckskin and tied with many strings of wampum and beads. The priests directed the girls as they took their places facing east, and then sprinkled the ground with sacred meal, typifying snow-clouds. Finally another girl came in, carrying the very fetish which the original Wood People brought with them. She wore white moccasins and a white wrap; the others walked awkwardly in the pointed-heeled shoes and the stockings of purple or orange silk which seem to be favored for general wear in Zuñi. Their blankets were from the stores, but they were gay in color and comfortingly warm-looking on this cold morning.

The chanting and praying lasted about an hour, while the kneeling musicians made rhythmic growlings with the bones on the sticks, and the sun gradually warmed the walls to rose, and the houses around the plaza woke. A tiny boy slipped round the corner and leaned his shoulder against the wall with grown-up nonchalance. A blue-framed window parted its pink ruffled curtains and a baby peeped out. Then a woman tied the curtains back, showing herself in brilliant silk scarf over her black dress, and a fire crackling temptingly behind her. The baby, in pink, stood framed in that blue window until the end of the ceremony, which oc-

curred when the sun reached a certain point. During this
time the girls holding the heavy fetishes were relieved by
twos, each pair at once leaving the plaza arm-in-arm and
giggling. When they had all gone, the directors lifted one of
the boxes and took out from under it a small purple basket
holding a snowy mound of meal. They passed it from hand
to hand, breathing over it to gain its virtue. Then they replaced the basket and went, leaving only one man on guard.

. .

During the morning a sand painting must be made in
the house of the Bear clan and only when that is done do
the dancers appear, probably in the early afternoon. The
visitor knows when to go to the sacred plaza because he
sees the whole village moving that way. Men stalk along,
their eyes glinting between their high hats and black
blankets held across their faces. The women wear
their gayest shawls and scarfs; even the children are as
gaudy as possible. All movement is quiet; the crowd
seems to materialize on the roofs around the plaza,
not to walk there, certainly not to push and force themselves in. There is low talk and laughter, but no loud
noise.

The Bow-priests enter quietly, carrying their wands,
slender sticks the length of the two arms extended, and
painted in the colors of the six directions. Seeds are tied
at the bottom of each one, feathers at the top; and in the
middle, which is supposed to come directly over the heart,
are miniature shield, war-club, and bow and arrows. As

the men take their places on the north side of the plaza, they
are joined by women. Each man and each woman grasp
a staff with each hand, so they all form a continuous line.
They dance in the intervals of the sword-swallowers' dance,
their circle never being closed. They use a curious step,
crossing their feet, which is very unusual in Indian dancing. An attendant, gorgeous in black velvet jacket, with
gaudy bunches of ribbons floating from the shoulders, goes
about begging young people to enter this dance. There used
to be two men and two women to perform this office, and
the circle would enlarge until it filled the plaza with giggling girls holding back to be urged and with eager youths
dancing beside the chosen ones. Now we see only one dis-
couraged man who makes half-hearted efforts to interest
these Indian school-children, all of whom refuse him.
Finally he gives up with a hopeless gesture and sits down,
watching the dancing of the small group of priests and
women. It is a good example of the passing of an old
folk-custom.

As the sword-swallowers enter, they present a very different picture from the practice group of the night before.
A drummer leads, wearing a velvet shirt, much jewelry,
and a red headband. The woman leader is dressed as before, but the man is now brilliant in snowy shirt with full
sleeves, white kirtle and sash, and dance moccasins of red
and turquoise-blue. Feathers float from his long hair, which
has been braided to make it wavy. The other officers and
the dancers are all painted yellow; they wear white kirtles, fox-skins pendent behind, and yucca wreaths on their
heads. In addition to the noise of the rattles, we have today

the jingle of the bells tied under each man's knee with black yarn. There is also a hank of black yarn around the neck, among innumerable strings of turquoise, wampum, coral, and silver beads. They dance with precision and beauty, picking up and setting down their feet with the delicate strength of a pianist touching the keys. The women wear the black dress, as before, but masses of turquoise hang from their chins to their waists, their hands and arms are heavy with silver and turquoise, they wear white moccasins, and they hold their swords erect, so that the feathers seem to float above their heads. They dance and swallow as before, but individuals now show more virtuosity. One woman swallows two swords at once, several men dance several vigorous steps with the swords in them. The sun is brilliant and the roofs are crowded with an intently watching crowd in every color of shawl and blanket: saffrons and reds, magentas and purples, blues and reds; and there is always the sharp accent of the tall young men in black.

After four appearances with circle dancing in the intervals, the sword-swallowers disappear for the last time. When the plaza is empty and most of the spectators have gone, the leader and the old warrior come in alone, carrying armfuls of swords. Then follows a queerly impressive ceremony. The leader, taking long steps, moves first to the east of the boxes, where he stamps hard on the ground, hoots aloud, and swallows two swords, his own and a feathered one. Then he makes similar steps in each direction, repeating his hooting and swallowing, while the old man follows to hand him swords. The old man finally

swallows his arrow-pointed sword and another, and the
two solemnly leave the plaza.

. .
.

Just before sunset two members of the Bear clan enter
the plaza, which is again filling with its colorful audience. They make crosses of meal on the ground and place
baskets on them. They overturn the boxes so that they
open upward, and move the notched sticks and the bones
to the baskets, where they make music, chanting all the
time. Almost at once a group appears at the southern
entrance: a leader carrying a meal-filled basket hanging
from a stick, and eight girls. The first four carry the wands
which the corn-maidens brought from the underworld, and
the others the four fetishes. They wear ordinary dress and
store shoes and they are wrapped in blankets; but their
progress is stately and the feathered wands are beautiful.
They scatter meal into the boxes as they slither slowly
along, followed by a chorus of men, who move their feet
in time to a richly melodious song, unaffected by the
other singers. When this group reaches the north side of the
plaza, they stand, and attention is again turned to the south
entrance.

There appear the three virgins, lovely as great white
chrysanthemums in their ceremonial garb. They move sideways into the plaza. The girls wear white ceremonial robes,
draped to give the effect of a full skirt with ruffled peplum,
and a blouse which leaves one brown shoulder bare. Their
feet are in white moccasins with shiny black soles turned

up at the toes in tiny triangles. Each girl wears all the turquoise she can carry, a solid mass from the chin to the
waist, ears and arms and hands laden. Each is topped by
a head-dress of shining black fur, under which her own hair
hangs to the waist behind, to the lips in front. The head-
dress bears bunches of yellow and fluffy white feathers, but
its special beauty is in a tall slim *tablita* of rose and
turquoise-blue which is cut into the shapes of sun and
moon and stars. They carry wands daintily feathered with
white down, which enhance the beauty of the lovely floating movement in that part of the dance. The youth is a white
figure also, in kirtle and sash and full-sleeved shirt. His
hair must be long, even if it requires the use of a wig. He
carries a *mili*. The dancing is the same as the night before,
but extraordinary in the evening light and in the beauty of
the white costumes. This group moves very slowly, while
the other groups go out before them. Finally the virgins
leave the plaza at the west. They cease dancing there and
walk almost to the ceremonial chamber, where they begin
again and enter it dancing. Within they are received by
their directors, who remove their costumes and wands.

The evening is a busy one in Zuñi, for all these dancers,
singers, directors, and priests must be feasted. All night
dancing continues in the house of the sword-swallowers,
who outdo themselves in swallowing more swords, swallowing them deeper, and in dancing harder while they do so.
Visitors are welcome, but, as always in Zuñi, getting into
the room is a problem, as the whole village is there. The
dancing ends finally at sunrise, when the leader recites in
an impressive tone the tale of the original wanderings.

Then officers carry all the sacred things to their appointed places, prayer-plumes are planted in the fields to assure good crops, and the ceremony is over.

..

### THE SUMMER RAIN-DANCE

Zuñi sits on a low hill in the midst of a fertile valley, which is rimmed by flat-topped hills. Its fields of corn and beans, squash and chile are watered by the little Zuñi River, a most inadequate water-supply. Recently the government has put in a dam six miles away, which usually conserves enough water to last through the summer. Ultimately, however, that depends upon rainfall, and, as every Zuñi child knows, rainfall depends upon the proper observance of ancient prayers.

During the lengthening days when the crops are high and vigorously growing higher and men put in long hours of cultivation every day, the Sun-priest withdraws from the village. In his absence women know that their best pottery can be made. So they mold and paint their choicest vessels, for " then we think of the best things to paint." This is also the best time to fire pottery, because unseen forces minimize the terrible danger of cracking a fine piece in the heat; so in front of almost every Zuñi house women tend the low smudging fires in which the beautiful painted jars are brought to perfection. Also this is a time when everyone must keep his mind and heart pure, for the sun is making a turn as the priest sits there in his shrine, watching.

When the first beams of the rising sun strike in the same place on five successive mornings, the Sun-priest knows that the time has come, and he returns to tell his people. Thus is the summer solstice established in Zuñi.

Then all who will appear during the Shalako in the masks of gods go to the proper shrine. In some years they go to the Sacred Lake through which the Zuñis emerged when they came, ages ago, from the underworld. In alternate years they go to the Hot Spring. In either case the boy who impersonates the Fire-god must light his cedar brand ceremonially and set fire to dry grass or brush. The smoke-clouds which rise will certainly bring rain-clouds. Then the dancers return to the village and retire into the fraternity room to prepare altars and otherwise make ready for the dance. In the evening they dance, unmasked, and visitors may come.

The dancers are painted with a yellow mud from the Sacred Lake, even those who appear as women. No women take part in this dance, but eight men wear the squaw dress and white mantle, with their long hair done in the elaborate swirls which are the Hopi squash blossoms, emblem of fertility. They wear anklets of spruce, which typifies life, and carry cat-tails as symbols of moisture. The men, long-haired too, wear topknots of macaw-feathers and three fluffy white eagle-plumes on a string down the back. Their bodies are saffron-yellow above the white kirtles, spruce is tied to their bare ankles, and they carry live tortoises, as many as may be. Those who do not have tortoises carry gourd rattles. Dancing continues all night, as is the Zuñi custom, with only occasional rests. None of the dancers may eat anything and they drink only " medicine water " prepared by the priest.

In the morning, very early, the Mudheads gather in the Sacred Plaza, where they entertain with many kinds of sleight-of-hand tricks, guessing-games, and frolic. They bring cat-tails, which are presented to one of the men who dances as the one woman who typifies the spirit of fecundity. He carries them into the ceremonial room, and soon after the dancers emerge. They are masked now in flat false faces of turquoise-blue, with long, black beards. The color effect is striking: yellow bodies, arms, and legs, bright-blue faces, black hair and beards, and tall waving green cat-tails. The men and women figures meet and pass and turn, performing complicated involutions like an old-fashioned quadrille. Four times they dance in the morning, in a different place each time, and four times in the afternoon.

On a hot and dusty afternoon it is a thrilling thing to see. Zuñis follow the dance group, seeking shade and standing against the houses, with one eye on the dancers, the other on the sky. It is not unusual, certainly, to see the great stationary white puffs of clouds begin slowly to draw together. As the dancing goes on hour after hour with its reiterated pounding beat, those clouds may suddenly turn black, rush, in sweeping waves, across the blue sky, meet with thunder and lightning, and pour long, black lines of rain upon the fields. Thus it should be. If it does not come, the Zuñis know that something has been done wrong and they will patiently try again.

This dance is repeated at any time, and any number of times during the growing months, though the coming-in of the gods does not occur again.

## THE DOLL-DANCE

ZUÑI'S ONLY CONCESSION TO THE CATHOLIC INFLUENCE IS its Doll-dance, given some time in the fall; but that has been modified until it bears very little resemblance to the semi-Catholic affairs of the Rio Grande pueblos. The doll is a carved wooden saint kept by a certain family who claim to have had it for three hundred years. Probably the original figure was the Virgin, but the one now used certainly looks masculine, judging by the cut of its hair. However, it is dressed in blue silk, hung with jewels, and referred to as " she." A part of her equipment is a leather bag hung around her neck, into which her custodian drops a coin every time she is exhibited. If he collects a dollar and drops a dime into the bag, who should notice or comment on that fact?

The date of the dance is set in various ways. In 1929, Zuñis who had attended the Laguna *fiesta* on September 15 promised a dance in return, and the Doll-dance was given on October 12. Other years, other reasons. On the great day the image is carried, reverently enough, but with no Catholic participation, and set in a shelter built out from a house in the big plaza. The shelter is converted into a shrine by hangings of fine cloth, woven garments, skins, and anything of value. Two men guard it with ancient muskets.

Slowly the people dribble in until the house-tops are loaded with them. Among the Zuñis, in their gayest shawls and blankets, are many Mexicans, for this is the one Zuñi festival which Mexicans are permitted to see, and they have been known to come from as far away as El Paso. They hold the image in great reverence, they kneel before it, murmuring prayers over their beads, and they greatly enrich the family that owns it. Often nuns and priests come.

On that October day, as I sat baking on a roof in the New Mexico sun, Flora Zuñi told me the story of the doll.

"They said that a long time ago Mexicans brought the doll to Zuñi. She was a queen and she was in the family way. She was not married, but the sun gave her a baby. They brought her to the old church which was used then, and there she had a baby. Her baby was a doll too.

"When she got up, after four days, the Acoma Indians came to Zuñi to dance, and the mother liked their dance so much that she wanted to go to Acoma. So she asked her daughter: 'Do you want to go to Acoma, or do you want to stay in Zuñi?'

"The daughter wanted to stay in Zuñi. So the mother went to Acoma, and the daughter stayed in Zuñi, and the Zuñis were so grateful because she liked Zuñi better that every year they have a dance for her!"

Dancing goes on all day, beginning in the morning "when they are ready." The dancers, boys and girls, are attended by a chorus of about ten men and one drummer, beating the staccato rhythm on a huge jar with a taut buckskin top. There should be an equal number of boys and girls, but that varies. The costuming is careful and effective, its prevailing tone being that of the white Hopi kirtles. Each girl is a study in black and white, for the kirtle is draped over her black dress, her white wrapped moccasins are black-soled, and her black hair hangs to her chin. In each hand she carries turkey-feathers, and on her head is an arrangement of blue macaw-feathers, white down, and long streamers of bright ribbons reaching to her knees. The boys wear the white kirtle and sash, with the upper body bare, and blue moccasins. Both boys and girls are loaded with jewelry after the Zuñi manner.

They dance in the usual Corn-dance formation, but with a quicker movement than usual; the twenty-minute appearance may be a real test of endurance. If the dance is well liked, a repetition is asked for, and then it may be repeated on the following day. If enthusiasm mounts high, men join the chorus until a nucleus of ten grows to a hundred or more, stamping and singing vociferously and holding on until the alternate group almost has to push them out. Everybody has a good time, nobody stops until he has to.

### THE SHALAKO

THE SHALAKO IS ZUÑI'S GREATEST FESTIVAL, AROUSING THE most interest and activity in Zuñi and bringing most visitors from outside — for it is the culminating event of the ceremonial year and has been in preparation since the winter solstice preceding. At that time the personators of the gods are appointed, and all during the year they perform rites at certain intervals. However ordinary the life of Zuñi may appear to the superficial observer, it is underlaid with a rich ceremonialism. Men who on the surface are occupied in farming, trading, driving cars into town, working on road gangs or about the stores or Indian schools slip away when no white man sees them and quietly perform their duties as those in whom the gods will for a time abide. Once a month they meet to practice songs and to make pilgrimage to some sacred shrine, usually a spring; and once during the last quarter of the moon they make and plant prayer-plumes.

Forty-nine days before the coming of the Shalako the personator of Sayatasha (the Rain-god of the North) and the leader of the Mudheads are each given a string tied in forty-nine knots, one of which he unties every day until the arrival of the gods. After this ceremonies take place every ten days until the Mudheads come to announce the arrival of the gods in four days, of the Shalako in eight. The announcement is made in the large plaza, where a large audience is gathered to hear the news and to greet the jokes with chuckles of delighted laughter. The Shalako does not occur on a definite date, but at any time from late November to late December. The Koyemshi also announce that the Zuñi dead will come, though only mediums will be able to see them. Long ago, when hearts were pure, both the gods and the dead used to come openly, but now the dead are invisible and the gods are present only in the persons of those who wear their masks. After this appearance the Mudheads retire to their own house, where they chant and pray until the gods arrive.

After four days all the performers make a pilgrimage to six shrines, at each of which the boy who is to personate the Fire-god lights a fire with a cedar brand. This group then returns to the village, announces the arrival of the Shalako in four days, and goes into retreat. Early the next morning the governor calls from the house-top, reminding the people to give food to the dead; and in every house food is burned in the fire-place, that the ancestors of that family may eat.

.   .
.

During these last days activity in the village increases steadily; activity, but not hurry. Indians seem to know that all will be done, and they work along quietly without much conversation, everyone seeming to know his job and doing it. Watching, one sees no committees hurrying from place to place, no strident-voiced bosses speeding up the work; but it gets done, the houses get finished. Properly there should be a house to entertain each of the six Shalako, one for the Council of the Gods, and one for the Koyemshi. Actually there are often two Shalako in a house; and often none of the houses are new, but they are merely replastered for the occasion.

Entertaining the Shalako is expensive, though honorable. One man killed thirty sheep and twenty cows and spent or contracted for three hundred dollars besides. Often a family faces years of slim living after entertaining the Shalako. All through the year the host is assisted in his farm work by the dancers who will use his house, and the whole village helps him to garner his crops and to build his house. Nevertheless the brunt of the expense falls on him. Beams must be brought about twenty miles, stones hewed and hauled, the house erected and finally finished by the women, who plaster and whitewash the walls and make the fire-place. At this point the effect is fine. Honey-colored beams top the softly gleaming white walls, and the corner fire-place, tall enough to take a two-foot log standing upright, flares to throw its heat in a generous circle. Shalako rooms are long, sometimes as much as sixty feet.

On the last day activity is intense. By this time the women are baking day and night, the outdoor ovens flaring their banners of flame long after dark and then smoldering to a dull glow when the bread is put in and they are closed for the baking. Men climb ladders to hang yards of calico or challis against the walls, while others sit on the floor dismembering sheep held in the lap, and women do unmentionable things to their insides. Odors of fresh bread and freshly killed meat and cedar fires and close rooms are indescribable. Women are grinding in many houses, where maidens dance with a perfect ear of corn in each hand, and old women sing the grinding-songs. Other women are making paper-bread on hot flat stones, and girls move stately from house to house bearing on their heads jars or baskets of food. Children are everywhere, but never in the way. On a sunny day it is an unforgettable sight.

Toward the end there is some change toward secretiveness. Doors that stood open are shut. Men wrapped in black blankets and wearing moccasins instead of store shoes move in quiet lines from place to place. They greet nobody and are not greeted. They are the personators of the gods going to appointed places for prayer. With luck one may see the boy who will be the Fire-god. He will be wrapped in a blanket too and he moves as solemnly as the men, only his cropped hair showing that between times he is merely an Indian kid in a government school. He must be a member of the Badger clan, and he is invited to assume this distinction. One little boy who was invited in 1923 cried, so his mother said, for days because he knew the dancing was so hard. Finally he consented, and now that he is sixteen and about to be graduated from a government school, he is glad. Ten is the average age, though sometimes an older lad is chosen.

When the morning star rises on the great day, the personators of the gods and their attendants slip quietly from the village, bearing their masks and other paraphernalia hidden under blankets. The masks have all been newly painted and feathered in the ceremonial chamber. This is a task that only the initiated may see. Anyone else chancing on it is beaten by the whippers, who bear yucca blades for the purpose. This is very necessary, as otherwise the Shalako would fall while running. A personator of the gods who spoke to a woman would be given the same punishment.

During the last day everything is finished. Every ceremonial chamber is hung with bright cloths, blankets, brilliant silk shawls, feathers, and skins. A hole has been dug in front of each house; and a causeway of stones and dirt has been made across the river. Everything has been swept, food is ready, and people begin to appear in their best clothes. All day visitors drift in — long-legged Navajos on ponies, the women sitting astride in their voluminous skirts,

the men wearing beaver-skin caps; Indians from the Rio
Grande pueblos with turquoise to trade; Hopis with ceremonial garments; and a complete assortment of white-man
types, from families of Mormons from the near-by towns
to the Greenwich Village æsthete and Eastern tourists in
stiff city clothes.

. .
.

About four in the afternoon one feels that electric something in the air which means that big things are coming.
What comes first is a little thing — the small Fire-god,
Shulawitsi, deputy to the Sun-god. He crosses the newly
built causeway, his nude body painted black and spotted
with red, yellow, blue, and white, the sun colors. His head
is hidden under a close-fitting helmet of the same effect,
and he wears enough jewelry, one would think, to beat his
bare body sore as he dances. A fawnskin filled with seeds
hangs from a strap over his shoulder, and he carries his
smoldering cedar brand. He is attended only by his ceremonial father, dignified in white cotton shirt and trousers,
a white deerskin wrap, and moccasins. This man carries a
basket of prayer-plumes. The two visit every ceremonial
house, and in each the boy mounts a ladder and leaves in
a box nailed to the beam two prayer-plumes, which typify
the original man and woman. They finally stop in the Sayatasha house.

Meanwhile a distant bony rattle is heard, and the Council of the Gods enters the village from the south. Many
Zuñis wait to greet them, standing reverently in line as

the dancers approach and sprinkling each one with sacred meal from the bag hidden under his blanket. First comes Sayatasha, the Rain-god of the North. He is draped in white buckskin, weighted with jewelry of turquoise, shell, and coral, and his boot moccasins are beaded and painted red and blue. His mask of black and white stripes has a long horn of vivid turquoise-blue on the right side and shining black goat's hair atop. He carries a bow and arrow in one hand, and in the other a bunch of deer-bones, which he shakes sharply at every step of his measured advance. Hu-tu-tu follows, the Rain-god of the South, in a similar costume, except that his mask has no horn. They are attended by two Yamukato, warriors of the East and West, and two whippers. The Yamukato's masks are small turquoise hoods, given a silly expression by round holes for nose and mouth. The whippers, armed with their yucca rods, may represent any two of the six directions, but usually they are Zenith, in a mask of many colors, and Nadir, in black. They are alert to punish not only dancers who fail to observe the rules, but anyone who drops to sleep watching the dancing.

This party makes the same round the Fire-god has made. In front of each house Sayatasha and Hu-tu-tu make elaborate passes at each other, shaking their bunches of bones and crying: " Hu-tu-tu," as they do a queer stamping dance. Finally they enter the Sayatasha house, through a hatchway in the roof, and are greeted by the householder and his family, who sprinkle them with sacred meal. The ceremony within takes place before a newly built altar and consists in marking each wall, the ceiling, and the floor with meal in recognition of the six cardinal points. A long litany is intoned by members of the fraternity, the Fire-god places food for the gods, and finally all may eat.

Thus the Council of the Gods comes annually to Zuñi and is received with the reverence due those in whom the divine is actually present.

We call these figures gods probably because Matilda Stevenson did so when she first wrote of them in 1879, but my informant, a very intelligent and well-educated Indian woman, refuses the title absolutely.

"They are not gods," said she; "that word is wrong. The Zuñis have no gods; they are Ko-Ko."

"Just so," said I, expectant pencil poised, "and what is the English word for Ko-Ko?"

"There is no English word for Ko-Ko. I do not know. It is something different. I cannot tell you how it is to the Zuñi, but they are not gods."

So there it is, as inexplicable as everything Indian must always be to the white man. They are not gods; they are Ko-Ko, and for Ko-Ko there is no English word, and presumably no English idea. It seems likely, from many similar conversations and a sincere effort to get the Indian point of view, that the Indian has no anthropomorphic gods. Yet such creatures as these of the Zuñis impersonate something divine: possibly merely an aspect of the great hidden spirit, which in one manifestation is so brilliant that the sun is a shield to hide it.

So these spirits who bring rain from all the directions are not, after all, gods; but they are greeted with rever-

SHALAKO

*Photograph by the Museum of New Mexico*

[M. WRIGHT GILL]

ence because they represent the divine, and we call them gods because we have no word and no exact idea which are better.

. .

As the Council of the Gods disappears, interest is transferred to the Middle of the World, where the Shalako will enter. By this time it is sunset, and Corn Mountain glows like an opal, reflecting the brilliance of the west. The drab pile of rocks which marks the world center is filled with prayer-plumes, and the ground before it is white with scattered meal. White people have lined up their cars behind the barbed-wire fence, and hundreds of Indians filter slowly in among them, blanketed against the cold, eager to see how well this year's Shalako will perform their difficult dance. Guards hold all these spectators back from the field, keeping it clear for the Shalako and their attendants.

In a breathless moment of the swift winter dusk the Shalako appear. They come into sight round the shoulder of a hill, looming, as it were, on the far side of that deep impassable gulf which forever separates the mind of the Indian from the mind of the white. The six magnificent figures tower above their attendants; the eagle-feathers of their fantastic head-dresses raying like the sun, their flat turquoise faces and upper bodies swaying, their feet looking incredibly tiny under the hoop skirts of the double Hopi kirtles. They are about nine feet high, the tallest masks recorded, with the exception of a sixteen-foot feathered spire worn by a savage masker of New Guinea. The

turquoise face is matched by a breast piece, and the white
and blue are accentuated by a ruff of shining raven's feathers and by long, black hair. The mask is carried on a long
pole hidden under the draperies and steadied by a man
who also manipulates strings which roll the great bulging
eyes and clack the wooden beak as the figure moves. Each
Shalako is attended by two: his manager, wrapped in a
blanket, and the man who will relieve him. The task of
dancing with the heavy superstructure is so great that no
one man could stand it; even with two it is a test of endurance and skill which the whole village watches intently.
The Shalako dancers wear only a black-velvet jacket, a
close-fitting white buckskin cap, and a string of bells tied
under the bare knee. Only the bells sound as the party
approaches the Middle, where a group of priests wait to
greet them with sacred meal. There the Shalako move
through a brief but intricate ceremony, changing the images
from man to man behind blankets held to conceal them.
This care to screen the actors is due to the fact that children
do not know that these are not really the gods, and that their
faith must be preserved until they are initiated.

Here one first sees the smooth running motion typical of
the Shalako. A mis-step and especially a fall would indicate that the dancer had not been true to his vows, and
the whipper would be called upon — a contingency not
within the memory of man, for it is a point of great pride
to balance the mask adroitly and never to miss a step.
Usually the running is perfect, the graceful figure swaying
over the tiny feet, the beak clacking, queer cries between
and finally the daring swoop as the man bends his knees

and the Shalako precariously dips and rights itself. When each dancer has performed his part, the party moves to a sandy stretch by the river, which is sacred as the last resting-place of the Zuñis before they found the Middle. Finally, about dark, the Shalako cross the causeway, carefully steered by their attendants, and each one enters the house which has been prepared for him. Within, there is a ceremony similar to the greeting of the Sayatasha, the principal point being the announcement of the god that he is present, and that in return for his entertainment he will bring plenty of seeds for the ensuing year.

A deep student of comparative religions watched this ceremony intently, following the Shalako and their attendants as they retraced the wanderings of the Zuñis from the center of the earth to the resting-place on the river and finally into the modern village, where the great feathered heads bent to enter the house-doors. He saw the high seriousness of the people following, the sometimes almost despairing efforts of the guards to prevent intrusive whites from profaning the event; and finally, as the last great figure disappeared into the house, he said:

" No wonder missionaries have had no luck in converting these people to Christianity. It will never be done. The essential mental rhythm of the two races is too far apart. You could imagine reducing that Shalako figure two feet or even four; you could not possibly turn it into Christ on the cross."

∵

Dancing lasts all night in all the houses, and many people go from house to house. In the early evening the Koyemshi house begins to fill with spectators. A group of men sits beside the altar, chanting to the accompaniment of a wooden flute and a pottery drum. The Mudheads are out, to visit the other ceremonial houses, where they perform sacred rites, varied by the monkey-shines and jokes which always bring laughter from Navajos and Zuñis. They enter their own house, all solemnity again, and are greeted by the householder, who leads each man to his place, and seats him. Here too the ceremony of the six directions is performed, and then the Mudhead masks are taken off, the deerskin pouches are hung against the wall, and everybody settles for a ceremonial smoke. Each Koyemshi is faced by a man, some sitting on chairs, some on upturned boxes, one I saw on a piano-stool, and one on the top-box of an old-fashioned sewing-machine. These men remove their shoes, and after the smoke they begin the long prayer, which lasts a couple of hours.

In every house similar praying is going on: a low, sing-song chanting of men who sit with bowed heads praying unceasingly for hours. Meanwhile the rooms fill with visitors, who enter quietly, paying no attention to the praying. Every ceremonial chamber has large window openings into adjoining rooms where favored spectators sit, dressed in their gaudiest, like the *élite* in opera boxes. Others occupy chairs in the dancing-room, which is packed so close that only a narrow lane is left for the dancers. Zuñis occupy the chairs, mostly bright-shawled women carrying babies. The rest of the space is jammed with unwashed Navajos, who sit or stand stolidly all night — the men smoking, the women nursing babies — moving only when food is brought by Zuñi girls and placed on the floor in bowls and baskets. Then the Navajos hitch along the floor, to break off great hunks of bread and to dip their fingers into the bowls of steaming stew. All guests are welcome to eat as much as they wish, and Navajos proverbially wish to eat a great deal.

Packed in among these people, one is reminded of the Zuñi legend that when their ancestors came from the underworld, they were protected by such a strong smell that no enemies could prevail against them. Nowadays only the most intrepid white, or one well protected by smelling-salts, can bear it long. Generally white visitors drift in and out; in when the cold without seems unbearable, out when the thickness of the indoor air forces them to face the cold again. A few young Indians also drift in and out, visitors from the other pueblos, and Zuñi youths muffled to the eyes in black blankets; but aside from this movement near the doors, the audience sits all night, quiet and attentive. By midnight many of the restless whites have left and deterioration has begun to attack those who remain. Ladies' city hats are riding at queer angles, figures which started alert and trim have settled awkwardly among the aborigines, men in proper clothes and spats are huddled into the welcome warmth of borrowed blankets.

About midnight the dancing begins in earnest. As an endurance test it is wonderful; each dancer takes about four times as many steps a minute as a Marathon runner and keeps it up much longer. Rest intervals are short. In the

Shalako houses the men alternate, yet the dancing is so difficult, with the heavy swaying superstructure to manage, that dancers have been known to fall under it, to be carried out, rubbed into strength, and returned. Nobody really gives up. The dancing is beautiful in the precision and grace of the steps, the striking costumes, the effect of high seriousness. Forgetting the men under the costumes and remembering only the gods, one is enthralled with the impressive gorgeousness of the scene, in spite of painful incongruities everywhere. Men in bright-blue trousers, silk shirts, and thick-toed collegiate shoes wait solemnly on the altars, the rooms are lit by the hideous glare of gasoline lamps, children snuffle, men spit, the odors are terribly thick. Yet when the Shalako rises and clacks his beak, when the chanting grows stronger and the great feathered head of the god moves with smooth stateliness the length of the room and gives its clear staccato call as the figure dips and sways — even the most cynical white man must feel that the god is there.

In the Sayatasha house the dancing is most varied. Sayatasha and Hu-tu-tu dance together, the East and West join them, Zenith and Nadir flash in and out, and always the little Fire-god strains his tiny body in the endless stamping of the dance. When the chanting stops and there is a moment's rest, he may droop with fatigue, but as soon as the music begins again, he snaps into vigor and pounds his blackened feet on the earthen floor as though nothing could weary him.

The wildest dancing is in the Koyemshi house. Relieved of their masks and moccasins, the Mudheads dance with their deerskin pouches bouncing against them, their bodies glistening with sweat, their feet never faltering in the many changes of rhythm, their faces grinning whenever the song calls for a certain yell of triumph or defiance. In their hands they now carry feathered wands, one blue for the Sun Father, the other yellow for the Moon Mother.

Dancing lasts until dawn. White people have nearly all disappeared before that time, and those who remain are facing complete disintegration, all the symbols of civilization having been abandoned. With faces ashen with weariness and with staring eyes, they hold on only by the force of a determination to see the thing through. Navajos sit imperturbably. Zuñis never move. About dawn a group usually appears to do a Yebetchai, presenting the Navajo dance in honor or derision of the Navajo visitors; it is hard to say which. Every detail of costume is correct, and Navajos say that the Zuñis perform it better than they do.

At dawn the dancers are sprinkled again with sacred meal by all in the house, final prayers are chanted, and the doors are closed so the dancers may rest and eat. Nothing more may be seen until the going-out of the gods, about noon. The final ceremony is on the sandy stretch south of the causeway, where holes have been dug, six at each end of the runway. First the Council of the Gods comes, headed by the Fire-god. Seen under the brilliant midday sun, the figures are even more gorgeous than at night. Each one places prayer-plumes in the holes, and then they leave the village, passing long lines of Zuñis, who scatter meal on them. All during this ceremony Zenith and Nadir prance by the river, and the Shalako have been steered across the causeway and seated on blankets south of the dance field.

When the Council of the Gods is gone, the Shalako rise for their final and most difficult race. They also deposit prayer-plumes in the holes, moving always with their peculiar running swooping motion, bells jingling, beaks clacking, voices calling, and all the people standing reverently with their meal ready. This is the final prayer for rain to fructify the earth and to fill all the watercourses, wells, and springs. It shows also how the Shalako, couriers of the gods, run back and forth all the year carrying messages, bringing moisture wherever it is needed. Finally the last plume is planted and the Shalako go, every boarding-school girl in high-heeled shoes, every mechanically trained youth standing as respectfully as the oldest blanketed Zuñi. At last Zenith and Nadir cease their prancing and go too. Nobody is irreverent enough to follow. The gods are gone. It is ended.

At this point most of the visitors leave, both whites and Navajos, and yet the days following are filled with fine dancing and most impressive ceremony.

### THE LEAVING OF THE GODS

FOR FOUR DAYS AFTER THE DEPARTURE OF THE SHALAKO, there is dancing every night and on the last two days. The night dancing is in the Shalako houses and the day-time ceremonies in the Sacred Plaza. The Mudheads remain in their house and dance as before, only more vigorously, if anything. In their house the altar stands, but in the other houses the altars are removed and most of the decorations taken down. More chairs have been placed for spectators. Dance groups are small the first night, but they increase in numbers until those consisting of three men on the first night may contain twenty on the last. This is because during these days every man in the village must dance. Every night the dance is the same, but the men are different. Each group has masks, but often they do not appear masked until the last night.

The first group are Bears. When they wear no masks, their hair hangs long, a floating orange feather over the right ear, a white one over the left, and in the back a couple of eagle-feathers. They wear the usual dance garments and jewelry and carry a yucca wand. Every dancer in this and every group wears a yucca fillet around the head. There is no chorus, the dancers singing. Their masks, when they appear, are enough to frighten any unsuspecting observer. The top and back are of bearskin, and attached to the crown is a real duck, his head sticking rearward, the rest of him consisting only of feathers assembled from many birds. The face of the mask has an open mouth with terrible teeth such as Red Riding-hood knew, a long beard of black or gray, depending probably upon the complexion of the family horse, and a long, red leather tongue. One man may wear moccasins of bearskin or bearskin mittens on which the claws have been retained. Such a figure may dance alone, soloing up and down with angular gestures of fright or rage, leering with his hideous mask and swooping and turning until his buckskin skirt stands out like a ballet girl's. There are two groups of Bears, one dancing with no accompaniment, the other accompanied by the beating of a stick on a large roll of sheeting, which must in its day have been a roll of buckskin.

The second group is " mixed ": dancers who all wear the usual kirtle and moccasins, but whose head-gear are masks from many dances. One sees the woman figure from the summer Rain-dance, masks copied from the Rio Grande pueblos, Navajo and Hopi masks, and many of Zuñi. One group of twenty men may have twenty different masks, all weird in conception, but beautiful in color and in workmanship. In this and all the dances the song is the same every year, we are told, but the words are new.

Asked who makes the new words, a Zuñi woman said: " Well, a man going for wood might think of a new song, and then his group would sing that."

Often the audience laughs heartily, as though the man going for wood had thought of a good one. Every dance lasts the length of the song, though if anyone living in the house, or anyone of importance, asks for an encore, it is given without question and at the turn of the hand of the leader. These leaders are men of the fraternities, and each carries his *mili* and bowl of sacred meal. His dress may be anything — even bright-blue trousers, thick-toed tan shoes, and striped silk shirt — but his manner is utterly solemn. He enters first sprinkling meal from his bowl, which should, of course, be the ancient ceremonial vessel. Actually it may be a pressed-glass compote or a blue china pitcher. As a dance group enters, it is met by the headman of the fraternity, who sprinkles meal in a line and retires. The leader stands facing his dancers and gives the word for starting and for stopping. At the end they are again escorted out. Often before one group finishes, another will be heard outside, stamping with the cold and uttering the raucous bird or animal cries indicated by their masks. Sometimes as the night wears on and the groups are larger, two groups may dance at once in a house, while another champs impatiently outside. Every group dances in every house, even the Mudheads who come led by a woman as well as a man.

In their own house on the last night the Mudheads may perform magic, such as making a small bowl disappear and reappear somewhere else. It is very clever sleight-of-hand.

An interesting group is that of the Tadpoles, who come from the Sacred Lake bearing tall poles which look like bamboo, but which the people call cane. This group wear close-fitting masks, painted with a many-colored butterfly on a black ground behind, and turquoise-blue in front. Bright-yellow spines stick out where the ears and mouth should be, and over the brow is a yellow lily made of feathers. They dance in a line facing the wall, each man holding his tall pole, which has a feather at the top, and they turn only for an occasional flashing view of the turquoise face and yellow lily. Often small boys appear in this group.

Late on the third afternoon and again on the fourth the dancers appear for an hour or so in the Sacred Plaza. Both times Mudheads come first, standing about, uttering their queer crowing comments, some of which cause mirth, others not. When the dancers come, each group is met by a Mudhead and escorted to position. When two or three

groups happen to dance at the same time, the effect is bewildering to a white eye and ear, but apparently not in the
least disturbing to the dancers, who chant and stamp and
dip and turn, each in his own rhythm without reference
to the beat of his neighbor's time. The last night, dancing
continues until dawn, but about eleven o'clock it is made
clear that women and outsiders will be graciously allowed
to depart. This night the Mudheads have their last meal
until the very end of the performance, sometimes as much
as forty-eight hours later.

.·.

On the fifth morning the Koyemshi are paid off for their
appearances in every ceremony of the whole year. By nine
o'clock they appear in the Sacred Plaza bearing their big
rolls of sheeting. An intricate ceremony is performed, in
which sacred meal is scattered over their hideous bent
heads, priests climb solemnly in and out of the kiva, and
slowly the people gather on the roofs. After this preliminary ceremony the Mudheads go out, each to the house of
his maternal aunt, where his head is ceremonially shampooed and where he chants the appointed prayers. Meanwhile the plaza has filled until its roofs are gay with color,
its doors and windows spilling babies, its one narrow entrance jammed.

Finally the Mudheads return, each one bent under a
load of food stacked in a stiff sheep's carcass, which he
holds by a couple of legs over his shoulders, the other legs
being upheld by followers. Those carcasses are filled with

every sort of thing: bread, package goods from the stores, apples and popcorn in strings, yards of calico, even pink silk underwear trimmed with lace. Following each Mud-head come his clan people in a long procession, the men bent under more dead sheep and sacks of flour, the women bearing bowls and baskets of food on their heads. Each sheep is strung to the beams, where it hangs like a fantastic horn of plenty, spilling apples and packages and cloth while the rest of the food is piled on the ground against the wall.

At the point of greatest activity the scene is indescrib-able: smoothly gliding groups of men and women bring-ing gifts; busy groups stringing and piling the offerings; women kneeling beside soft piles of yellow, blue, and white corn-meal and scooping it into sacks; priests moving here and there; and all the people interestedly attentive, but never noisy. There is never a sense of confusion. Everything is done in order with quiet voices, deft handling, unhurried movement, until the whole plaza is filled with the ten great piles. Meanwhile the Mudheads stand, wrapped in their Navajo blankets, their ugly heads demurely bent, their arms filled with the feathered corn they have collected, looking like nothing so much as fantastic travesties of brides, and watching this accumulation of wealth.

During the morning an impressive figure appears from the kiva. His hair is brushed forward into a stiff horn over the brow, heavy white lines are painted across his eyes and mouth, and he is wrapped in a heavy blanket, his bare arms protruding. There are feathers tied to his wrists and knees, and bunches of feathers in each hand. This is a member of

the Galaxy Fraternity. Climbing solemnly down the ladder,
he crosses the plaza, apparently unseen by anyone, and
goes out by the narrow passage; only the shrill whistle
held between his teeth is heard as he disappears. Watching
from the roof, one can see that he goes to the river and
plants prayer-plumes. He returns, still unnoticed, and with
the stately tread of a Chinese mandarin, mounts the ladder again and disappears into the kiva.

When the offerings are all arranged, the people withdraw and leave the Koyemshi, still fasting, guarding the
huge tantalizing piles of food, which they must not touch.
Shadows — sun — finally dance groups. The dance groups
enter for their final appearance, and again the dancing is
bewildering in its varied figures and rhythms. It ends with
the dismissal of the dancers by the appropriate priests, who
make the final prayers, take from each dancer the ceremonial objects of the fraternity, and retire to the kiva.
Finally each dance group makes a pilgrimage to the river,
there to plant prayer-plumes before disappearing for the
last time. Only the Mudheads remain in the plaza, where
they must stay all day, guarding their gifts, and neither
eating nor drinking until the end of the day, which may
be very near the next morning.

At sunset the final act of the long drama occurs. Boys
who personate the corn-maidens go out to the river, carrying watermelons and many seeds as emblems of plenty.
On the river-bank they await the racing of a group of real
girls and then take their places in line according to the
rank of the racers, each boy taking the rank the girl of his
clan has won for him. In this order they return to the

Sacred Plaza to be greeted by the leader of the Galaxy Fraternity. This group, entering when the sunset light is most lovely, is one of the most beautiful sights of all the Zuñi ceremonies. Each young man is dressed like the virgin of the earlier dancing, all in white, with floating wavy hair, brilliant moccasins, and masses of jewelry. They are attended by the Director General of the Gods, who now makes his first appearance. His general costume is like that of Sayatasha, white buckskin wrap, dance moccasins, and mask. His mask, however, is turquoise-blue, with two large flat ears, black top, yellow feathers, and a boa of fur. The general effect of this group is white with daring dashes of turquoise-blue and black. They perform serious rites in the plaza and finally disappear into the kiva, received at the top of the ladder by the Galaxy priest, who greets them with the shrill note of the whistle held between his teeth. The rest of the ceremonies are secret.

Late into the night the Mudheads wait, but finally they are given permission to gather up their goods and depart to their house, where at last they may break their long fast.

This ends the Zuñi ceremonial year and brings them again to the fast with which the winter solstice must be ushered in.

WALPI                                    [ANDREW DASBURG]

# IV: The Hopis

ONE SUNNY SUMMER MORNING WE STROLLED THE LENGTH
of the First Mesa in Hopiland. The few people we met responded to greetings with quick flashing smiles and friendly
words, usually in the musical minor notes of their native
Tusayan. Most Hopis are short, with broad faces, and they
move with a queer effect of stillness. The men wore overalls and shirts whose original brilliance the fierce Arizona
sun had faded to the soft tones of mesa and desert. They
wore moccasins or store shoes, but the women padded over
the rocks barefooted. Their broad hips and bosoms were
confined in the old-time squaw dresses, or blouses and full
skirts of gingham, and their hair hung in knotted queues
over the shoulders. An occasional boarding-school girl
came along in American dress of cotton or cheap silk.
These girls spoke to us in English, either curtly or with
hidden resentment. Only the older women murmured the
pretty Hopi " Lo-lo-mai " as they fingered a white woman's
Indian jewelry or offered pottery for sale.

The houses were cool, dark, and quiet within. In one
doorway I saw an old man, still unhampered by the trousers of civilization, carving a Katchina doll while he

115

chanted an ancient song. A naked baby played near him.
Small children run quite naked, even up to the age of ten,
playing in the sand or making shining bronze images of
themselves as they whoop and splash round some stagnant
pool left by the last rain.

In another house we saw the supine body of a man lying
on the floor, as blissfully relaxed as a child. Working
hours in Hopiland are from dawn until noon heat, and
from late afternoon until dark. All summer the men are
forever busy in the tiny fields, which are terraced into the
rocky mesa-side to catch any underground flow of water,
and which follow every hidden stream in waving patches of
brilliant green far out on to the arid plain. For centuries
they have forced a living from those deserts with no weap-
ons more powerful than sharp sticks and the invincible
human spirit which is born of need, and of faith. So every
year they bring to maturity enough dwarf corn, round pale
watermelons, beans, and peaches the size of walnuts to
keep alive.

Looking out across the desert, I sensed the desperate
struggle which these people must make for life. No part
of the whole unconquerable southwest is more inhospitable
than this land of the Hopis. It is strangely beautiful, but
it supports only the occasional scrub growth and sparse
grass on which both Navajos and Hopis graze their sheep.
For the Hopi reservation is about five hundred square miles
in the midst of the Navajo reservation, a sharp reminder
even in these peaceful days, of how the gentler people were
driven by their enemies.

The Hopi villages cling to three rocky mesas, where

these gentle people took refuge from their foes in a pitiful huddle of desperation. The entire Hopi population is less than two thousand, most of whom still live on three mesas in nine villages, and in Moencopi, which makes the tenth. Americans first called the Hopis Mokis, a Navajo word meaning dead. Naturally they resented that; they prefer their own name for their country and their musical speech, which is Tusayan.

The finest pottery is made on the First Mesa, tall honey-colored vases and squat bowls decorated in dull red and brown-black. We looked into one house where a group of chattering women sat on the floor molding or painting pottery. An old woman knelt, bending over the grinding-stones set in the dirt floor. The house was scantily furnished, and swept clean, but smelly with that persistent unsanitary smell so typical of Hopi houses. The American influence had extended to one screened window, but the door stood hospitably open to swarms of flies, buzzing the fat contented buzz of the well-fed. One of the women cordially invited us to come in, and we sat on the floor watching the work. Food was simmering in the corner fire-place. Bunches of herbs and Katchina dolls hung from the smoky rafters, and depending from a pole were a few ceremonial garments. Hopi men are the weavers. During the winter they weave cloth of white cotton and wool and decorate it with free-hand embroidery in red and green and black, the colors of sun and growth and rain. A few families still have bits of prehistoric weaving, made when rabbit-skins were twisted into soft woolly robes with thongs of buckskin.

The First Mesa is a long, narrow peninsula of rock,

dropping off sheerly to the desert. It is as though the world ended there, as though the Hopis were the only people in the world, with the exception of the long-legged Navajos who come in on ponies for every feast. Looking westward, one sees clearly the Second Mesa, which curves in a lovely crescent from Mishongnovi, clinging to its perch above Corn Rocks, to Chimopovi on its western tip. In Shipaulavi, on the highest tier, they weave the largest coiled baskets, sometimes as tall as Ali Baba's jars. These villages are the least touched by any modernizing influence. Incredibly dirty, they still have great charm; Mishongnovi and Shipaulavi seeming to grow out of the rocks, and Chimopovi dusty white on its dusty plain. In Chimopovi one day I saw a burro, dusty white like the houses and the plaza, drooping half asleep; three naked little boys scuffling through the sand; and an old weaver, his only garment a dusty white shirt, his skinny legs dusty from sitting on the floor, the oldest type of spindle in his hand. Chimopovi might have looked like that on a hot July day three hundred years ago.

From First Mesa one can hardly see the Third, but it is there: abandoned Oraibi, which died when its people moved to Hotevilla, on the other end of the mesa. Later a group split off from Hotevilla, where the old men tried to stand out against government schools and missionaries, and founded the village of Bacavi, most modern of all, with a few tin roofs, a store, and no terraced houses at all.

Our stroll brought us to Walpi, which perches on the western point of First Mesa where the peninsula is so narrow that there is room for only two solid rows of terraced houses. They step down to the south, where the kivas are built into the very walls of the cliff, their roofs only a few steps higher than the lane, their ladder-poles reaching irregularly above them, the taller one for the man, the shorter for the woman. The snake kiva crowds into the plaza about half-way the length of the village, where the hour-glass-shaped Snake Rock stands. In a crevice of this tall bowlder is a shrine where one always sees prayer-plumes and freshly scattered meal, and in front of it they dance the Snake-dance.

Like other Pueblo peoples, the Hopis are divided into fraternities, which control all ceremonial life. The priesthoods seem to be hereditary in the family which carries the clan name and whose legendary ancestor brought the fetishes and altar paraphernalia. Their government is less democratic than that of the Rio Grande peoples. Each village has a hereditary chief. There is no council and no appeal from the decisions of the despot; hence the many splits resulting in the settlement of new villages under new chiefs. Each village is independent, recognizing relationship with the others, but no union, either for government or for ceremony.

Now rapid changes are coming about under the American influence. At the foot of every mesa is a group of government buildings: a school, houses for employees, a laundry in which an effort is made to clean up the Hopis. Children wear government-issue clothes of gingham and blue jean, and heavy shoes; and in the entrance to the school-building are rows of tooth-brushes hanging on nails labeled: "Geraldine," "Percy," "Hortense," and "Clyde." At First and Third mesas the Percys, Hortenses, and Clydes have moved down from their ancestral homes and built houses on the American pattern, in which they live more or less on the American plan. Here are found the people dressed in store clothes, cooking on stoves, listening to Victrolas, otherwise conforming to what they have been taught. The missionaries of various Christian faiths have much to do with these changes, and even more deep-seated ones. Several important ceremonies have been abandoned because of the conversion to a Christian faith of the one man who could carry them on. Probably a few more generations will see the abandonment of the beautiful villages and the old beliefs, and the submergence of the distinctive Hopi in such typical American homes and lives as these.

## KATCHINAS

LIKE ALL PRIMITIVE PEOPLES, HOPIS PERSONIFY EVERY-thing. Not only men and animals, but plants, stones, mountains, and storms, astral bodies, clouds, sky, and underground have spirits which may be evil or beneficent toward human beings, and which may be propitiated or defeated by certain prescribed acts. These spirits are personified as Katchinas, who come into our modern world trailing the tatters of everything historical or legendary in the Hopi past. Their pictures are found carved on stones in various parts of Arizona; their prototypes are found in Zuñi and the Rio Grande pueblos; they carry implements like the most ancient ones found in ruins; they chant in languages older than anyone knows; and their costumes, though they are prescribed by ancient ritual, still show the effects of the modern store, for a felt hat may be the basis of the god's head-dress, and the priest who serves the underground altar often appears in overalls.

Katchina may be the man who dances in a mask; the spirit which the man represents; or a doll, carved of cottonwood and painted, dressed, and feathered exactly like the dancer. These dolls are seen everywhere in Hopiland: children carry them about in play, they stand on the altars.

The Katchina, meaning the spirit, is similar in idea to the Zuñi Ko-Ko. It is not a god; it is merely one manifestation of the great all-powerful being, which is infinitely higher and greater, but which may somehow be reached through appeals to these Katchinas. Prayers are primarily, of course, for blessings which are of advantage to the whole group: rain and sun, plentiful growth, many children. The Hopis are still in the cultural stage of group consciousness, and the government schools, trying to make twentieth-century Americans of them, find themselves up against this enormous gap between the primitive and the civilized mind. The Hopi, dirty at home, dirty in his person, careless of everything which the white man considers of greatest importance, is deeply concerned about all the things of tribal significance. All ceremonial objects are exquisitely made, all ceremonies are conducted with truly prayerful attention to detail.

When the Katchina appears as a masked man, it is in the dramatization of a myth or a legend. Often much of the significance has been lost, and often the ceremonies, borrowed from other peoples, are conducted in a foreign language which even the participants do not understand.

The ceremonies may vary from year to year, only certain masks being constant, and the appearance of others depending upon the whim of the actors or upon hidden causes. The masks, less beautiful than those of Zuñi, are even more numerous. Dr. Fewkes, who spent years among the Hopis, studying their ceremonies, collected, in 1900, more than two hundred pictures of Katchinas drawn by Hopi artists. Most of these probably appear in the dances in the course of several years; some of them appear annually.

Before a Katchina dance very important business is the refreshing and repainting of the masks, which fit closely over the head, completely hiding it, and are finished at the neck with a ruff of feathers, fur, or spruce. The face may represent a bird, a beast, a monster, or a man, or every combination of all these, with many variations in the use of color and the misuse of feature. The rest of the costume is usually the white ceremonial kirtle and sash, with turtle-shell rattle under the knee, moccasins, and jewelry. The man often carries some object especially associated with the being he represents: bow and arrows, a yucca whip, pine, or feathers. Women figures, Katchinamana, are represented by men. They always wear wigs of long hair dressed in the flat swirls over the ears which typify virginity and which are usually called squash blossoms.

The Katchina dances, generally thought to have been introduced from the eastern pueblos, cause a queer division in the Hopi calendar. The Katchinas come between late December and February. A few appear in Soyaluna, a ceremony of the winter solstice, but the " coming-in " is usually considered the Bean-planting dance in late January or February. From then on there is a continuous succession of masked dances until July, when, with the Niman Katchina, the " gods go out," returning to their home near San Francisco Peaks. After that the more ancient ceremonies of the Hopis are given: the Snake-dance, the Flute Ceremony, and others which have no masks.

This division in the ceremonial calendar is further emphasized by the fact that every summer ceremony has a winter counterpart. Fewkes suggests a belief that the gods who preside over the summer retire underground in winter and may be reached there. So the fraternities in charge of summer dances always meet in mid winter for ceremonial smoking and the planting of prayer-plumes. In the case of the Niman Katchina, a runner goes every December to a certain shrine on San Francisco Peaks, where he scatters meal and plants plumes to be brought back at Niman time, in July, by another runner. The winter run is no easy task, for the runner has to cover about a hundred miles in two days across cold and snowy country; yet the summer man has always found the plumes properly planted there under the snow peaks.

Clowns appear in both masked and unmasked ceremonies. Sometimes they resemble the Zuñi Mudheads and sometimes the Koshare of the Rio Grande pueblos. They are notable in both cases for gluttony, obscenity, and an absolute license in their fun-making, which often makes for real wit, and sometimes for less desirable results, as in all fun-making.

# V: Hopi Dances

THE REAL RETURN OF THE KATCHINAS IS CELEBRATED IN Powamu, the Bean-Planting Ceremony: an elaborate ceremony, lasting eight days. On the first day, masks are brought to the kiva and renovated. Flat color is applied from the mouth, as a Chinaman sprinkles clothes; design is painted with a yucca brush. On the first day, also, messengers visit all the kivas and announce the ceremony quietly. This variation from the usual Hopi custom of making announcements at the top of the lungs is due to the convention that the names of the Katchinas must not be spoken aloud. The priests, in the kivas, are chanting the myth on which the rites are based. They emerge only to visit every home in which there is a *tiponi*, feathered wands which are owned by certain priests, or by women through whom the legendary family descends.

During these days the clowns are much in evidence. They are like the Zuñi Mudheads, with their clay-daubed bodies and their heads hidden in knobby sacks. They dash about, calling jokes, many of which are said to be in Zuñi, trip each other up, and cause laughter wherever they go. A part of their play is concerned with a basket plaque piled high with wooden cones. They challenge the girls to lift the plaque without spilling the cones, a feat none of them can accomplish. Finally a youth does it; the clowns fall over as though dead from the shock, and must be revived by methods even more shocking to the few white people who have seen this rite — probably a sexual pantomime. Dr. Fewkes, always discreet, says that anyone of scientific attainment may learn all — presumably by proving an interest purely scientific. The treasure of the tray turns out to be seeds, which are distributed to the women to plant in the fields and so assure fertility.

On the third day youths bring in baskets of wet sand which they leave near the kiva hatchways. Later, as the actors enter, each man fills a basket or bowl with the sand, carries it into the kiva, and plants his beans in it. From then on, hot fires are kept going, attendants keep the sand constantly wet, and blankets are stretched across the opening so that every kiva becomes a regular hothouse in which the seeds are forced to an unseasonable sprouting.

Late on the fifth night Hahawuctqi, " mother of the terrifying monsters," appears upon the kiva roof and announces in her weird falsetto call that she has arrived and wishes to see the children. An answering voice responds that the children have all gone to bed and urges her to postpone her visit until morning. Thus are the children warned of the presence of the horrible and thrilling beings who bring gifts for good children and punishment for naughty ones. It must fill with trepidation many a little brown Hopi snuggled into blankets and fearfully eager for the coming day.

Yet the monsters and their mother do not emerge until

late afternoon, when they appear in procession. The mother, a man, leading, wears the black dress and a white mantle and leggings. Her mask is a flat black face, with hair in pigtails such as the women wear, feathers raying from the crown, and a fox-skin ruff. She carries a long juniper whip, a whitened dipper, and a flat tray covered with gifts for the children: ears of corn, seeds, and bundles of sticks for little girls, and tiny snares of yucca fiber for little boys. The other woman figure, Soyokmana, is such a terrifying old witch as every people in the world seems to have invented to scare children into virtue. She is dressed like the "mother," but her hair is straggling, her clothes are old and dirty, and she carries a crook in one hand and a knife in the other. The others (Natacka) usually appear in Navajo velvet shirts, belted around slim waists with heavy silver belts, and with white buckskin mantles over the shoulders. They all wear terrifying masks: great snouts, bulging eyes, and horns. Each carries a bow and arrows in his left hand, leaving the right hand free to receive gifts, for this is a begging expedition.

There are three such groups, one for each village. They visit every house in their own village, and every house in the other two villages into which one of their men has married. For in Hopiland the custom still lingers of a man's going to his wife's people. So one meets them everywhere, hooting as they pass along the crooked streets and as the "mother" calls at every door or at the top of every ladder. Her queer cry always brings out women with food or children to be admonished. Children cling to their mothers or to each other, bright black eyes peering bravely over blanket folds, or they stand sturdily to face the fearful being, determinedly not afraid.

During the following two days all sorts of queer happenings take place, all significant for the reception of the great spirits, but unaccountable to whites. Men run naked the length of the mesa, hooting, or lie full length on kiva-tops, making nosing motions at each other, grunting and groaning; they dash in and out of the kivas, naked and painted, feathered and jeweled, dance a few steps, and rush off again. Even Fewkes, the insatiably curious investigator, could not find out what it all meant.

∴

Every fourth year, during Powamu, occurs the initiation of children, which is a whipping administered by the Flogger Katchina (Tunwupkatchina). The ceremony takes place in the late afternoon, when Tunwup enters the village from the west. His mask varies from year to year, but it always has bulging eyes, horns, and a mouth full of red tongue and teeth. His body is painted with stripes or zigzags, and he carries a bundle of yucca for a scourge. Arriving at the plaza, this creature prances up and down its limited length, making no sound except the weird inhuman cries of his kind. Children, both boys and girls, are brought in by their god-parents, stripped, and led up to the monster, who, still prancing, wields his whip vigorously, striking each little bare brown back until the child shrieks with pain and fright. Usually he gives five or six such strokes; sometimes, if a child seems unduly frightened, he merely waves his whip and does not strike at all. Sometimes adults present themselves for the punishment, which is thought to have healing properties. In these cases the beating is apt to be vicious. Sometimes, especially if there are many children of suitable age, there is more than one flogger.

This is the Hopi revelation of " the secret of life ": the knowledge that Katchinas are not really spirits, but men dressed to represent them. It is noticeable that younger children, who have not been flogged, are never permitted to look at the Katchinas when they come begging, though when they dance this care is not observed.

. .

The final act of Powamu, the dancing, takes place in the nine kivas which dot the mesa. Every one has been freshly plastered for the occasion with a thin mud from a sacred spring, and each job of plastering has been signed with the print of the slim hand of the girl who did it.

We were permitted, one year, to enter one of the kivas and witness all the ceremonies of that last night. Our host, stopping on the kiva roof, spoke down the hatchway and was answered in Hopi words. Then we descended the ladder. Leaving the cold star-spangled air, it was like dropping into the very bowels of the earth, where there was a hot thick stench of unwashed people, and where the only light came from a smoky oil-lamp and a smoldering fire. Once inside, everything outside seemed impossible: there could be no crystal freshness of an Arizona night, no biting air that would cleanse the lungs. We were back in a time when people lived underground in a darkness varied only by shifting gleams of a false light, when the only hope was in weird rites designed to reach incredible beings, themselves hampered by ignorance of the real powers.

Then, as we settled on our blankets, nonsensical notions gave way before the sight of familiar things. We sat at the eastern end of the kiva on a slightly raised platform, probably a foot higher than the floor at the fire-place end. A few women were there when we went in, and others drifted in from time to time, muffled in blankets, which they dropped as they sat, showing flat heads and faces with untidy twists of hair falling down their cheeks. Many of them were barefooted even on that cold winter night, and as they loosened their blankets, some of them brought to light perfectly naked babies. Men came down the ladder too, but they usually sat at the ceremonial end of the room, squatting on their haunches near the fire, stooping to pick up coals and light corn-husk cigarettes, exchanging remarks and chuckles with the men already there, busy with the manufacture of corn-husk flowers.

They smoothed the pale gold husks on their knees, tore them into the right shape, and then, dipping twisted yucca fiber into shallow pottery bowls, they applied a light-red paint to one half of each leaf. The work was apparently negligently done, while conversation went on, but the results were beautiful. Soon four petals were ready, and then they were quickly twisted into the shape of a big open flower, like a squash blossom, tied, and laid aside. Without any apparent effort or hurry each man soon had beside him a pile of pale-gold and red blossoms.

Then they began to dress. Lazily they rose from where they sat and, without the slightest embarrassment, removed their shirts, trousers, and shoes, neatly folding their things and laying them in corners. That left their smooth brown bodies exposed, the demands of propriety being satisfied by those modest curtains, front and back, which are the gee-string. Each man then painted his own body, making one leg, one arm, and one half the torso red, and the other one white, the same color scheme as that of the flowers, though the thin wash of white paint over the brown skin gave a different effect. Then each man gave a helping hand to others, painting the backs like the fronts. Chatter and laughter went on all the time. Each man loosened his own hair, and with a grass brush he curried and shook it until it lay in a shining black mane to his waist behind and fluffed out in bobbed puffs over his cheeks. Then he tied three of his flowers to his crown, making a chaplet of the big gay blossoms, most effective against shining black hair. Somewhere in this process white kirtles and sashes were adjusted, turtle-shell rattles, strings of shell and turquoise, and silver-studded baldrics were put on; and those ordinary young men in faded overalls and dirty shirts were suddenly brilliant and beautiful figures, studies in all the possible shades of red and gold and ivory-white.

Then, obeying the hints of the leader, given usually with the slightest bending of the head, they moved into two facing lines, shifted, stamped, rattled their gourds, and swirled into the dance. It was thrilling how quickly that hot underground room was transformed into a chamber of mystery as those gay creatures stepped and turned and

swayed with graceful precision. Shining brown skin slipped
over muscles which were hard but never strained, hands
and feet moved rhythmically, voices chanted one of those
compelling songs so characteristic of the Indian. Then it
seemed that there was real force in that underground
prayer, a real relationship with all the glory of the starry
night outside.

The dance was soon over, and the dancers left, climbing
the ladder into blackness and departing in a dying jingle
of bells. They had gone to visit another kiva, and soon another group entered ours, calling first at the top, and then
dropping down the ladder with rattle of shells and sound
of voices. During the night every kiva group visited every
other kiva — a long succession of different dances and various costumes.

The night wore slowly on. The atmosphere in the kiva
thickened, and we were frequently glad to accept our hosts'
invitation to visit other kivas in order that we might breathe
outside air and save our puny lungs from succumbing to
the fetid reek, which apparently did not affect the Hopis
at all. Going along the mesa on those expeditions, we en-
countered groups of dancers, jingling along under the
stars, voices always musically gay and laughing, kirtles
swishing softly, and bodies smelling of sweat as they
brushed past us on the narrow stony path.

. .

Early the next morning, all too soon after getting to
sleep, we were roused. We lay in a row of bed-rolls on the

floor of a Hopi house in Polacca at the foot of the mesa.
A kitchen stove, a box with a pail on it, a mirror, several
lithographs, a row of Katchina dolls, and a phonograph
were its furnishings. The dawn was just turning from pale
gray to pale rose, and above us on the high point of Walpi
rose a musical cry. It was, we knew, the call of a priest
announcing that the Katchinas were in the village and
would soon appear. Very soon the children in our house
excitedly pointed to one of the Katchinas leaping down the
mesa-side. Against the dun-colored rocks he was a brilliant
figure of turquoise-blue and dull green. As he came closer,
uttering his queer hoots, we picked out the detail of his
costume: a turquoise-blue mask with snakes painted under
the eyes, feathers sticking out of the ears, feathers on top,
a collar of spruce. His body was painted green and yellow,
and his moccasins were brilliant blue. Tousled youngsters
trooped out to meet him, still struggling with sleep, but
alert enough to hold out little brown hands for presents.
He had brought dolls and gay-colored rattles for the girls,
bows and arrows for the boys, and for both the long, pale-
green sprouts of the beans which had been forced out in the
over-heated kivas. All the time the dancer kept his feet
moving in short jerky steps, a little as though to fight the
cold; but we knew that this constant motion and the high
falsetto hoots were to create the illusion of a being of another world. All through the three villages such figures
were moving, and nearly all the morning they were busy
bringing gifts to every child, especially the long, trailing
streamers of pale green which were seen in every house,
in every child's hands.

Later performances were not so pleasant for the children, and very upsetting for white visitors, filled with notions of the lasting effects of terror on the child mind. About noon the procession of monsters again came out of their kiva, the mother leading, six other ogres in animistic masks, and the witch-like creature with crook and bloody knife: Soyok-mana. This group visited every house, hooting their request for food, presenting bean-sprouts, and receiving gifts, which they put into their huge bags. If the food offered was not enough, the Soyok whistled indignantly through her teeth, and the others gave hoots amounting to disgusted groans. Usually the racket worked and more food was forthcoming. At many of the houses Soyok, hideous old witch, used her crook to hook some child around the neck and hold him there, screaming in terror, squirming with horror, and clinging to his mother in an agony terrible to see.

Protests to our host were met with his quiet, gentle Hopi voice: " But that is our way. He has been naughty. His mother asked them to come." Altogether it was too much for the white visitors, and they left the mesa.

There was no dancing during the day. The masks disappeared into the kivas before mid afternoon, and we were told that when the final acts of smoking and the disposal of ceremonial things were properly attended to, there was great feasting. Certainly in every house big pots were stewing up messes in which the bean-sprouts were an important ingredient, that there might be great fertility in the coming spring.

So the Katchinas come in, every year. From that time

HOPI MASKS                    [FRANK APPLEGATE]
(Niman Katchina Dance)

until the " going-out," in July, there are masked ceremonies constantly in all the Hopi villages. White people who have lived there say that there is hardly a week without its ceremony. They differ greatly from year to year; some are dying out, some new ones, so they say, are being brought even now from other peoples. Any and all of the gods may come and disport themselves as they, or their impersonators, please, until the season of the ancient gods comes round again.

## NIMAN KATCHINA:
### THE GOING-AWAY OF THE GODS

WE WOKE IN OUR BORROWED HOPI HOUSE AS DAWN WAS breaking over Keams Canyon, and low-hanging clouds parted to let the sun rise. Indians were coming out of their houses in Polacca and starting up to Walpi, afoot over the trails, and up the road on horses or in wagons. Our car followed them, picking up several walking Hopis until we were well loaded. Everyone wanted a smoke and did not mind mentioning it if we seemed forgetful. Burros moved aside to let us pass, a Navajo couple on two wiry ponies whooped into a gallop and passed us on the rocky up-grade, breaking all the rules of horsemanship.

On the mesa, people were beginning to stir. As we passed along through Hano and Sichomovi, we saw people performing the most intimate details of toilet in the open, no more abashed than the scratching dogs and the chickens ruffling in sand baths. A few women were sweeping out, a few family parties were sitting on the ground around pots of food, breakfasting. The inevitable Hopi smell hung heavy, even in the cool morning air. Blue sky, cloud-streaked, was reflected in the muddy water-holes. Many men and small boys were drifting slowly toward Walpi, and as we reached the narrow bridge, we heard chanting.

Peering over the rocks, we could see the dancers gathered on a flat stretch of sand sheltered by an overhanging rock. They were already dressed in dance kirtles and sashes, fringed brown moccasins, and flaring skirts of piñon boughs. Their bodies were smeared with corn-smut, a sort of dare to the gods to send rain and wash it off. On each torso were interlocking crescents done in white paint, symbols of friendship. The gaudy masks sat in a row on the rocks, waiting and looking curiously human.

Among the men were women figures, whose white buck-skin legs made sturdy pedestals for the black squaw dresses, the red-bordered white blankets, and, finally, the masks which they were adjusting. The women's masks were flat painted faces hidden under red fringe, and parted black hair done in the squash-blossom swirls of virginity. To twenty-three men, there were seven women figures.

As they finished dressing, they chanted; whether in worship or in practice was not clear. A group of men sat on the rocks above, watching; but no women were there, as a Hopi woman is not supposed to look upon a Katchina without his mask. This convention is relaxed only when women come bringing food, women with food being welcome anywhere. Finally every man had adjusted his mask and they started up the trail, moccasined feet falling softly into the prints worn in the rock by many generations.

The Niman Katchina celebrates the going-away of the Katchinas, who are thought to return to their home on San Francisco Peaks. The ceremony is celebrated every year on all three mesas, but it varies greatly, as any Katchina fraternity may present any one of several ceremonies. The one we saw in 1930 was Humis Katchina, a favorite dance for Niman, as Humis is "the one who makes the corn grow high ": a valuable gift in July, when first-fruits are ready to gather. Besides bidding farewell to the gods the ceremony is a grateful recognition of the good which has produced the crops. After its serious rite is over, young people picnic in the fields, gathering the crops and making merry.

As the dancers climbed over the rocks, we saw first the feathers and spires of headed grass which topped the masks. Each mask is in itself a cloud symbol and bears many symbols of cloud and rain and rainbow on its terraced top. At the back of each one a small Katchina doll stood on a carved ear of corn or on another Katchina. Around the neck was a ruff of spruce, a Katchina symbol, and each man carried spruce in one hand, the inevitable rattle in the other. Jingling and talking, they appeared, first the gay-colored masks, then the men, a long line. They stopped a moment at a shrine built of slabs of rock, added their quota of meal to the white scatterings already there, and then moved on across the causeway. In the middle of that narrow passageway lay a long cotton string to which were tied a white and a yellow feather: the traditional trail-marker to lead the gods and future blessings into Walpi. Every dancer's arms were filled with green corn-stalks, and several carried musical instruments: large hollow gourds painted yellow and green, notched sticks to lay across them, and the deer-scapulæ which are the bows for these primitive fiddles.

Two priests in ordinary dress led the group. One carried a feathered stick and a bag of sacred meal, which he scattered before the dancers; the other a corn-cob. One called all the orders, repeated the words of the song, directed the shifting for position, gave the word for the dancing to start. The maskers danced first in the narrow plaza in front of the first house in Walpi. The first movement was simple: rhythmic pounding of the feet in perfect time, as the bodies swung now right, now left, showing front and back views of the weird masks, the swishing skirts. All the time the dancers sang, catching without error the frequent changes of tempo. To and fro they swung, to and fro, following the leaders' chant, intoning the deep droning prayer, curiously muffled under the masks.

Then they stopped and stood at ease while the leaders prepared for the second movement. First they arranged on the ground a row of folded blankets, dirty quilts, whatever they had or whatever women threw down from the housetops. On these the seven women figures knelt, facing the men. In front of each woman was a hollow gourd, and each one wielded the deer-scapula to bring out a hollow squawking, so perfect in rhythm as not to be unpleasant. Chanting, the Katchinas danced to this music, the steps a little more vigorous than in the first figure.

Finally the priests signaled for the end, sprinkled meal to indicate the line of march, and led their troupe to the second plaza. There the figures were repeated in front of the Snake Rock, where for this occasion a small spruce-tree had been planted and decorated with a few floating breath feathers. The priests, as they scattered meal upon the dancers, threw pinches of it also at the tree. The dance was the same. A few more spectators had gathered. A woman, following the priests, quietly threw meal on all the dancers, especially upon the kneeling women figures, whose wigs were becoming well powdered with it. Then the whole party moved to the western plaza, where an interesting ceremony followed the dance.

At the end of the second movement the dancers rested as a procession of about ten men and women approached them from the kiva. Evidently they were priests and priestesses; I wondered if they were the chiefs of all the Katchina clans, coming to bid farewell to the gods. They were all in some sort of ceremonial garb: the women in white mantles, the men bare-legged and either in velvet shirts or in very new ones from the store. Everyone had a breath feather floating from the crown. Two were blind — old men who came gingerly to the top of the ladder, felt with bare feet for the stepping-stones, were handed canes by men following, and got themselves to the edge of the kiva and off the short step to the ground. Then, when they had located the waiting line of dancers, they laid down their sticks, put their hands into their bags of sacred meal, and followed the line in its slow progress round the dancers. All sprinkled meal and murmured prayers. One man carried an ancient water-bowl, from which he flipped drops of water with an eagle-feather. One had a ceremonial pipe, from which he blew smoke, suggestive of clouds. The women, instead of scattering meal, took hold of each dancer's hand and put the meal into it. All during the ceremony and until the priests had returned to the kiva, the dancers stood at relaxed attention. Then, following their director, they turned and filed back to the Snake Rock, where they danced again. So they danced their way back to the first plaza and retired to their dressing-shelter under the rock. Women with food followed them.

This dance was repeated at intervals all day. Once in the late morning the dancers brought gifts: gourd rattles and bows and arrows for the boys, Katchina dolls for the girls. The rattles were painted turquoise-blue, the bows and arrows feathered and well balanced, the dolls perfect in every detail of costume — lovely gifts, such as children anywhere might enjoy. Every dancer had his arms full of these things, and many brought also bowls, baskets, or wash-pans of food. Traditionally these should be the first-fruits from the fields, and they did include small ears of corn, little red-cheeked peaches, melons of various kinds. But in the piles were also hard-boiled eggs, terrifically pink store cakes, iced with coconut, sticky chocolate, and pop-corn balls. Some brought *piki* bread, colored a delicate pink and tied in flat bundles like the pipes of Pan. Every dancer, peering with difficulty through the narrow slits in his mask, offered his gifts. Children came shyly forward, but only when they were sure they were called; there was no pushing or snatching, no effort to get more than was offered.

During the day the audience steadily increased, people following the dancing group or sitting on roofs to watch.

Older women still wear Hopi clothes, black dresses and bright shawls, with their hair falling over their breasts in twists. One woman, who spoke excellent English and had been to school, was dressed as one could hope all Hopi women might be. Her hair, done in the old-time queues, was shining soft instead of dull and stringy. Her skin looked clear, her garments fresh, but entirely in the traditional style. As well-groomed as a white woman, she retained the beauty and distinction of her Hopi dress. Looking at her, I wondered that the usual effects of civilization in Walpi are so curious. Usually, unfortunately, everything Hopi is being supplanted by everything American; yet the underlying ancestral dirt seems untouched.

The beautiful head-dress of the marriageable maid is no more, all the girls having been bobbed in the schools. Katy, a Walpi matron, told me about it, as I sat on her roof above Snake Rock.

"No more we make those squash blossoms," she said. "I wanted my daughter's hair to grow long, but the teacher won't let me. It don't have time to grow after she comes home. Too bad!" Katy sighed, probably thinking of the great day when she was a giggling *débutante*, stepping out for the first time with her hair in squash-blossom swirls, daring the swains.

From where I sat, I could see the modern virgins. They appear now in badly made calico dresses or sleazy silk ready-mades from the stores. Instead of well-fitting moccasins they wear French-heeled slippers of patent leather or imitation reptile-skin. A couple of young Carmens, draped in flowered shawls, sat on roof-edges, dangling silk stockings and high heels and turning giggling away from the boys. The white woman's brand of coquetry is only beginning to supplant the more subtle quiet of the Indian maid. Katy's little daughter and her best friend trotted about wrapped clubbily in one shawl. Other little girls, eight or ten years old, carried babies hanging in shawls. There are no naked children on feast-days now.

The influence of modernity seems to stop, however, with dress. Food is handled in ways incredibly dirty. A woman ladled a steaming mess of corn-meal out of a buried pot with hands which had handled everything else. A mother with a child in her arms absently chewed up a mouthful of food and when it was well predigested, poked it with a dirty finger into the baby's mouth. Women and small girls occupied their fingers, as they watched the dance, with the Hopi woman's fancy-work of picking lice out of the baby's head. The whole village is always redolent of filth, a menace which only an Arizona sun could cope with.

As the day went on, the sun grew hotter, and more and more people gathered until the house-tops were loaded. A man from Winslow brought a traveling salesman out. They stood about for a few minutes in shining straw hats, gray summer suits, and left. A car from Ohio drew up, bearing a load of young people in overalls, high hats, and painful-looking sunburn. No other white people came, this being a little-known dance. Nothing modified that terrific burning sun, though great stationary clouds stood in the quivering blue sky, waiting. A few moved leisurely, making purple shadows across the dun mesas. An emergency landing-field was marked by a sock, which was too hot and too unstirred by any breeze even to flap.

The dancers entered more frequently now, the leaders looking drawn and tired. The dancers must have been approaching exhaustion; yet the dancing was as lively, the chanting as quick as ever. Each time they brought presents, more and more presents, until every child in the three villages must have had piles of them at home. Finally, the children all being burdened, the dancers began making gifts to grown women. A matron sat near me, in black satin, with bobbed hair. She told me that she was Tewa and lived in Polacca. Her English was excellent and we talked. Then she was called to receive a Katchina doll that a masked man held up to her, which she accepted graciously.

By five o'clock the light had changed. Instead of clanging back viciously from a hot sky, it fell softly across the plain and caused the roof-beams to drop cooling shadows along hot walls, and the houses to make curtains of shade in every plaza. A breeze came to raise puffs of dust and to bring a different smell. About six o'clock the dancers made their final appearance in each of the three plazas.

"The brides are out," my Tewa friend whispered to me, and I saw that the crowd was making a quiet shift to the western plaza.

Each Hopi bride of the year, I learned, has been barred from seeing any dance until this Niman Katchina, which she may see, and her attendance is a rite. We reached the upper plaza in time to see them come out: four demure little Hopi girls, looking very young. They all had bobbed hair, but they wore black squaw dresses, wrapped leggings, and the huge pure-white wedding-blanket. Each groom makes this for his bride, spinning and weaving the native cotton and wool; she wears it on certain ceremonial occasions after her wedding, and it finally serves as her shroud. The girls looked tiny in the huge blankets, gentle, shy, rather Japanese. Beside each bride stood her sponsor, an older woman, wrapped in a bright shawl in which bobbed the bride's baby: a bright-eyed little mite in a white store dress with coarse lace. This group stood quietly on the low portal of a house just above the kiva, surrounded by a crowd, but still apart: the honored spectators.

The dancers finished their last figure, the priests and priestesses came out again to sprinkle meal and to remove the turtle-shell rattles. Then the Katchinas departed, leaving the village by the trail which goes down over the rocks to the west. Silently they moved now, a weirdly beautiful procession like a ballet which might by some enchantment have been condemned to wander forever over those gray rocks.

∴

Still the gods were not altogether gone, for the next morning there was a short ceremony at sun-up. It seems to be a ceremony which is always performed at Niman Katchina, no matter what dance may be presented the day before.

Very evidently we saw only half of the rite, the rest of which was hidden in the kiva. First appeared four figures, three of them dressed like the dancers of the day before, with the addition of white mantles. The fourth wore a white shirt, knitted leggings, and the usual kirtle, sash, and fox-skin. He carried a digging-hoe, such as may be seen in the oldest pictographs, and a small water-jar. He also carried a small green bush from which dangled four tiny disks colored to represent the points of the compass and decorated with puffs of down. His mask looked like a flour-sack with holes for eyes and mouth, and a sprig of green on top. This man stood at the north, the others at the other cardinal points.

Then a priest appeared at the kiva hatchway and there followed a complicated business of moving from point to point, throwing meal, pouring water down the hatchway from the bowl. Finally the bush with its disks was handed into the kiva. Then the rest of yesterday's dancers, the priests, and the priestesses all came out of the kiva, silently climbing the ladder and moving in solemn parade around the plaza. The whole ceremony was in utter silence with the exception of the steady droning prayer of the priest who stood at the top of the ladder.

At the end of the prayer the whole procession moved away, following yesterday's path over the rocks, disappearing just as the sun rose. The gods were gone.

## THE SNAKE LEGEND

### *(following J. Walter Fewkes)*

THE SNAKE PEOPLE AT WALPI TELL THIS STORY.

Once a chief's son sat on the edge of the Grand Canyon, wondering where all that water went. He thought that he might be able to help his people if he should follow it; so, on the advice of his father, he built a boat, inclosed like a box, and set off down the river. He had many adventures as he floated on toward the ocean, and finally he came to the home of the Spider Woman, who gave him food and good advice and who finally went along with him, hidden behind his ear.

They met, in turn, a panther, a bear, a wildcat, a gray wolf, and a rattlesnake. Each of these beasts tried to stop the young hero, and each was pacified by the gift of a prayer-stick which the Spider Woman gave him. At last they came to a snake kiva, over which stood the bow standard, just as it stands over the snake kiva nowadays when the priests are praying within.

Inside there were both men and women. The chief gave the young man a pipe, saying: " Smoke, but swallow the smoke." This seemed impossible, but the friendly Spider Woman, still sitting behind the youth's ear, removed the smoke from behind, thus making it possible for him to pass the test. Then the men and women all dressed themselves in snake-skins which hung on the wall, and were at once, miraculously, changed into snakes. The hero was instructed to catch one; and, encouraged by the Spider Woman, he made a set at the youngest and prettiest maiden, who had been changed into a yellow rattler. She was vicious, but the Spider Woman gave him medicine to spit at her, and so he caught her. Immediately she became very meek and pleasant and brought him *piki* bread, melons, and peaches to eat.

This seemed to end the young chief's initiation, but he

still owed his initiation fee of beads. So he and the Spider Woman set off to get it. They went to the house of an ugly old hag, to whom the youth gave prayer-sticks. She then changed herself into a lovely young woman, with whom he spent four happy nights. At the end she gave him a bagful of beads and shells which she said would increase all the way home if he did not open the bag. If he looked, they would all disappear. So the youth returned to the snake kiva, where he wed the snake maid, and after four days set out with her for his home.

Like all legendary heroes, the young man, terribly tempted in the matter of beads, peeped into the bag, which had been steadily growing heavier. The beads, according to the prophecy, disappeared; and that is why — so the Hopis say — they have so few beads now. He observed all the rules regarding his wife, however, and got her home safely; whereupon she bore many little snakes. These baby snakes were not popular with the Hopi children, whom they bit, so the young chief and his wife were forced to move. Thus they came to Walpi. After that the snake maid bore many human children, who were, of course, related to the snakes, and so founded the Snake clan.

The young father, who had brought all the paraphernalia necessary for the snake ceremonies from the original kiva, then made the " *tiponi.* " For four days he hunted snakes, bringing one from each direction. Then he found a hollow cottonwood root, in which he placed one snake, and the rattles of the other three. He bound the bundle with buckskin, tying on eagle-feathers and the plumes of the oriole, bird of the North, the blue-bird of the West, the parrot of

the South, the magpie of the East, and the feathers of two
other birds, typifying above and below. This is the marvelous *tiponi* still owned by Harry Shupela, the chief Snake-
priest at Walpi, and carried by him in every snake-dance.
It is about twenty-seven inches long, including the feathers,
and it is so potent that the dance, to this day, is wilder and
more fervent at Walpi than in any of the other villages.

### THE SNAKE-DANCE

#### *Preliminary Ceremonies*

OF ALL SOUTHWESTERN INDIAN CEREMONIALS THE HOPI
Snake-dance attracts the most shivering attention. Everyone wants to see it, and every year more white visitors
crowd the villages, threatening the frail roofs, making
crude and loud comment, squirming in an agony of pleasant horror to see men handle venomous snakes. Thousands
see the dance every year, in spite of threats on the part of
the Indian Office to put a stop to it. One Indian commissioner went so far as to threaten its suppression on the
ground that handling snakes was a " loathsome practice "
— presumably to him. Friends of the Indian protested,
and the dance was saved.

If it had been stopped, it would have meant the end of
a pure totemistic rite, dating from the earliest era of human life. Undoubtedly the Snake-dance is the most ancient
ceremony we still may see, for it is the direct worship of
the clan ancestor, who is the snake. Fewkes, who holds this
opinion, says that the dance was also originally a water
ceremonial, snakes being the traditional guardians of

springs. While all dancers are not members of the Snake clan, probably the important priests are presumed to be descended from the legendary pair who introduced the rite, and are actually descendants, through the female line, of the people who brought the cult to Hopi. They are always assisted by the Antelope clan, whose ancestors came at about the same time. The Flute Ceremony, which follows the Snake-dance, is performed by members of the Horn clan, who, in legend, married girls of the Snake clan. Those mythical youths lured their maidens by playing on flutes, as they still do in the Flute Ceremony.

The Snake-dance is performed on all three mesas: in odd years at Walpi and Mishongnovi, in even years at Hotevilla and Chimopovi and Shipaulavi. The Flute Ceremony is held on the mesa which does not have the Snake-dance.

The dance itself is the final act of a sixteen-day ceremony, which begins a few days after Niman Katchina. The last nine days are filled with open and secret rites, both snake and Antelope-priests meeting daily in their kivas. As the men are very busy in the fields, usually only a few conduct the earlier ceremonies, the kivas filling up toward the end. The usual preparatory activities go on: the making of prayer-sticks, the preparation of dance paraphernalia, the erection of an altar, and the drawing of sand paintings.

The altar in the antelope kiva tells the whole story of the significance of the dance to one who understands something of Indian symbolism. The painting is of lightning in the form of snakes, and clouds in the colors of the four directions. The altar, also in symbolic shapes, is finished with bowls of water from a sacred spring, tall green corn-stalks, and trailing vines of melons and beans. Anyone, god or man, ought to know what it means. "We wish," it says quite clearly, "storm and rain from every direction, that our springs may be filled, that these life-giving plants may grow, that there may be plenty of food for our children." It is notable that in all prayers food for children is mentioned first: "then, when our children have eaten, may there be food for all."

On the last four days the Snake-priests hunt snakes, often very small boys going with them. Teachers in the Indian schools say that boys of the Snake clan catch and handle snakes without fear from the time they are tiny tots. The trick is to find your little brother, be he whip-snake, bull-snake, or rattler, under a rock or bush, stroke him with a feather until he straightens out of the dangerous coil, and then nab him just behind the head. Brother though he is, this is wise, for then he cannot mistakenly turn and bite you. The priests, stripped to the loin-cloth, leave the kiva before dawn. Each man's face is painted a light rose-red, a line of the same color runs from the shoulder down over the breast, and a red feather is tied to his crown. He is armed with a digging-stick and a snake whip, a rod to which are tied two eagle-feathers. It is used to make the snakes straighten, and the digging-stick comes into action if enough snakes are not found above ground, but must be dug out of their holes. Each man carries a bag of sacred meal with which to sprinkle the snakes, and a buffalo-skin bag to put them in. The hunters stay out all day, going in a different direction each day: first north, then west, then south, and finally east.

On the sixth day, before dawn, the Antelope-priests present a brief drama in their kiva. Few white men have seen this, but Dorsey, writing for the Field Columbian Museum, describes it most effectively. When the morning star rises, priests begin to stir about their altar, and two of them go out and return leading two children of about fourteen years old: a boy, who is the snake youth, and a girl, who personates the antelope maid.

Working quickly, the priests remove ordinary garb from these two, who stand quietly relaxed, moving and turning as told, yielding themselves like dolls to be dressed. The girl's arms and legs are whitened and her lower face is painted black, with a sharp white line running from lip to ear, and she is dressed in white ceremonial garments, with loosened hair and much jewelry. She holds an ancient ceremonial jar filled with trailing bean and melon vines. The boy is similarly painted, with the addition of white lines on his bare upper body. He wears a white kirtle and sash, and his hair hangs loose. He holds the *tiponi* on his left arm, and a live rattlesnake in his right hand.

Standing at the head of the sand painting, these two make a lovely picture as the flat white morning light steals down the hatchway, bringing out the beauty of the painting, the sinewy bare backs of the priests, the drifting blue smoke of the ceremonial pipes. The ceremony consists only in blowing smoke wreaths to the six directions, sprinkling meal and water over the painting, and chanting the long legend. It is a matter of several hours, during which the young people stand quietly and the light changes gradually to day, as represented by a patch of sunlight just under the hatchway, and sharp black shadows from the ladder-poles. The service ends with a solemn prayer for rain, growth, and fertility. At the end the children are disrobed by the same priests. Each one takes water from a gourd and blows it into his hands to wash. A woman comes to dress the girl's hair in squash blossoms. Then the two leave the kiva, and the priests resume the endless business of making prayer-plumes.

On the eighth morning before dawn two priests emerge from the kivas and place the standards. Each is an ordinary bow, about three feet long and decorated with horsehair stained red, skins of the skunk and the weasel, and eagle-feathers. This takes the place of a short eagle-feathered stick which has been the earlier announcement that the priests were within. Two strange figures then come out. They are the warriors; their bodies are painted black, their faces red; and they wear brown leather kirtles painted with snakes and edged with metal bugles. One carries the whizzer, which typifies thunder, and the other a contrivance which shoots out like lightning. The whizzer, or bull-roarer, is merely a shaped stick which is whirled on a string to make the humming, roaring sound of low thunder. The lightning is simulated by a more elaborate device: a jointed frame which folds down close to the man's hands or shoots out in a long zigzag like lightning. Gravely they turn to each direction, making thunder and lightning. Then a priest, in a long, musical call, summons the runners, and the warriors trot off into the darkness, going to a sacred spring about two miles from the village, where the race is to start.

At the spring, cloud symbols of meal are made on the ground, ceremonial smoking is indulged in, the feet of the runners are rubbed with mud from the spring to induce the rain to come more quickly, and finally the warriors signal for the start.

Races occur on the last two mornings. Racers may be any man or boy of the villages, though usually members of the Snake and Antelope clans do not enter. Sometimes as many as sixty or seventy runners appear. They make a fine sight as they streak across the plain just before sunrise, their naked brown bodies straining and shining with sweat, their bells jingling, white teeth flashing as they give occasional yells, panting up the last difficult slope to the mesa.

Meanwhile boys and girls have gathered on the lower terraces, usually dressed for the occasion in their best. Boys are stripped, painted, and hung with jewelry. Girls wear ceremonial wraps or bright blankets, and their hair, until the late epidemic of bobbing, was always in the swirls of virginity. The boys carry armfuls of green corn-stalks, and as the runners reach the mesa, the girls scramble for them. Often the outcome seems uncertain, but eventually the girls get the corn and carry it to their homes. The winner of the race, as he passes the priest, is handed a ring and a prayer-plume, both of which he plants in his field to assure a good crop. He is then received at the kiva, and a short ceremony is performed inside.

. .

On each of the last four mornings the priests visit certain springs, a different one each day. One year I was fortunate enough to see this rite. As I slept in camp at the foot of Second Mesa, I woke just before dawn, when that early stir calls people awake. I lay still a moment, and then I heard, in the dark, voices and a low faint jingle. Slipping from my blankets, I moved to the edge of the rock and sat where I could look down on the spring, guarded by its rude stone terraces. There I saw six Snake-priests, their dark bodies defined by white loin-cloths. One, the leader, bent over the water, casting sacred meal upon it while he chanted a low prayer, which was repeated or replied to by the other men. Then, solemnly, they moved around the spring, one of them flipping water with his aspergill at each cardinal point.

They turned then and came rapidly up the trail toward me. I sat still as they passed through our camp, threading their way between blanketed figures. They made no sound except the jingling of shells and their low voices, which replied pleasantly to my greeting. Later, when we went down to the spring, we found, just as we expected, prayer-sticks planted there, and the ground white with sacred meal.

### The Antelope-dance

On the eighth day the village is busy getting ready for the Antelope-dance, which will occur in the late after-noon. Every dancer and nearly every inhabitant of the vil-lage is shampooed. All priests are now spending all their time in the kivas, occupied in serious preparations, or sleeping either within or on the roofs. Some time during the day a patient little burro will be seen trotting into the plaza almost hidden under a load of leafy cottonwood. From this is built the *kisi*, the shrine which will hold the snakes. Supported on four uprights driven into the ground and tied at the top, it is a conical bower, open on one side, where a blanket, a skin, or a piece of canvas is hung. In front of this opening is dug a shallow hole, possibly a foot deep. A board is laid over it, and the ground smoothed until the board is hardly visible. This is *sipapu*, the entrance to the underworld, where dwell the spirits whose attention must be attracted during the dance, and to whom the snakes will finally carry the prayer. Some time during the afternoon a long bundle of greenery is carried into the *kisi*, thus completing arrangements for the arrival of the priests.

The plaza of Chimopovi on a hot August afternoon. The houses, so soft a gray as to be almost white, are dusting off at their edges and leaving protruding stones which make odd broken stairways to the roofs. Every house is a study in broken lines; all together they make a beautiful unit. The plaza is dusty, only the green *kisi* relieving the dull tone. All doors stand open, and most windows are unglazed. If one looks into a house, it is cool, but smelly, and light voices usually speak an invitation to enter. By mid afternoon people begin to gather on the shady side of the plaza. Compared with the brilliance of an Indian audience in New

Mexico, these people seem poverty-stricken almost to sor-
didness. The same Indian freedom from confusion prevails.
Women nurse their babies without concealment. One fills
her mouth with water from a gourd and bathes her child
by squirting water over the wriggling little brown body.
Older children play quiet little games in the sand. A few
white people show up, but as most of the crowd goes to the
more advertised dances at Hotevilla or at Walpi, Chimopovi is usually predominantly Hopi. Navajos come in, a
few at a time, drinking pop from bottles. Sometimes Zuñis
or people from the Rio Grande pueblos bring turquoise to
trade for ceremonial garments.

A little before sunset the performers appear. First the
chief Antelope-priest emerges from his kiva and calls a
greeting, which is probably in Keresan, a recognition of the
Antelope clan at Acoma. He speaks down the hatchway of
the snake kiva, asking if all is ready, then re-enters his own
kiva. When he comes out again, he is in full ceremonial
regalia and carries his *tiponi* and his rattle. His chin is
blackened and outlined by a sharp white line from ear to
ear, his body is painted with the zigzag lines of lightning,
and his legs are whitened to the knees. He wears feathers in
his hair, white kirtle and sash, fox-skin, beaded arm-bands
holding feathers, and beaded anklets. The other priests are
the same, except one who wears a wreath of cottonwood
leaves on his head and carries a bowl of water resting on
another wreath. The men who do not carry special objects
carry two rattles. These costumes vary from year to year,
from village to village, even from man to man; but in essentials they are the same.

The antelope men stand near the kiva until all are out. Then they rattle vigorously, and, following their leader, they advance quickly into the plaza, which they circle, almost touching the walls of the houses as they pass. As each man reaches *sipapu*, he stamps hard with one foot, not missing his step, and producing a hollow sound. He sprinkles meal as he passes the *kisi*, his rattle calling, his kirtle swishing with the rapidity of his movement. Four times the men circle the plaza, each time making a smaller ellipse, and finally lining up in front of the *kisi*, where they stand in relaxed immobility, as effective as their former rapid movement.

By this time the Snake-dancers are ready to enter. Their chief, coming out of the kiva, takes down the bow standard, which he carries with him. His assistant brings the antelope standard. The general effect of the snake costume is dark brown and black. Dark-brown bodies are spotted with dirty white, the dark-brown kirtles are painted with the snake symbol in white and black, the hair is smeared with white and feathered with red-stained feathers. Each man wears a turtle-shell rattle below the right knee, but otherwise anklets and armlets, jewelry and bandoleers are worn without absolute uniformity. Each man carries his snake whip and bag of sacred meal. Their entrance is even more thrilling than that of the antelope men, probably because of the dark forbidding effect of the costumes, and the dense silence and solemnity of both actors and audience. Four quick circuits of the plaza, every man stamping upon *sipapu*, and the snake priests line up facing the Antelope-priests, the chiefs being at opposite ends of the lines.

One of those tense moments of suspense, which all Indian dancers manage with theatrical skill. Then the antelope men rattle rapidly, and the snake men make angular movements with their whips. Then begins a sonorous, growling chant, so low as to be scarcely heard. It seems to come from the earth, rather than from those two lines of men, whose bodies move back and forth, their feet not leaving the ground, except as each man raises his right heel to shake his turtle rattle with a nervous insistence. Then the singing is suddenly stilled, while the antelope men rattle and the snake men shake their whips. It is a queer alternation of sound: now the rattles while the snake whips rise and fall, then the deep-voiced, almost inaudible chant accompanied by the very different note of the turtle rattles. Eight times this is repeated.

Then the snake men move back from the *kisi*, keeping their line as before, and one snake man and one antelope man leave the group, the snake man's arm resting on the antelope man's shoulder as they move in small circles in front of the *kisi*. They are followed by other couples, and all make the circle four times. Then one antelope man ducks into the *kisi* and comes out carrying a bundle of corn and bean plants, which he holds in his mouth as the snake men will tomorrow carry the snakes. The snake man holds up the end of the bundle in his right hand. The rest of the men, again in line, move rhythmically back and forth, and the antelope men chant, their first low mutter growing louder and louder and wilder and wilder until the act is over and the bundle passed back into the *kisi*.

Suddenly then the Snake-dancers wheel in unison and,

reversing the movement of their entrance, make four circles, each one larger than before, until they leave the plaza
and retire into their kiva, the jingling of their bells growing fainter as they disappear. The priests restore the bow
standards as they go. Then the Antelope-priests leave with
the same ceremony.

Later women come to both kivas with food. This is the
Snake-priests' last meal until after the next day's ceremony.
An interesting touch is the appearance of men to hang fox-
skins on the ladder-poles. This is not ceremonial, just sar-
torial, for the fur is said to stand out more fluffily when
well aired.

### The Day of the Snake-dance

On the ninth, as on previous mornings, ceremony
begins in the kivas before dawn. By this time all the
dancers are spending all their time in the kiva, and work
in the fields has been suspended for the time of this more
important observance. At dawn eight prescribed songs are
chanted, ashes are taken from the fire-place, spat upon, and
thrown up the hatchway by each dancer, who thus exorcises
any evil charm which may lurk about. Before dawn, as on
the day of the antelope race, the runners are called by that
clear musical cry which flows from the kiva-top over the
desert. The priests make their last ceremonial visit to the
spring, and the race is run. This time the winner's trophy
is a jar of water, which he later pours over his field to bring
rain. Traditionally the racers should run naked in order that
they may be seen by the gods, who see only the essential man, never his trappings. The hair should flow loose,

symbolizing the falling rain. Both these customs are changing under the tendency to wear underwear instead of bare skin, and to have short-cut hair.

It is a busy day in the snake kiva. Priests enter carrying bags which are said to contain herbs for making the emetic. Some of them go out to the fields to catch black beetles for the same stew. Ceremonial smoking, chanting, final work on their costumes, keep the men busy all day. Their principal business, however, is the lustral washing of snakes: a ceremony described by both Dorsey and Fewkes, who are among the few white men who have been permitted to see it.

The reptiles are washed in a large jar into which water is carefully poured in six gourdfuls. A herb is added, but neither scientist could identify it. The men all wash their hands before handling the snakes, which they take in wriggling handfuls from their bags, dip in the bowl, and then throw upon a bed of clean sand, which young boys have prepared for them. The boys then guard the snakes, squatting on their bare haunches around the sand-bed and making a great game of keeping the reptiles where they belong. It is all fun; there is no sense of fear or revulsion. Using their snake whips to prevent coiling, the youngsters, some of them no more than nine or ten years old, keep the snakes within bounds, allowing them to crawl about their naked bodies, between their legs, over their bare feet. Finally the snakes are gathered into a huge bag, in which they are carried to the plaza and placed in the *kisi*, where they are left in charge of the warrior who will hand them out to the dancers. The water in which the snakes were washed is carried out and poured off the mesa in the four directions.

There are other rites in the kiva, which no white man has seen. Certain traders who have seen the dance many times believe that the Indian's apparent immunity to snake-bite is due to the fact that the poison is extracted from venomous reptiles before they are used in the dance. A snake could be rendered harmless, biologists say, by forcing him to strike repeatedly and so exhaust his supply of poison. Certainly something, whether practical or mystical, frees the Snake-priests of all fear.

A feature of the last day is the initiation of new members, usually small boys, who are ceremonially shampooed, given a white ear of corn and a snake whip as symbols of their new dignity, seated at a corner of the sand painting while prayer and smoking go on, and finally greeted by terms of relationship and the new names of their membership.

By mid afternoon all this is finished and the men dress for the dance. Each man makes up and dresses himself, exchanging brotherly assistance at getting at the middle of his back. Bodies and faces are blackened with soot, the chin is whitened in an effect unaccountably weird, pinkish spots are painted on forehead, arms, body, and legs. Owl- and eagle-feathers are tied to the hair, which is also whitened. Snake kilt, bandoleer, arm and ankle bands, and moccasins are all dark brown. Altogether these dancers are the wildest figures to be seen in any southwestern dance. Everything about them, even about the smallest boys, is darkly forbidding, wildly straggling.

## The Snake-dance

All day the audience has been gathering. The crowd is worst at Walpi, for the plaza there is small and its dance is the best-known. Yet it must be described, for only Walpi has the original *tiponi;* only Walpi has the Snake Rock, which plays no direct part in the service, but which has appeared in almost every painting or photograph of the ceremony. Many people come for the Antelope-dance; as many, one would think, as that small plaza could hold. Yet all the day of the Snake-dance the roads across the plain are black with cars, scuttling along like so many beetles, each one bringing its load of white visitors. "Dudes" come in droves, usually shepherded by professional "dude-wranglers," who wearily answer question after question, who fight a hopeless fight against dust and heat and glare and tepid drinking-water to make comfortable people who cannot be made comfortable short of real comfort. Parasols and wide hats, fans and thermos bottles of clinking ice-water, venders with pink pop; the clashing Navajo jewelry, which is almost the badge of an interest in the Indian; loudly called greetings between Arizona townspeople who come every year to see each other; Indian Service people, knowing everybody. Long rows of Indian wagons coming up the road which is closed to automobiles, dudes rocking precariously on chairs tipping in wagon-beds, scrawny little horses tugging terribly, being beaten. Navajos arriving on horses, always haughtily aloof, always quiet, always laden with the most beautiful turquoise and silver, specially priced for eastern buyers. The mob gathering slowly,

*Photograph by the Museum of New Mexico*

SNAKE-DANCE                                    [OLIVE RUSH]

crushingly, in the little plaza, bulging against the inadequate rope which has been strung along the edge; small
boys squirming through, fat women sweating unpleasantly,
men coatless, fanning themselves with straw hats, Hopis
selling the same roof-space again and again, collecting before delivery, and then calmly disappearing when rival
parties of swearing, jangling whites arrive to claim their
" reserved space." Men boosting fat old ladies on to roofs,
occasional prehistoric beams giving way and tumbling a
struggling mass of human beings into dusty debris, unpleasant, but soft enough to prevent broken bones. Movie stars
in white veils, women novelists picturesquely distributing
peacock-feathers among good-looking young Hopis, tall
drivers in international costumes of English riding-boots
and breeches, cowboy hats, and Russian blouses. Bitter
complaint from women without parasols against women
with parasols. So the white man comes to see the Snake-
dance.

..

In time, a long time, the warning rattling is heard and
the antelope priests appear, walking quickly. They repeat
the evolution of the day before, and their costumes are the
same, but the effect somehow is much more tense. The
whole crowd is held silent, watching for the snake men, and
also watching the clouds in the sky, for traditionally it always rains after the Snake-dance, bringing an immediate
response to the prayer.

When they finish their four turns round the plaza, which

they make by actually pressing against the crowd, the antelopes line up before the *kisi* and, swaying slightly, await the arrival of the Snake-priests. By this time the tension is vibrant and no sound is heard as the Snake-dancers enter with a long swinging step, definite, quick, hard, and circle the plaza the appointed four times, stamping their insistent call upon *sipapu* and scattering their sacred meal each time. Finally they come to rest, facing the line of antelope men, and link arms. Then the two platoons sway from side to side, making only enough motion to cause the rattles to sound, and chanting that terrible low thunderous murmur, which never sounds as though human beings made it, but seems to come from the very bowels of the earth. Louder and louder it grows, as the bodies rock. Then suddenly it ceases, the men release each other's arms and swing into a rapid vigorous dance which shakes all the rattles and which is paralyzing in its unexpectedness. Time after time this transition is made from the low humming growl to the insistent beat of the dance, and back again. Finally it is over, and the groups break into dance formation for the handling of the snakes.

The line of antelope men breaks, leaving the *kisi* entrance open, and a Snake-priest stoops into it and emerges with a snake, which he places between his teeth, and sets off. He is accompanied by another priest, whose left hand rests on the carrier's shoulder, his right hand holding the snake whip to stroke the snake and prevent the dangerous coiling. Dancing in unison, this pair starts on a circuit of the plaza, stepping rhythmically to the accompaniment of the antelope chant. Other pairs follow until the plaza is

crowded with them. A third man trails each couple, unob-
trusively. When the circle is complete, the dancer drops
his snake, which at once tries to get away. Then the third
man, the gatherer, comes into action. Quietly, with alert
mien, he watches his snake. Sometimes with his whip he
stirs up a little puff of dust which causes the snake to turn
away from the crowd. He never lets it get among the people,
though many squealing women anticipate it. Then, when
the time is exactly right, he touches the snake with his
feathered wand, accurately drops meal on it, and, making
a graceful swoop with his whole body, catches it just behind
the head. Swinging the undulating reptile the length of his
arm, the man's body and the snake make a flashing bronze
statue for one unforgettable moment. Then, nonchalantly,
as a woman carries a shower-bouquet, he lays the snake
across his arm and goes after another one. Meanwhile the
whole group of fifteen to thirty men has broken up into
similar threes. The plaza is filled with dancers who follow no regular line. Snakes curl about men's necks, their
heads are often seen against a man's cheek as though biting
it; sometimes a small whip-snake makes a rosette of itself
on a man's ear, sometimes a long bull-snake is so heavy that
the two men have trouble holding it. Sometimes a small
boy priest gets his legs all tangled up in a snake longer than
he is and has to be released by a kindly antelope man. Rat-
tlers are handled with no more concern than the smallest
whip- or garter-snake. Gatherers never lose sight of their
particular snakes, even when the dance is at its height and
the ground is covered with wriggling reptiles trying to
escape, being turned back and finally caught. When a

gatherer gets more snakes than he can conveniently handle, he honors some man in the crowd by handing him an armful, or he gives them to the swaying, chanting Antelope-priests, whose arms are soon filled with them. Each dancer handles many snakes, sometimes fifty or sixty being used in an afternoon.

At last, when the bag of snakes is emptied, the chief Snake-priest makes a large circle of meal on the ground. Moving with the quick definiteness of the whole ceremony, he strews meal from the six cardinal directions toward the center of his circle; and then the gatherers approach and throw in the snakes, a writhing mass. Women and girls, covered with white ceremonial mantles, have been standing ready with plaques of meal. They approach and scatter meal on the wriggling pile, their quickness lacking the careless fearlessness of the priests and having more the quickness of nervousness. They disappear, losing no time. Then the snake priests all dash into the circle, gather up the snakes in great armfuls, and rush out of the plaza. Way is made for them with no hesitancy and they disappear down the four trails and out on to the plain, carrying the snakes to certain shrines where they are released to carry their message to the underworld.

Meanwhile in the plaza the Antelope-priests make their four circuits again in reverse, the asperger puts meal, water, and his cottonwood wreath in the *kisi*, and they all go out. This ends their participation and they return to their kiva merely to undress and to eat the meal which women have been bringing in huge steaming pans and bowls and in piles of *piki* bread.

The snake men come straggling back, panting from their race, and one by one they reach their kiva, where they openly strip and bathe. Women of the Snake clan bring bowls of the emetic, whose taking is the final public act of the ceremony. The men not having eaten since the previous day, the results are not so loathsome as might be expected. Every dancer drinks and leans, retching, over the edge of the kiva until he is entirely purified. This is said to be to purge the dancers of any snake-charm which might be dangerous to other inhabitants of the village. As each man finishes vomiting, he enters the kiva, where ceremonial smoking is the prelude to a feast, which must be eagerly anticipated.

Meanwhile, if the gods are good — and if all has been done well, the gods are good — rain is coming. As the late afternoon light wanes, dusk is usually hastened by the gathering of huge clouds, streaks of rain appear over distant mesas, dude-wranglers marshal their charges into cars, eager to " cross the wash " before floods fill it, Hopis from neighboring villages get themselves and their families loaded into cars; and then comes the long, swishing, sweet-smelling rain, pouring in cleansing floods from the roofs into the streets and over the edge of the mesa, bringing hope and confident assurance that hearts were pure and the work was pleasing in the sight of the unseen ones.

The Snake-dance always brings rain.

## LALAKONTI, A WOMEN'S CEREMONY

WE SAT OUTSIDE THE GOAT KIVA IN WALPI ON A DARK
night. It was September eleventh, and the Lalakonti was to
be danced the next day. Percy had squired me up the mesa
— Percy, my Hopi host, short and bandy-legged and with
a steady flow of incorrect English.

"White people call it Basket-dance," he told me, "but it
means hail. It brings hail and cold wet for the ground, so
things grow next spring."

A few women passed us, stepped up on the kiva roof, and
disappeared down the ladder. Then a man went in. All the
time we could hear chanting: a low melodious singing,
with women's voices predominating, but men's voices dis-
tinguishable too. It sounded curiously like a Catholic chant,
as though blue nuns might be singing somewhere underground.

A head appeared over the roof edge behind us, dimly
outlined against deep-blue sky. "Hello," said my friend
Norman. "Did you bring parrot-feathers?"

I had brought parrot-feathers, so that was all right.
Norman and his family were all sleeping on the roof, they
explained, the chicken-bugs having taken the house. They
rolled out of blankets to come and sit on the edge of the
roof and chat. They preferred not to discuss the ceremonies
going on within the kiva, so we talked of other things.

From my reading I knew that the kiva ceremonies of
this women's rite do not differ much from those usual in
the men's fraternities. Most village people of the southwest
have women's dances, conducted by women priests, with

just a man or two around, as a Mason attends the doings of the Eastern Star. Lalakonti is celebrated by women of many clans, headed by four priestesses, whose office is heredi-tary. One Hopi said that they must always belong to the Bear, the Sun, the Spider, and the Eagle clans. The kiva ceremonies are the same as in the men's rites: the making of prayer-plumes, the erection of an altar, the painting of a sand picture, the preparation of costumes, even ceremo-nial smoking. The participants stay in the kiva day and night, and during the last four days they eat no salt or meat and nothing raised within the year.

About three o'clock, while it was still dark, the chief priestess, an old woman, emerged from the hatchway. Her roughened hair and blanket-draped figure were outlined for a few minutes against the starry sky as she considered it intently. She was, I knew, making sure that Orion had reached a certain position. Then she backed down the lad-der, and soon a procession came out of the kiva, twenty-six women and two men. They filed silently into the little plaza in front of the Snake Rock and formed a circle open to the east, that nothing might come between *sipapu* and the point of sunrise. About a half-hour of chanting, very low and ghostly in the darkness. Then the man moved; and, without quite seeing, we knew that he was digging out the hidden board which conceals *sipapu*. He carefully cleaned out the hole under it and put in freshly made prayer-plumes, and then the whole procession filed round, chanting all the time, and every woman dropped in a feathered twig. Then *sipapu* was closed, the ground was smoothed and stamped hard, and the party returned to the kiva. The few watchers on the house-tops disappeared like wraiths before the earliest streaks of dawn.

Just before it was light enough to see clearly, one of the men and a slim little girl of about ten years old came up the ladder and went away over the edge of the mesa. We could see that the child was wrapped in a white blanket which was fastened around her waist with a white sash. Four black feathers were tied to the blanket on her back, and one floated from her bobbed head. Her feet and hands were black and so was her chin, outlined by a sharp white line from mouth to ear. She carried a plaque, her trophy as the winner of yesterday's race, which we had not seen. She and the priest were going to a shrine in the near-by foot-hills, where they would make medicine with meal and water, and where the man would give the starting-word for the race of young men.

Since earliest light the runners had been trotting off down the trail to the starting-point: all slim and all excel-lent runners, as Hopis always are. At sunrise they started at a point hidden by the trees around the schoolhouse, so we did not see them until they appeared well along the trail, swiftly moving dots, running in close formation and show-ing well their training, especially when they came to the steep pull up the narrow rocky trail.

Just as the runners reached the foot of the mesa, the women came out of the kiva. All were barefooted and bare-headed, and all wore their hair parted and twisted, except the schoolgirls, who were bobbed. The older women wore black squaw dresses and some sort of wrap, white ceremo-nial mantles or bright shawls. A few girls were in gingham dresses. Each of the four priestesses carried feathers in addition to the plaques or baskets which all had. The plaques seemed to be of no special design: butterflies and wind symbols, the lightning and various Katchina patterns were among them. There were seventeen mature women and ten girls. Forming an open circle as they had the night before, they waited for a signal from the chief priestess and then began their chant. They are said to have fourteen different melodies, to which different words may be sung each year, if poetic fervor runs so high. As they sang, they raised and lowered their baskets with a quiet even movement, making two downward gestures from each shoulder in recognition of the four directions. As they sang, the whole group swayed slightly, eyes downcast, feet still, voices faultlessly following the soft cadences of the song.

Then the first runner appeared, coming in from the west end of the plaza. The tradition that a runner must be naked in order to be seen by the gods was modified to the extent of long, white underwear. Yet the youth was slim and graceful, a little taller than most Hopis. As he entered the plaza, the men gathered there murmured approval. He was immediately followed by the little girl in white with the winner's plaque. She presented it without ceremony and went on into her kiva, while the winner disappeared through the archway into the north street. The chanting women paid no attention to this or to the arrival of the other runners, except to open a break in their circle through which all passed as they came panting in — about twenty of them. Then, at the end of the song, the women turned and went into their kiva.

"Breakfast now," said my Hopi friend. "You have breakfast now too."

So we went down the mesa to the home of Hopi Baptists which had been rented to us for the day. It had many religious texts on the wall, one especially suitable for a guest-house. "Even Christ," it assured us gently, "pleased not Himself." So, trying to be becomingly meek, we went across the street to the nearest kitchen stove, made our coffee, broiled our bacon, then washed up, brought fresh buckets of water, and swept our crumbs off the freshly plastered floor with a Hopi besom. Our hostess, speaking no English, made up for it by repeated use of " *Askwal, askwali,*" the Hopi, " Thank you," and by chuckling delightedly at everything we did.

· ·

On the mesa again about ten o'clock we found waiting Hopis getting impatient because the priestesses came so late. Women and children sat on roofs, leaving the plaza to men and boys. We were warned that we should be safer above ground, and space was hospitably made for us on a roof. Only two Navajos came to this show, a tall young man, made taller by high heels and a very high hat, and his squaw, in a brilliant orange and black skirt and a dull-green velvet blouse. Everybody was chatting. Men were smoking and leaning over the edge of the mesa to watch a group of small boys who had chosen that as their point of vantage. Finally, about eleven, word went forth: " They are coming." Many more Hopis suddenly materialized from nowhere until the plaza was crowded. We were the only white visitors.

Then the women entered, formed their open circle as before, and began chanting. Still all eyes turned to the kiva, and then we saw Lakone and the two Lakonemana. Lakonetaka was a yellow and white figure: his face, body, and arms and legs were painted yellow with the sunflower pollen, and he wore white ceremonial garments. He carried a small plaque piled high with yellow corn-meal. They told us that yellow was the color of the North. The two women were similarly dressed in skirt and bodice made of ceremonial kilts. Their faces were yellow, with black lines drawn across the eyes from temple to temple and across the mouth from ear to ear. They wore anklets of yarn, masses of jewelry from the chin to the waist in Zuñi fashion, and hair hanging loose. Their head-dresses were coronets of turquoise-blue and black, with rain-cloud symbols above, symbols of the sunflower on the right, and a horn on the left, tall eagle-feathers and headed grain, and a fluffy mass of small feathers at the back. The faces were so thickly covered with yellow paint and so impassive and the head-dresses were so elaborate that the effect was mask-like.

The man, advancing, strewed yellow meal on the ground to make cloud symbols, which were like the figure used to play tit-tat-toe. Then the two women, standing side by side, each threw two ears of corn at it: a white, a blue, a yellow, and a red. Each was feathered with two eagle-quills like the shuttles for battledore and shuttlecock. The man picked them up, handed them back, and, advancing a few steps, made another cloud. The figure was repeated four times, which brought the group into the circle of women, who had steadily continued their chant.

When the Mana were well within the circle, we could see that each one had on her back a bulging pack. She eased it down to the ground, assisted by her companion, two men followed with more bundles, and the throwing began. Then we knew why young men and boys had so eagerly crowded the plaza. This was their game. Each woman took from her pile article after article and pitched it out into the crowd, maintaining her impassive expression, but hurling vigorously. We saw packages of popcorn flying through the air, tin pie-pans, boxes of matches, scattering their contents as they broke, Hopi plaques, store dishes, sacks of salt, bags of candy, yards of calico or gingham weighted with a stone and flapping like queer long-tailed birds. Once in a while one of the women, picking up something precious like a pottery bowl or a pressed-glass dish would shamelessly hand it to a favored man in the crowd. Sometimes one of them would cast a canny eye round the crowd and pick out some man to whom she would toss a bundle of Bull Durham. One woman especially was a hard, straight thrower, and she spun her tin pans flashing through the air to the very house-tops. Occasionally something flew so close to the edge of the rock as to make the breath pause for fear some eager young man would go over. But no: Hopis learn to balance on the edge of that rock in very early youth. Once in a while something did go over, to be caught by the foresighted youngsters who had been waiting among the rocks on just such a chance.

Finally the sacks were empty and the two Mana withdrew, the crowd giving place quietly to let them pass. This performance was repeated eight times during the day, with intervals for rest and food. The gayest episode was just after noon, probably because the Mana made more of a game of it, feinting a throw in one direction and then hurling the gift in another. One plaque seemed to make an especial appeal, for many men grabbed it. In the confusion it was several minutes before we realized that about twenty men were struggling. They made a hard compact mass above shifting feet and below heads thrown back openmouthed and gasping for air. They staggered from one end of the plaza to the other and were pushed back by bystanders just before they pitched over the cliff or knocked down a house. Back and forth, round and round, they fought, choking out guttural calls, welded to each other as though they never could be pulled apart. Occasionally bits of plaque flew through the air, long straw bunches, torn loose in the fracas. Finally the struggle narrowed as man after man fell off, looked himself over for torn shirtsleeves and lost hat, wiped his wet face, and joined the spectators. At last only three or four were left, grunting, straining savages, holding on with amazing endurance. Then the most powerful one began throwing his body back and forth in his final effort to throw off his opponents. They hung on like bulldogs, coming away every now and then with more straw. At last the winner was acknowledged, Harry Shapala, a store-keeper in Polacca whose very modern truck stood at the causeway. What he had for his pains was a small remnant of battered plaque, a shirt torn half off his body, a face running with perspiration, and a sharp triumphant grin showing white teeth under his keen aquiline nose. Everybody seemed satisfied.

Meanwhile the group of women continued their singing. Sometimes they were bumped by the fighters, sometimes little girl chanters had to be rescued by men standing near. Always they kept the chant going, eyes down, hands moving regularly and softly from shoulder to shoulder, shaking down the snow for which they prayed. In the midst of the rioting they kept on with their fundamental task as women must always be concerned with fundamentals while men struggle about them, testing their strength in exhausting, exciting, but not-so-necessary fights.

A friend from Shipaulavi sat next to me on the roof, smoking my cigarettes. He had been overseas, he had written several Hopi legends which I must see. I had evidently picked up one of the Hopi intelligentsia. He watched the dance closely, giving me bits of information about the chanting, the meaning of the dance, various matters.

Finally he sighed. "I don't see why they do it so early. This dance brings hail and snow. They shouldn't do it so early. Walpi should not do this. What if we got a cold storm now?" he asked me anxiously.

What indeed? Here was Walpi, quite inconsiderate of her neighbors, regardlessly calling for hail and winter storms before the crops were in, before a suitable time. I was worried myself for fear there should be a storm and spoil things. Walpi, obviously, shouldn't do that.

Soon we had a horse-race; not that it had anything in particular to do with the day's activities, but any kind of race any time is always welcome to Hopis. This one started a good half mile from the foot of the mesa, where the ground had been cleared for a landing-field. We saw the men going out, sitting easily on their barebacked ponies, bare-legged or in the ubiquitous underwear. They gave their mounts little try-outs up and down the field while waiting for all to get there. Meanwhile their grandstand was full of comment. They sat along the edge of the mesa, dangling a fringe of tennis-shoes, moccasins, and stiff boots. Behind them stood another row of men, a few youngsters were on the very tops of the houses, and women were on all the terraced roofs between. A gay and happy crowd, calling, as the race started, greetings in both Hopi and English. " Get going! You'll have to do better than that! Keep it up! Stay with it! " When the racers reached the trail, they slid off their horses and made the rest of the way afoot, abandoning their steeds where they stood and letting later comers get around them anyway. The winner of this race had a plaque too.

By six o'clock the women had made their last appearance and the day's ceremony was over. Most young men in the three villages must have had gifts. But they were not destined to keep them. The girls who had sat so demurely all day watching the struggle were going to get those things yet. The next day, I learned, would be held one of those Hopi free-for-alls, when the girls would race the young men and get the yards of calico, the plaque or basket, the shiny tin pan, the beautiful bowl. Old people sitting on roofs love these games, and they shout encouragement and criticism as the race goes on. Young men dash round houses, dodge from side to side of the kivas, disappear through an opening, shout tauntingly from upper terraces; and the girls swarm after, giggling, grabbing, tearing shirts, taking the same swift turns and dashes; finally and inevitably getting the spoil.

NAVAJO TRAVELERS                    [GERALD CASSIDY]

# VI: The Navajos

### "DINNE," THE PEOPLE

A NURSE, NEW TO THE NAVAJO RESERVATION, WAS TRAVEL-
ing to her station, almost two hundred miles from the railroad. Sitting beside the mail-man in his Ford, she watched
the broken country unfold. First they passed through a
patch of pines on a high upland. Then for miles came the
weird pale colors of the Painted Desert; then miles of
strange tortured rock shapes where even scrub cedar could
not grow. They halted at a trading-post and she saw her first
Navajos.

Two men sat on the steps of the store, chatting. One wore
a dirty red sweater, a Stetson hat, and brown moccasins.
The other had no hat; his long hair was held under a red
silk handkerchief, and a blanket fell from his shoulders.
A slim pretty girl passed, her very full skirts almost touching the ground in front and bobbing high behind. Beside
her trotted a tiny child, also in a long, full skirt and a dirty
velvet jacket; her hair, like that of the women, was tied
with cotton string into a heavy chignon.

They delivered mail at two such posts before they
stopped for lunch at Red Lake, where a flat pond lay in a
hollow of the desert. The store, which is one of the oldest

179

on the reservation, was obviously built for protection as well as for business. An octagonal stone building with high windows, it would still make a very worthy fort. In the one living-room upstairs two New England women in fresh gingham served lunch and gossiped about their neighbors fifty miles away as easily as though they lived in the next house.

They drove on between the great stone " Elephant's Feet " and off over miles of stony roads along the brink of canyons where no water ran. They saw a few irregular fields of stunted corn. Once they passed an empty hogan. It was the typical Navajo home, built of logs laid lengthwise and rising gradually into a low dome. The one door faced east, as rigid convention prescribes, and the only other opening was the hole at the top to let out the smoke from the fire in the middle of the floor. Near by was a brush shelter, which the mail-man said was the Navajo summer home.

The road bumped and scraped and struggled along. Once they stopped to speak to a small girl herding a bunch of sheep, but she spun her long skirts out into a fan and ran for cover like a wild thing. Once two men crossed the road on ponies, their slim shanks riding close as though a part of their horses. They accepted cigarettes, but had no English. Once a wagon pulled elaborately out of the road to let the car pass. The driver beamed, the woman seated on the bed of the wagon smiled demurely over her striped blanket, children stared with amazed black eyes. These were the only people they saw on that long drive.

The nurse was silent. Then she said:

"This is magnificent country, and there seems to be more than enough of it. But why do they need a nurse? Where are the people?"

Yet on that reservation there are more than forty-two thousand Navajos, supporting themselves by marketing their sheep, their blankets, and their silverware. They come into the trading-posts to exchange these things for what they need, and disappear again into their mysterious desert. One sees them in numbers only when they meet for their great "sings." Then often more than a thousand will gather in response to that strange underground summons which travels faster than the white man's telegraph.

Navajos are marked by mystery, by arrogance, by a strange sardonic humor which no white man has ever analyzed or even much noted. In appearance they are very different from the other southwestern Indians. One would say, offhand, that Navajos are a tall people, slim-waisted, both men and women, with high cheek-bones, narrow hands and feet. Yet on closer acquaintance they are seen to represent every human type. They are short and fat as well as long and lean; high aquiline noses and narrow faces are varied by flat faces and almost Negroid features. Probably Jewish traders could contribute little to the Navajo's gift as a hard and close dealer, but Jewish features are not infrequent. A stunning sheik of the desert may have gray eyes; they are probably due to the fact that the American Army passed that way. Whatever his physical appearance, the Navajo's outstanding characteristic is his hauteur. He is dignified to the point of superciliousness; and he looks upon the white man as upon a strange interloper whom he tolerates because it is his own high pleasure to do so, and not because he has to.

That the Navajos consider themselves the aristocrats of the southwest they tactily admit by calling themselves " *Dinne,*" *the* People. They are of Athapascan stock, and ethnologists are generally agreed that they came from the north, drifting into the area they now occupy less than a thousand years ago. In earliest historical times they were found wandering over what is now western New Mexico, eastern Arizona, and southern Utah and Colorado. Their present reservation, while much smaller than their original range, is in the same region. Navajo legends in general bear out the supposition that they came from the north, except one very picturesque one which tells that the People came from the south, bringing their four sacred plants: tobacco, corn, squash, and beans. They occupied all the country, but, finding the Pueblo people better fitted for agriculture, they generously gave them the valley lands and kept the high grassy uplands for themselves. This legend has the great advantage of justifying the Navajo habit of appropriating the crops raised by the Pueblo people.

The Navajo also appropriated women when it suited him to do so, with the result that his race is probably a compound of all the southwestern Indian stocks, with accretions of Spanish blood, whatever racial amalgam the Spaniards had acquired in Mexico, and later additions from the American Army and American traders. What was most vigorous, most alluring, most enduring of all races the Navajo has apparently taken and made his own.

The name " Navajo " was first " Apaches de Navaju," a designation first used by Alonzo de Benavides in 1630 to distinguish these people from other related bands of Apaches. " Navajo " is a Tewa word meaning " broad cultivated fields." Not that the Navajos condescended to cultivate the fields, but that they were found living near and preying upon those who did.

## NAVAJOS AND SPAIN

THE NAVAJOS WHOM THE SPANISH EXPLORERS KNEW WERE a nomadic fighting race, clever, acquisitive, keen to take whatever appealed to them. They wandered in small bands, probably related groups; they dressed in skins, and their legends mention garments woven of cedar fiber. They probably made shelters of brush or logs as they do today; they fought, hunted, sang, and danced. They made baskets, often very fine ones, but as time went on, they learned that Piutes could make as good or better baskets, so the aristocratic Navajo let the Piute do it. They made woven waterbottles covered with pitch, and a crude pottery for cooking. As soon as they found a weaker people from whom they could acquire pottery, however, they abandoned that craft also.

The Spanish never conquered the Navajos, and they remained a constant menace to the little settlements widely scattered over the province of Nuevo Mexico. But the Spaniards probably saved the Pueblo people from complete extinction at the hands of the Navajos. The Navajos claim that they conquered the people who lived in the Canyon de

Chelly, and in Chaco Canyon; and there is sufficient record of how their encroachments caused the abandonment, within historical times, of the Piros villages in the Manzano Mountains, of Pecos, of villages near Socorro.

Though the Spaniards never conquered the Navajos, they gave them, perforce, certain arts and other gifts. Captured horses multiplied rapidly until a horse was almost a part of every Navajo. Every man's wealth was estimated by the number of horses he owned; he bought his wives with horses; children rode as soon as they could walk. With the horse went the sheep, and with the sheep went the art of weaving. Before the Spanish conquest all the Pueblos wove cotton. They learned wool-weaving rapidly, and probably passed it on almost as rapidly to the Navajos, who knew how to make good use of their captives. Navajo women now became sheepherders, owning their own flocks and bringing the wool through all the processes to the final blanket. They had the natural white and black, which combined to make gray; *bayeta*, which is the red raveled from Spanish uniforms; certain yellows made from vegetable dyes; cochineal, which they got from the Yaquis; indigo from Mexico. Many of these old blankets, treasures for collectors, have marvelous fineness of texture and beauty of soft faded color and definite, balanced design. Blankets must have made a great difference in Navajo life. Every man, still in fringed leggings and no shirt, now wrapped himself nobly in the comforting folds of a blanket; every woman now wore, instead of a skin tunic, which must be chilling to the body, a woven squaw dress, such as Pueblo women still wear on feast-days.

By the end of the eighteenth century Spain's glory was past, and the distant province of Nuevo Mexico was left to the mercy of its enemies. Navajos, Apaches, and Comanches grew ever more aggressive. There are records of bands of Navajos advancing to within twenty miles of Santa Fe, pillaging little ranches, taking what they wanted, including the likely women, locking the rest of the family into the house, and setting fire to it before they rode away.

The Mexican Republic proved even weaker than Spain, and it is no wonder that whites and Pueblo Indians were equally glad to welcome the American Army when it came promising protection.

## THE AMERICAN CONQUEST
## OF THE NAVAJOS

KEARNY, BEFORE HE PASSED ON TO CALIFORNIA, APPOINTED Colonel Doniphan to give the Navajos a sharp lesson, which he promptly did. The chiefs readily entered into a treaty with the United States, but they could see no reason why they should not go on fighting Mexicans as usual. The fact that the United States, having fought Mexicans itself, now claimed and protected them did not seem reasonable to the Indian mind. So Colonel Doniphan's treaty was the first of many. The Navajo continued his ancient policy of maintaining a friendship with the Mexicans and the Pueblos during the growing-season and of inaugurating a war when crops were ripe. Over and over governors of the province, which was now called New Mexico, appealed for aid against the " blood-thirsty Navajos."

Mexicans, for their part, soberly advocated a state of continuous war with Navajos, who, they pointed out, had many sheep and horses and many children. Mexican gallants liked the sport of capturing Navajos for slaves, and the ease of having them. It was estimated in the sixties that from two to four thousand slaves were held in New Mexico. Even one governor was said to own them, though ownership was legally vested in his wife. Prices varied, but a promising girl of eight sold for as much as four hundred dollars.

So whites were probably quite as much to blame as Indians for the constant fighting. It was the period in which " the only good Indian was a dead Indian," an assumption which would hardly make for friendly feeling. Kit Carson, the little, wizened, almost illiterate mountain-man who finally conquered the Navajos, understood this very well. He said once:

" I think, as a general thing, the difficulties arise from aggressions on the part of the whites. From what I have heard, the whites are always cursing the Indians, and are not willing to do them justice."

He also said: " I believe if Colonel Bent and myself were authorized, we could make a solid and lasting peace with those Indians."

A distant and warlike government, however, could not be expected to listen to such moderate words, nor to turn the conduct of its affairs over to a simple mountaineer and an Indian trader. So the wars went merrily on, and they proved to be a tedious business. For eighteen years an army of over three thousand men was constantly in the field; every general who later came to fame served an apprenticeship fighting Navajos or Apaches; the expense became appalling. Treaties multiplied, until in 1863 Brigadier-General James H. Carleton, in command of New Mexico, put an end to that farce. After a skirmish he made the unexpected move of refusing to make a treaty with a deputation of Navajo chiefs. He told them that they could have peace at once and without the bother of a treaty by simply ceasing to molest the Mexicans. He said that they had always been more apt at promise than at performance, and that he was giving them a chance to perform. The bewildered Navajo statesmen retired, promising to do their best, but cannily reminding the General that their young men were hot-blooded and hard to hold.

Depredations began again within a few months. Carleton was ready for this. He sent word that he had no desire to fight friendly Navajos, and that any of them could show their friendly feeling by reporting at once at Fort Wingate. He agreed to move them to the Bosque Redondo, where they would be given land, including six thousand arable acres on the Pecos River. The Navajos, always invincible, could not believe that they had at last met their match, and practically none responded. The Navajos have a tradition that a removal east of the Rio Grande would ruin them. If as wise a man as General Carleton had known and respected this ancient belief, might he not have been more successful?

Carson, known to the Navajos as " the Man Who Talked One Way," met the chiefs in council and told them what they were up against. He explained that the American

Army was invincible; that however clumsily and helplessly they lurched about over the desert with heavy equipment and unseeing eyes, white men would never stop coming, because they were inexhaustible. But the chiefs would not listen.

A venerable Navajo told his white friend one day how his band eluded the great Carson. There was a faint gleam in his watery old eye as he recalled the trick they played. Then he stopped and meditated. " If we had listened to Carson," he said, " we'd have been all right. As it was, *do-so, do paizh;* it was just too bad."

It was, indeed. Carson was a soldier, and, both sides having refused his excellent advice, he had no choice but to go out and get them. Knowing the country and with an uncanny ability to get about over it in a short time, Carson was not long in penning most of the tribe in the Canyon de Chelly, which the Navajos considered sacred ground. But that thirty miles of twisted sandy canyon, with thousand-foot walls of colored sandstone, proved to be not a haven for them, but a trap.

Carson reported: " In the main Canyon de Chelly they had some two thousand peach trees which were mostly destroyed by my troops.

"When I first captured the Navajos, I first destroyed their crops, and harassed them until the snow fell very deep in their canyons, taking some prisoners occasionally.

" I took twelve hundred sheep from them at one time, and smaller lots at different times."

One does not like to think of what months of such warfare meant to women and children. Strange, wild, hunted creatures they must have been, facing starvation or the even worse horrors of surrender to an unknown and relentless power. In the end, trusting the word of " the Man Who Talked One Way," about two hundred men, women, and children surrendered in the canyon. Other bands came in so rapidly that by February of 1864 several thousand had been moved to the Bosque Redondo. They could not know that the man who promised them food and protection and fair treatment was not powerful enough at Washington to make a great civilized government talk one way also.

## THE BOSQUE REDONDO

AT THE END OF FEBRUARY 1864 GENERAL CARLETON REported the surrender of over three thousand Navajos, more than half the tribe. He demanded food and clothing for them all, and while waiting for Washington to act, he put his troops on half rations and ordered that no grain be fed to cavalry horses until the Navajos were fed. In appeal after appeal he pointed out that it was cheaper to feed Navajos than to fight them, and that the lands captured from them were worth more than any cost the captives could be.

" For pity's sake," he urged in one report, " if not moved by any other consideration, let us, as a great nation, for once treat the Indian as he deserves. Otherwise," he prophesied, " this interesting and intelligent race will diminish and disappear." The People had friends, even at court.

The whole tribe was never captured: a few old men still

boast that their bands never surrendered. Still, enough of them were exiled to the Bosque Redondo to make an effective object-lesson. Many died on their way there. The first winter, when food came slowly and there was a shortage of firewood, killed many more. Many contracted diseases, especially children. Near-by tribes of unconquered Indians attacked them, and the government gave inadequate protection. Agents paid government money for good flour and fresh meat, accepted wormy flour and tainted meat, split the difference with the traders — and did not increase Navajo respect for government.

Worst of all, the Navajo could not farm. He had, during the Spanish era, made the dizzy leap from wild marauding savages to a pastoral people. He could not compress an equal development into three years and become, on demand, a farmer. When the Navajos first reached the Bosque Redondo, they had no idea what to do with the spades and hoes issued to them. They knew nothing of irrigation. Naturally, their crops failed.

So it became apparent, even in Washington, that the noble experiment of the Bosque Redondo was a failure, a commission was appointed, and in 1867 a new treaty was signed with the Navajos.

## THE RESERVATION AND THE GOVERNMENT

THIS TREATY PERSISTED IN THE DETERMINATION TO MAKE the Navajos skip a few centuries of normal development and become at once peaceable Christian farmers.

To this end every man was to be given land, seeds, agricultural implements, flocks and cattle, and even a hundred dollars with which to get started. A school was to be established for every thirty children, and attendance made compulsory.

Most of the terms of the treaty were never carried out, the government, like the Indian, being more apt at promise than at performance. The Navajo returned to his gorgeous deserts, resumed his pastoral and nomadic life, and hid his children as well as he could from government agents who came to take them to distant schools. His next advance into a sedentary group was going to take at least another century, and he could not be hurried. The Navajo had learned that the United States was stronger; whether it was smarter, time would tell.

With their usual quick adaptability, the People had made good use of their captivity. Women, deprived of their sheep, got Germantown wool from the traders and learned to make a new blanket, smoother than the old. Owing to lack of wool and the influence of white women, they gave up their short wool dresses and went into calico bodices and skirts fifteen yards round, as the mode prescribed. Men went into calico too: shirts, and straight drawers slit up the sides. Velvet did not take its important place in the Navajo wardrobe until Mormon traders introduced it, years later. Silver not being available, smiths made jewelry and horse-trappings out of sheet copper which the government gave them.

.·.

The original reservation was twelve thousand square miles, roughly between the San Juan River in New Mexico and the Little Colorado River in Arizona. It offered scanty grazing for flocks, and almost no water for agriculture; yet the adaptable Navajo has increased his flocks and developed herds fast enough to keep up with his own amazing increase. More land has been granted from time to time by executive order, and slowly the government is developing water for irrigation. The lordly Navajo is working with pick and shovel, helping government engineers to make dams and ditches and reservoirs; he is even bending his proud back to force a plow through his deserts. They say he is a natural mechanic and can do anything, once he is satisfied that he wants to. Through it all he manages to maintain his dignified aloofness. He is not yet a white man's Indian.

Government is administered by the agent, who appoints Indian judges and policemen to assist him. If he is wise, he chooses medicine-men or clan or district headmen, and he gives them as much latitude as possible. The Indian judge holds a court somewhat like a justice court; he gets at the facts in his own way, and he hands down judgments often as penetrating as Solomon's.

Within the last fifteen years oil has been scented, and some has been discovered, on the Navajo reservation. Oil-companies leased land from the Indians, and a couple of new problems appeared. Old men were afraid that drilling might offend the gods. Fortunately, several of the early structures produced water instead of oil, so the shamans were assured of divine favor, and advised their people to lease lands to strangers who, whatever their purpose, produced ever-useful water. How to use the prospective oil-money without corrupting the Indian was the other problem.

About this time, providentially, there came into the government service a man who understood the Navajos, and who met them as one gentleman may meet another to discuss their problems. As United States Commissioner to the Navajos, Herbert J. Hagerman called a council of twelve men, with twelve alternates. They met in 1923 — a very significant meeting, for it was the first elective group among the Navajos, the first time that the tribe had acted as a unit. The United States was represented by Mr. Hagerman, the presiding officer was Henry Chee Dodge, a gray-eyed Navajo headman, and hundreds of Navajos attended as intelligent and attentive listeners.

The council has now become an annual affair. The Navajos amaze visitors by showing themselves straight and able thinkers, well aware of their rights under the treaty, quick to distinguish between the valuable and the meretricious, and wise in their insistence that the oil-money be used for the benefit of the whole tribe. They have consistently opposed individual allotments. They realize that the greatest need of the tribe is for more land, and they are working toward that end.

In 1928 a new president of the council was elected: Dashne-Chis-Chiligi, who is a school graduate and speaks English well. He is about thirty-five years old — young enough to understand changing times — but he is conservative in his attitude toward the old ways; so he is pleasing to the old men.

## NAVAJO LIFE

IN SPITE OF ALL THESE CHANGES THE NAVAJO WITH FEW exceptions is born in the hogan; his mother is assisted by a tribal midwife, and a medicine-man chants suitable prayers. The baby nurses a long time, sometimes a couple of years, and is weaned on beans and coffee, or whatever the family has. Infant mortality is high and children beyond the nursing age often look undernourished. Yet the Navajo child who survives has the boon of a serene and happy home, with much less nagging and fussing than the ordinary white child is subjected to. Navajo parents are accused of over-indulgence, but their children greet visitors politely, proudly sing their little songs when asked, and speak only when spoken to. They belong to the mother's clan and she is the dominant parent, but the bond with both parents is very close. As a consequence old people are tenderly cared for and family feeling is strong.

As they grow, Navajo children share in the family work. Both boys and girls herd sheep, going out first with older children; but even when as young as ten, they are responsible for good-sized flocks. Life is largely conditioned by the needs of the sheep. The family drifts with them from water-hole to water-hole; in summer they follow good grazing into the high mountain pastures, in winter they seek sheltered spots in the lowlands. It is a nomadic life, but the ordinary family probably moves in an area of not more than ten miles.

Wherever they are, the woman is the head of the family. She owns her sheep as well as her home and her children, and if she tires of her husband he must go. No woman in the world occupies a more dignified position, and probably no woman in the world works harder. She is a wonderful shepherd; she shelters orphaned lambs under her wide skirts and even suckles them at her own breast. Her husband assists with dipping and marketing the sheep, but she handles the wool from shearing to the final blanket, and she is never far from her loom, hung in the hogan or between two cedar-trees.

The man may make silver, squatting on a sheepskin before his low charcoal fire, and chanting softly as he hammers Mexican dollars into adornment for all the tribes, including the tribe of westward-minded whites. His tools are simple, but as a craftsman and designer he can hardly be surpassed. He works without haste, as an artist must work, and he has the artist's quiet assurance of the value of his own work. There is much other business for the Navajo man. He buys, sells, trades, and races horses, in spite of the fact that the rapid increase in the herds has made them a liability instead of an asset. He, rather than the woman, is meeting changing conditions. He must make the necessary great adjustment to the modern world, and, in his own good time, he is taking over what suits him from the mechanical civilization of the whites.

Life in the hogan is as simple as a coffee-pot, a pile of blankets, a loom, and an anvil. Yet the Navajo child must from his earliest years be aware of great natural forces moving in color and rhythm across his desert, and caught now and then in the movement and cadence of the dance. Both boys and girls learn the tribal legends and are taken to the great religious ceremonies where songs are sung and prayers are danced to bring close whatever gods there are.

This life is interrupted by the business of schooling. At the age of six, children are taken from the hogans to the great barracks-like structures which are the government schools. There they are deloused, scrubbed, cropped, issued blue calico and blue jeans, and held sternly to an education designed primarily for white children. True to his aristocratic heritage, the Navajo child has not let this training affect him very deeply, even yet. He is secretive and aloof, he leaves the school as soon as possible, and he reverts with amazing suddenness to the life of the hogan and the clan.

The tribe is divided into about fifty clans, related groups which are loosely organized under a headman. Marriage within the clan is prohibited, so the young man, back from school, roves widely, looking at the girls. They meet at the great ceremonies and arrange their own affair, though marriage formalities are conducted by the families. The wedding is a ceremony. It takes place in the girl's hogan, a medicine-man presides, and the principal rite is eating corn-meal mush from a wedding-basket. Gifts are exchanged, everybody feasts, and the young couple move into a new hogan which has been built for them.

Wherever Navajos meet, for work or religion or play,

there is sport. Young men gamble, race, afoot or a-horse-back, dance, or sing. Always they sing, sing for hours, sing all night. They rehearse all the regular chants, being care-ful not to commit a profanity by singing winter ceremonial chants out of season; they sing love-songs, running-songs, and songs learned from other tribes. Sometimes a quick white ear will catch, in the midst of resounding Navajo phrases: " Hello, John! Hello, John! " This is a song to celebrate the big potatoes which the white man brought to replace the little wild ones.

Such a song brings laughter, and there are many others which cause the Navajos to rock with mirth, and which they refuse to translate. No doubt they would not pass any board of censorship. Neither would much of the burlesque which crops up impromptu. Their humor is caustic and keen, and it finds endless inspiration in the white people who cross the reservation. Names given to white people nearly always hit with cruel aptness upon some physical or mental peculiarity. " Old Parrot-feathers " was a woman who tried to feather her way into favor. " Big Mouth " is a man who talks too much.

Altogether, the Navajo is amused rather than respectful in his attitude toward white people. After he leaves school, he knows them mostly as traders, doctors, and missionaries. He does business with the trader, and he usually finds him and his family the sort of friends who are willing to help without undertaking radical alterations in one's ways.

Doctors and nurses try, sometimes cleverly, sometimes clumsily, to supplement the work of the medicine-man and to teach better ways of healing. A clever doctor was once called by a trader's wife to attend a pitifully undernourished baby. Medicine-men, who had been singing over the child for days, were naturally resentful. The doctor quietly waited on the conference, and the trader's wife, with quick understanding, made the convincing speech.

Said she: " You have been working hard here, calling upon the powers to help. So you have saved this baby. It is living, the doctor says it will live. Now it needs only good food, and its mother cannot nurse it. May we not take it to the doctor's hospital, where it will have good food, so your work will not be in vain? "

That was satisfactory, and the child was saved.

Among missionaries, too, there are many kinds. The government policy is to welcome any Christian missionary, coming to bring light to the heathen. Indians are usually persuaded to give them land, and then they are let alone to convert whom they can.

Once a Navajo headman came into a trading-post filled with anger. He thundered, his arms working like flails, his eyes flashing. He was a stormy man of wrath calling upon the gods of vengeance. He spoke in Navajo, but the trader afterwards gave me the burden of his oration.

" Why," he raged, " don't these missionaries go home? Why do they come here? Why do they bother us? We have a good religion. It is a religion of good. It teaches good. It tells us not to bother anyone. It is the same religion for all the People. Now come these missionaries with seven religions. They all talk different. They divide our people. They make trouble among us. Why don't these missionaries go home? "

Missionaries, on their part, point out that the tribal religion tolerates all sorts of superstitions, even sorcery.

Several years ago a medicine-man was accused of witchcraft. His wife's son had died of tuberculosis, that mysterious white man's disease which medicine-men are loath to treat. Another young man in the neighborhood sickened. Then a third. Clearly it was a case of bad medicine, for the victims grew weak and thin, lost appetite, and finally lost blood. There was a trial for witchcraft; and it took all the quick enterprise and daring of a trader to get his friend the medicine-man away before Navajo justice took a fatal turn. That medicine-man still lives far from his own people.

Among the superstitious fears with which even educated Navajos are filled is the fear of a hogan in which anyone has died. It is considered haunted and must be burned. Consequently a dying person is moved outside if possible. After he dies, the family, for four days, sit outside the hogan, facing east and chanting prayers to help the departing soul on its way. Friends wait on them and dispose of the body. Then the family undergoes a purification, which ends, as all Navajo prayers end:

" In beauty, it is finished.
In beauty, it is finished.
In beauty, it is finished.
In beauty, it is finished."

## CEREMONIES

MOST NAVAJO CEREMONIES ARE " MEDICINE SINGS OR chants." These are curing ceremonies given for one individual, but they have power to bring good to all who attend. The most important, Mountain Chant and Night Chant, occur during the winter.

There are two ceremonies which are not cures. A " prayer night " is held before grass comes in the spring. People bring seeds of corn, melons, beans, and squash to be blessed before planting. The rites take place in a hogan, with a medicine-man presiding. There are prayers for rain in dry years, which most years are. In both of these ceremonies the influence of the Pueblo people is evident. Neither includes a dance.

Other danceless " sings " are the Eagle Chant, which is a cure for sores; the Big Star Chant, which stops bad dreams or insanity; the Red Ant Chant, which used to be more important than it is now, for it is a cure for wounds received in war; the Feather Chant, for bad blood. There are special chants for child-birth and for farewell, and one called *In-dah*, a purification.

When I asked Clyde how In-dah was used, he said:

" Well, if my father was to suicide a Ute, they would have In-dah."

Staggered at the idea of so calmly and naturally " suiciding a Ute " — even a Ute — I failed to ask Clyde whether purification was for the crime of murder or to rid one of the contamination of the Ute. I learned afterwards that its purpose is to lay the ghost of the enemy, whose scalp used to figure in the proceedings. Now any trophy will do, whether it bears directly on the case or not.

Individual obligation in religious matters is apparently slight, though prayers indicate that everyone is expected

" to keep his heart pure," which is perhaps not so slight an obligation after all. Everyone, both man and woman, carries a personal fetish-bag, a small buckskin pouch. It contains a turquoise matrix, the blue typifying the sky, the matrix the rain and clouds. Small sticks and stones symbolize the male and the female, and fresh pollen, renewed each year, keeps the spirit alive.

Before taking part in any ceremony, at all important times in his life, or if he is ill, the Navajo takes a sweat bath. He chants while he bathes, and his heart must be pure.

Recently a Navajo came back from town drunk. He took a sweat bath, evidently too soon after the debauch, and in the close heated hut, he died. Traders who told me the story said that his neighbors were not at all concerned. They said he had not chanted properly, that his heart was not pure; altogether they showed no regret at his loss, and they refused to touch his body.

The bath is a low wattled hut, into which hot stones and wet grass or weeds are put to make steam. The patient sits inside, chanting, while someone heats more stones, brings more wet grass, and occasionally lifts the blanket over the doorway to let in air. After fifteen minutes or so the Indian, dripping dirty sweat, emerges, rubs his body briskly with sand, and returns for a shorter steaming. On the second emergence he is perfectly clean, glistening, smooth, bronze-gold. In winter he finishes with a roll in the snow. In summer the kindly friend dashes a bucket of cold water.

# VII: Navajo Dances

### MEDICINE-MEN

CEREMONIAL LIFE IS INTRICATE AND ELABORATE, AND THE medicine-man is its center and moving spirit. He is doctor as well as priest, and usually he is a dignified, honorable, and truly spiritual person. Here, as in all professions, a few misfits occur, a few crooks, a few fakes. It requires a long and arduous training to become a fully qualified medicine-man; sometimes a man serves an apprenticeship of twenty years before he is able to lead one of the great nine-day sings. If a boy shows an aptitude for the calling, such as a good singing voice, an unusual memory, or a spiritual quality, he begins training as assistant to a skilled medicine-man, often his maternal uncle.

They may be called to a home where the administration of a brew of herbs, with a few suitable motions and prayers, are indicated. They may be called to exorcise a devil, to cure a fever, to stanch a bleeding wound, to set a bone — an art at which the Navajo medicine-man commands the respect of white surgeons. Sometimes they fail, as all doctors sometimes fail. Often they succeed. Their methods would seem reasonable to a psychoanalyst in that they interpret dreams; to a hypnotist because they use suggestion freely; to an allopath when they turn herbs into medicines; to a yogi because they make passes of the hands accompanied by mystic words.

Often a highly respected medicine-man is called upon to render judgment or to settle disputes. Sometimes his psychic skill locates lost articles. In curing, the pupil does much of the work. He gathers herbs, learning their uses, as doctors once learned their trade in the apothecary's shop. He brings colored sand for the paintings and prepares it, and gradually he learns to make the great free-hand mosaics, dribbling sand through the fingers to draw pictures of such religious importance that there must be no single error. He learns hundreds of songs, in which he must be perfect to the smallest inflection. He learns the legends and traditions of his people. He develops whatever skill he may have in trance or in hypnotism.

A medicine-man is supposed never to refuse to answer a call, and never to stipulate a price. Like white doctors, he sometimes decides to be business-like. Ordinarly, if a person is ill and a sweat bath does not cure him, his family sends for the nearest shaman. The diagnosis may result from an interpretation of the dreams of the patient or his relatives, or the shaman may have a revealing dream. A very picturesque method is that in which the medicine-man sits, cross-legged, holding his fetish and chanting until he goes into a trance. Then someone mentions a long list of diseases, or of cures, and when the right word is uttered, the medicine-man shakes all over, and the diagnosis is made. Then the family decides upon what practitioner to call in to make the cure. Medicine-men are specialists in such arts as the cure of head diseases, of wounds, of certain kinds of bad magic.

The man chosen may come from a distant part of the reservation and he may, and often does, call upon several local shamans to assist him. No doubt the chant prescribed depends upon the wealth of the patient. It may be a matter of one night; it may be one of the lengthy eight-day ceremonies. Poor people, however, are treated; medicine-men often treat for no pay at all. Payment always includes the baskets used ceremonially in the chant, the ceremonial deerskin, if one is used, fifty dollars in cash, out of which the assistants are paid, and sometimes additional fees of sheep, goats, blankets, or cloth.

The ceremonies have marvelous unity, considering how large the reservation is and how sparsely populated. This and the astonishing coherence of the whole tribe are no doubt due to the medicine-men. They travel widely to assist each other's sings, to observe and criticize each other's magic; and they hold every new medicine-man strictly to the ancient conventions. So these wise old men try to hold together an ancient faith, in the midst of an alien and dominant civilization. They are certainly sagacious old men, experienced in the vagaries of weather and of human life. Looking at them anywhere, it is easy to believe that they are also wise with some deep occult knowledge of the hidden meaning and movements of life.

### THE SQUAW-DANCE

THE SQUAW-DANCE IS THE ONLY AFFAIR AT WHICH COUPLES dance. Navajos say that " Squaw-dance " is a white man's name for it; it is really a war-dance. It is also a curing ceremony, the disease figuring as the enemy to be defeated.

The whole affair lasts three days, starting at the home of the patient and moving each day a day's journey for a horse. The trek is made slowly in wagons or on horseback, and every day the crowd increases. On the second night a few men, daubed with mud, dance a wild shouting turn, as a prayer for rain. Only on the last night do women dance.

A summer ceremony, the Squaw-dance may occur at any time from the beginning of the rains in July until the peaches in Canyon de Chelly have ripened and been gathered, and the first frost opens the season of the great winter sings. One may be told any day on the reservation: " There's a Squaw-dance over by Lone Cedar," or " They're dancing tonight by Lukuchukai." Even as close to civilization as where a transcontinental train rushes by in streaks of orange light, and an air-line beacon swings a pencil of light across the plain, they dance.

Nearing the place, one sees the fire-glow in the sky long before the ear is struck by the rhythmic pulsations of the chanting. Dropping over a hill, one comes suddenly upon hundreds of people, gathered in an open space among the trees. Picketed horses snort as the car throws light on them. Babies are bedded under blankets in wagons. A few battered cars. Men stand in a circle of saddles thrown on the ground, and in that enclosure is the dancing.

A few girls, making their first appearance, may be shy and must be encouraged by their mothers; but, watching, one understands fully the independent, not to say dominant, position of the Navajo matron, who is truly a matriarch.

The woman approaches the man, standing resistant among his friends, links her right arm into his so that they face in opposite directions, and pulls him into the circle. Then they dance, up and down and back and forth, to the short staccato beat of the chanting voices. That is all; but it is quite enough to define the position of the lady. Sternly, firmly, relentlessly she holds him. Where she goes, he goes. She may seem to pay no attention to her particular quarry; facing away from him gives her a fine impersonal air. She goes forward while he goes back; when she backs up, he goes forward; but always when she goes, he follows. There is no escape. It is lady's night, and no mistake.

The only way out is pay. They say that in the good old days it was suitable for a buck to present a squaw with a white child brought back from his last war, thus neatly squaring the account with Mexicans who captured Navajos as presents for their brides. Then jewelry, skins, or horses. Now it is usually money, and the lady is not to be put off with a few cents. If he does not offer enough at first, they go on dancing, kicking up the dust as her skirts fly and his tall head bobs meekly along above hers.

Giggles, chuckles, and chortles run round the circle of watchers, and afterwards one often hears amusing bits of gossip, but the dancing is as solemn as a Quaker meeting. The business is dancing, and collecting. So they dance, and collect.

## THE MOUNTAIN CHANT

THE MOUNTAIN CHANT IS GIVEN ONLY IN WINTER, THE SEAson of hibernation: " after the thunder sleeps," which means the end of the thunder-storms; and before the spring winds begin. Navajos believe that if the ceremony were given, or even if the songs were sung and the legends told, at any other season, death from lightning or snake-bite would result. If during the ceremony an animal which should be hibernating is found out, they bring him in to the ceremony; so they say.

This chant is very important to medicine-men, as each shaman is given a chance to display his magic and to observe that of his rivals. Often several medicine-men from various parts of the reservation attend. There are said to be four ceremonies, all founded on the same legend, but differing greatly in detail of presentation and in the wording of the songs. When I asked one medicine-man how they decided which one to give, he said: " If the bear medicine ran against you, you would give the Bear Mountain Chant."

### The Legend of the Mountain Chant
#### (following Washington Matthews)

Six Navajos, father, mother, two sons, and two daughters, wandered from place to place. As they went, they developed spring water, discovered the uses of various seeds and berries, built a hogan and a sweat-house, and the two young men, coached by their father, learned the best ways of hunting and killing deer. They also learned much magic.

In hunting, the young men were warned by their father never to go south of their home, though they might hunt in any other direction. In time the elder brother, Dsilyi Neyani, showed himself akin to all the heroes of all the tales by deciding to take a look in the forbidden direction. Utes captured him and threatened his life. Assisted by a mysterious old woman, by a man in the mask of an owl, and finally by one of the gods (the Yei), he made a miraculous escape, carrying treasure with him. This was only the beginning of a long flight, during which Dsilyi Neyani was saved in one way or another by a mountain sheep, by a bush-rat, and by a whirlwind. When the dangers which beset him became particularly threatening, there was always a friendly Yei at hand to help him. Yei made bridges of ice or cloud or rainbow, lighted his way with lightning, gave him protective medicine, taught him magic words.

In time he came to a hogan where lay four bears the colors of the four directions. They taught him to make sacrificial sticks. Later he visited weasels, the Great Serpent, the lightning. Everywhere he learned magic or ceremonial acts.

One of the most interesting of the young hero's adventures was his visit to the House of the Butterfly, a beautiful place filled with butterflies and rainbows. There he was bathed and shampooed in a basin made of a white shell; and painted and dressed as are the couriers who announce the Mountain Chant even today. By this time Dsilyi Neyani was well up on the mountain. He visited many places, in each of which he met young men, four or eight, who taught him more rites in the great ceremony which he was to take back to mankind. By this time the hero himself had been molded by the Butterfly Woman into the shining likeness of the gods, and the places which he visited were roofed with light, upheld by white spruce-trees, lighted by rainbows, floored with sacred corn-pollen.

He learned all the sand paintings which are used in the chant, how to make feathers dance, how to swallow swords, how to make a weasel appear and do magic, how to play with fire unharmed, and the mystical " hu-hu-hu-hu," which is the cry of the dance.

Then Dsilyi Neyani returned to his people, who had apparently grown in his absence from a family into a tribe. He was met by a medicine-man, purified as is customary when one returns from foreign places, and then permitted to tell the tale of his wanderings. It took him four days and four nights, but he was so convincing an expositor of the new rites that at once runners were selected, adorned according to the new specifications, and sent out to invite guests to the ceremony. Among the guests were to be friendly Utes, distant bands of Navajos, and several tribes of Apaches. That is why the Mountain Chant is still a ceremony to which visitors are especially welcome.

The young men selected as runners were known as lazy and worthless youths; yet they went farther and quicker than was common and brought back objects to prove that they had done in one day what was planned for four. The rest of the time was spent by all the Navajos in gambling, and then the visitors began to arrive. Matthews, quoting the tale as he heard it, says: " After the guests began to arrive the young men set to work to cut trees for the corral, and when the sun had set the building of the dark circle of branches began. While the young men were making the circle, the old men were making speeches to the multitude, ' for the old men always love to talk while the young men are hard at work.' It was the greatest corral that has ever been built in the Navajo country. It was as broad as from Canyon Bonito to the Haystacks (about six miles); yet the visiting tribes were so numerous that they filled the circle full."

During the night there were many different shows and tricks, performed both by Navajos and by visitors. Some of the visitors proposed a race such as the young couriers had made. The course was to be round Mount Taylor, and the visitors were allowed to choose which runner they would back. They chose the one who had run to the north, and the Navajos got the southern runner. Then bets were laid: strings of coral, shell, and turquoise, shell vessels as large as the largest Zuñi bowls, tanned buckskin garments, dresses embroidered with porcupine quills, suits of armor made of several layers of buckskin.

When the race began, the fastest runners of both Navajos and strangers followed, but they could not even keep in sight of the contestants, those strange young men who had always been considered so lazy and worthless. The Navajos won, naturally, so they had all the wagered wealth of their visitors — a most suitable ending.

The strangers were dissatisfied and demanded another

race, this time on a longer course. So plans were made to race all round the foot-hills of Mount Taylor. This time the Navajos wagered only half their winnings. The strangers won, so they were satisfied, and the Navajos still had more than any of the other people, which is the reason they are still more wealthy than their neighbors.

After this, Dsilyi Neyani moved his family several times. Finally they settled in the Black Mountains, from which they could see Mount Taylor. Dsilyi Neyani knew that the Yei would come there for him, so he prepared his family for his translation. He said to his younger brother: "You will never see me again, but when the showers pass and the thunder peals, 'There,' you will say, 'is the voice of my elder brother,' And when the harvest comes, of the beautiful birds and grasshoppers, you will say: 'There is the ordering of my elder brother.' "

So was established the Mountain Chant, which celebrates these events.

### Going to the Mountain Chant

On our way to the Mountain Chant we stopped at a trading-post. A sunny winter morning. Patches of snow among the scrub cedars and piñon on the hill-sides. Within, a large glowing stove standing in a sand-box. Navajos leaning against the shoulder-high counter, trading. One large flat-faced man, who had just completed a trade for pelts, began the spending of his twenty dollars. With a few guttural phrases and many gestures he made his selections: two sacks of flour, three buckets of lard, two packages of Arbuckle's coffee, three tins of baking-powder. As each article was added to a pile in the corner, the trader made a calculation on a brown paper sack, deducting the amount of the sale, and telling the Indian what his balance then was. The grin on the broad face grew constantly more expansive as the pile of groceries grew, and especially as the white women admired his jewelry. He wore a magnificent turquoise necklace, which the trader assessed as worth fifteen hundred dollars, and a heavy silver hatband on a very dirty hat. The company watched with beady black eyes. Trading went on to shirts: white silk striped in colors, one for the big man, one for each of three or four attendant young men. Business progressing so favorably, the plutocrat indulged himself in a large cigar and in a bag of candy, which was passed to the young men. By this time his ideas seemed to be running out, and he moved more slowly the length of the counter, looking at the shelves and followed by the trader with his sack and his pencil. Well aware of Navajo psychology, the trader offered no suggestions; he just cannily waited. During a very long pause he handsomely presented a boy with a second bag of candy, which went the rounds. Another can of baking-powder was finally decided upon, a thin silk handkerchief, maybe for the woman in the hogan, another sack of candy, and finally, to wipe the slate clean, one sack of Bull Durham tobacco.

Meanwhile, in the course of an hour's trading, the big man had taken out of pawn a necklace, very inferior to the one he wore. He wore it for a few minutes, and just before the end of negotiations he repawned it to the trader, who put a new ticket on it and hung it in his case again. The whole transaction took place on the back of the brown paper sack, and no money changed hands. Everybody beamed with joy, seeing such important and wealthy matters going forward. A woman, her full skirts sweeping the floor, and her hair straggling from its cords, accepted a bit of candy. She munched a piece, fed some to the baby cuddled in her warm store blanket, and stood impassive, only her bright black eyes moving. Young men lounged, their lithe bodies balanced in high-heeled cowboy boots and supported against the counter. One sat in the broad window-sill, crouching like an animal. He knew a little English.

" Belicana ladies in chitti," he announced, as a rattling Ford drew up outside. It was labelled: " Jesus saves. Ask me. I love to tell the story." Two prim tight-lipped women came in, bought soap and calico, murmured patronizing words to a few Navajos, who did not answer, and left again.

The time came for us to move out to the medicine hogan, where the Mountain Chant was going on. The large purchaser, his money all happily spent, was engaged in loading his goods on to a truck, where his family already sat on piles of blankets. A fine old grandmother, with the face of a sibyl, held a baby strapped to a board. Two young women, glorious in amber and rose velvet shirts, squatted among their billowing skirts, their chignons topped with celluloid combs set with rhinestones, their bosoms and arms heavy with native jewelry. Children of assorted sizes, most of them in velvet shirts and jewels. A tall youth cranked the motor, and they snorted out of the enclosure and off up the rocky piny canyon toward the ceremonial ground.

It was a high lonesome place on a hill-side, where piñon and cedar were beginning to yield to a stand of yellow pine and spruce. A wash dropped off sharply at one side, a long lane had been grubbed clear for the races, and many shelters of piñon boughs had been built against the wind. Within their shelter sat women butchering sheep, tending babies, poking small sticks under bubbling pots, gossiping. The young men were racing, great piles of bets lying on the ground in blankets, cries of delight rising from the crowd as the tiny ponies dashed from one end of the runway to the other.

### Preliminary Ceremonies

The medicine hogan, facing east as always, was of the most formal type, with an extension for the entrance and a hanging blanket for a door. Smoke curled from the smoke hole, and men went in and out, raising the blanket and letting it fall behind their long legs. The ceremony had been going on for seven days, during which all the tale of Dsilyi Neyani's wanderings had been rehearsed in chants and in sand paintings. There are even short dramatic episodes described by Dr. Matthews, who has published a detailed account of every rite.

Most important is the making of sand paintings, an art most highly developed by the Navajos. A large space is covered with fine sand, which is smoothed with the batten used in weaving. Then the workers begin. Sometimes as many as twelve men crouch around the space, allowing colored sand to dribble through their fingers to make the pattern. Four colors are used: red, blue (which is really gray), yellow, and white. The chief medicine-man does nothing, but as he sits quietly watching, he is alert to catch any false move or incorrect line and to direct its change. Any error would nullify the effect of the whole ceremony.

We arrived, one year, during the afternoon of the eighth day and were met by Jeanette, our sponsor. Jeanette speaks very good English, and, as the daughter of the headman, she had influence. She had promised to get us into the hogan to see the curing and the destruction of the last sand painting. When we arrived, she was in the cook-shelter, a huge pavilion of boughs where the patient's family was providing food for all comers. Jeanette came out to meet us, wiping her hands on a purple shirt bound with orange. She wore a red plush blouse, her hair was smooth, and she was splendid with jewelry.

" I'm so busy! " she said cordially; " I've got to run this whole damned show."

Then she led the way toward the hogan. A few old men looked on us sardonically, their haughty scorn rather affecting our composure. Clinging to Jeanette, we murmured:

" You're coming with us? "

" Oh, no," said Jeanette, " ladies don't go in there. You go in. Ladies don't go."

So, our last bit of assurance completely washed out in true Navajo disdain, we meekly bent our heads under the blanket and entered. Inside was that dull gray light of a winter interior, only a square patch of sunlight wavering under the smoke hole as shreds of blue smoke drifted out. A sheet of iron hid the fire, which was placed at one side to make room for the painting. The chief medicine-man sat facing us, his fine old head bent, brown sensitive hands lying inert on thin legs in striped trousers, which ended in brown moccasins folded under his knees. His velvet blouse was purple, purple shadows lay about him on the dirt floor, his turquoise and silver hung loosely from his bent breast; his quiet was positively eloquent. Nobody spoke to us, but several men moved a little to make room for our blankets on the dirt floor. We sat. Nothing happened. Men simply sat, and the light shifted lazily round the drifting smoke and touched the sand painting.

This one represented the House of the Dew-drops, which was well up on the mountain that Dsilyi Neyani climbed. Four great figures lay parallel, probably to accommodate them to the space, for their coloration showed that they represented the directions. The whole was surrounded by a rainbow.

Finally the blanket over the entrance was raised and the patient came in. She was a large woman, looking well fed and not in the least ill. One thought of the splendor of the affair, the social distinction which must accrue from the spending of so much money; and one thought also of wealthy white women undergoing operations. The patient removed her blanket and sat down, south of the painting. Again nothing happened. Then the medicine-man began to chant, not moving or in any way announcing that he was about to begin. His voice was high-pitched and very true, the syllables he uttered were musical, with interesting harsh inflections and wailing minor notes. The song seemed interminable, as Indian chanting is apt to do. Finally he ended it, rose, and with a feather dipped in water he sprinkled the woman and the sand painting. Something was placed in the woman's hands and she sat on the painting.

Then the serious treatment began. The shaman touched parts of the painting with sacred meal, and parts of the woman, applying it first to her outstretched feet, then her knees, her hands, her abdomen, her shoulders, her back, her mouth, in which he placed a bit of meal, and finally her head. Touching her firmly with long, accurate hands, he kept his chant going and occasionally he whistled to blow away the evil. Others in the hogan watched intently. Incense was scattered over the fire, and the patient stooped to inhale the fumes as they rose. She also chanted, following the medicine-man line by line. Sand was taken from various parts of the picture and applied to parts of her body. At this point several spectators also took sand and touched their own bodies, undoubtedly getting their share of the mystic cure. Finally the woman moved away from the painting, which was then completely destroyed and the sand carried away.

Weary from the long sitting, half-hypnotized by the soft blue light, the chanting, the mysterious solemn movements, we followed the men out into the evening light. By this time many Navajos had gathered and snapping cedar fires were burning all around and sending long blue banners of fragrant smoke toward the west.

### The Ninth Day

All day visitors arrived on horseback and in creaking wagons, rattling Fords, a few large cars. Women sat like queens among their voluminous skirts, carrying babies. They dismounted unaided, built fires, cooked, cared for children; but always with that fine impersonal scorn of drudgery with which the Navajo woman asserts her supremacy. One feels that she does what she does because she wishes to, or that she accepts the task without stooping to it. Men worked too, chopping and dragging in an incredible amount of wood, picketing and feeding horses, clearing the ground of stumps for the great corral in which the dancing was to take place.

During the afternoon the lodge was filled with dancers, preparing the paraphernalia for the night. We were admitted, and we saw much work with small sticks, little circles of willow withes, feathers, down, paint. Just what they were doing we could not see in the dull light, but we learned from reading the report of the all-knowing Mr. Matthews.

Rings of a pithy wood were fitted on slim wands of aromatic sumac and decorated with fluffy eagle-down. Two rings for each wand. Arrows made of hard cliff-rosewood were made to run into false arrows of hollow wood. Spruce limbs were whittled down to slender bending sticks, such as the Zuñi sword-swallowers use, and painted red. We were gently excused before the actors began to rehearse the use of these and other properties.

Outside we found a great welter of activity. Eighty miles from the railroad, more than a thousand people had gathered to meet and talk, to be entertained, to win or lose money, to hear speeches, to trade, to be healed, or to acquire protection from future danger of fire or lightning. The great cook-house where Jeanette presided was filled with hungry ones; smaller fires everywhere were surrounded by family groups. A few young men, inveterate gamblers, were still following the sticks and stones of their favorite game in the failing light. Huge piles of seasoned wood were ready for the great central bonfire, and the sacred wood for making the mystic "dark circle of branches" lay ready in a rough ring near the medicine hogan.

About sunset the chief medicine-man came out of the hogan, allowing the blanket to drop behind his tall figure, and standing quietly until all were aware of his presence. Then he began to chant the mysterious words by whose power the evergreens rose, as though by magic, and formed themselves into a circular corral. Eight or ten feet tall, the trees completely hid the men who handled them; and the work was done so quickly and so smoothly that they seemed to rise of themselves behind the stately figure moving to the wailing chant. When erect and laced, the trees made a circular fence which inclosed a space about a hundred feet in diameter, quite regular, and with only one opening, that to the east. As soon as it was finished, the ground within was sacred and any intruding dog was chased out with yells and missiles. In the center they erected the cone of tall poles for the great fire which would be lighted later on.

People began at once to crowd in, always turning south from the east gate to make the correct ceremonial circuit, a convention rigidly observed by all the Navajos and by any whites who were quick enough to catch it. Soon the circle of branches was lined with an inner circle of small household fires, lighting swarthy cheek-bones and flashing red on silver. Piles of blankets concealed babies, watermelons, and boxes of food. Smells of roasting meat and corn mingled with the pungent smoke. It was a cold evening, frosty and still, and the ground was icy. Gradually the fires made small warm islands, very comforting in spite of stinging smoke which gentle winds spun round and into the eyes. The imperturbability of the Indian is never better exemplified than as Navajos settle themselves for a long winter night's ceremony. Women and children of all ages dispose themselves among blankets, with a blackened coffee-pot at hand, a pot of beans and meat stewing in the embers, a water-bag hanging in the sacred branches, a watermelon ready to be opened about midnight. Then they rest uncomplaining. Children are waited on as need be, fed from the pot or from the mother's breast, held while their bright black eyes shine like beads into the firelight, allowed to droop gently asleep, and packed away in blankets for a nap. Men crowd into the entrance, allowing only a narrow neck of space through which the performers have to force their way. Nobody stands against the outside of the corral wall, for that space is reserved for the spirits of the ancestral animal gods: bears and wolves, weasels, bush-rats, and others who might wish to attend. White visitors, not understanding this, are occasionally warned away, but without explanations.

### The Last Night

When a certain star rose, the night's ceremony began, with the entrance of a group of men bearing musical instruments. They settled on the west side of the corral, and as their rattling and scraping began, the huge fire was lighted. Well-seasoned wood, standing twelve or fourteen feet high, roared into a terrific blaze which sent flares of flame and smoke a hundred feet into the air, while showers of sparks fell back into the corral and caused a general patting of blankets. The scene was magnificent: an operatic glow on dark faces, striped blankets, silver and turquoise, gaudy velvets — all set against the dark mystery of the circle of branches.

Suddenly dancers came dashing into the circle; bare bodies whitened with clay until they looked like animated clay models. They leaped wildly, gyrating with arms and legs and yelling like lost souls. Cavorting in an irregular circle, they rounded the fire as prescribed, south, west, north, and south again. Twice they made the circuit, keeping a gingerly distance from the menacing waves of heat, posturing gracefully, but with dramatic pantomime of its horrors. The heat is indeed so terrifying that, sitting back against the wall of boughs, one often turned away or raised a blanket against the face. That those dancers could bear it was incredible except on the assumption that white clay is an excellent non-conductor. At last one man, yelling as in despair, nerved himself to approach the fire closer, holding toward it one of the sumac wands we had seen made in the afternoon. In the firelight it was a mysteriously beautiful thing, slim and white and tipped with delicate white down. Throwing himself flat and shielding his face with a bent arm, the dancer thrust his wand into the glowing coals; then he whooped madly and rose to dash about and to show that the ball of down was burned away. Others followed him until all were running round with downless wands. Then, yelling in wickedly false triumph, they shot out the little ring with its new ball, apparently renewing the fluff.

Everybody understood the trick, everybody was delighted to see it well done, and the dancers left, still whooping.

The second act was one which is said never to be omitted: the dance of the great plumed arrows. For this act, as for them all, the chorus entered first in a long line, headed by a medicine-man. They shuffled sideways, making a queer serpentining effect as their bodies turned obliquely, never looking in the direction in which they went, and always intoning their queer complaining chant. It was as though they approached the gods in a wily manner, refusing to look them squarely in the eye, making not so much a prayer or a song of praise as a querulous fussing. In nothing is the Navajo's essential strangeness more evident than in the tone he uses toward his gods. No white man could do it: no white man's god could understand it. Glancing aside, complaining, bitterly and solemnly complaining, they rounded the fire several times, taking no note whatever of the heat so devastating to spectators and to the former dancers. Finally they took their places on the west and the dancers entered.

This time there were only two, young men dressed as were the couriers, only without the beaver collars or the pouches of sacred meal. They danced leaping, carrying high the plumed arrows which are the most sacred of the healing devices, though everyone knows them to be faked. Finally they stopped before the singers, where the patient waited for them, sitting on a blanket, with outstretched legs. Each dancer stood before her and with cries of distress held his arrow up, marking with his thumb a point near the feathered tip. Then he threw back his head, placed the arrow-point on his lips, and thrust the weapon down his throat. Excellent acting made the spectators gag in sympathy as the dancer swayed and pranced, forcing the awful thing down his gullet. Yet everyone knew, and he knew that everyone knew, that he was merely holding the arrow-point between his teeth and running the hard shaft into the hollow tip. The curing was done by touching the patient with the arrows in the manner prescribed, which chased the evil from the body. Then the dancers left. The chorus always leaves too.

By this time a couple of hours had passed, and the fire had been replenished several times. A battered old moon was up, and long rags of cloud drifted across it, trying to work up a snow-storm. It was cold, but very still. The whole world seemed to center in this dark circle of branches from which a great red globe of light reached into the blackness, as though through it this human stir of prancing and yelling might convey its meaning to whatever gods there are. The great fire made a pulsation as the hours passed: roaring and snapping angrily when it was built up, then settling down into a steady consumption of dry wood until it comforted itself into a beautiful glow of flower forms among the leafy ashes; then being rudely broken up with more tinder wood and forced into activity. All the time the acts and the waits followed the beat of the fire: sometimes it was all vigorous howling and stamping; sometimes it was a still, cold night with a thousand or more people huddled around a circle of little fires in the middle of a desert, not sleeping, fighting discomfort all night long in answer to some hidden and incalculable urge for betterment.

The program may vary, depending upon what medicine-men are present. In 1929, near Two Gray Hills, we saw these acts. Singers entered, whining that nasal falsetto cry of the Yei, who, being gods, must never speak the words of man, but convey their messages in meaningless syllables. The leader was an old man buttoned tightly into a white man's coat, his long, gray hair gathered into a knot behind, his long, crooked legs ending in trim moccasins. Then another old man, with the mien of a priest, solemnly twirling the childish whizzer, which the Navajos call "the groaning stick," and which makes the noise of thunder. Then the Yei, in flat blue mask and raising in his hands the slim dead body of a mink as he gave his characteristic yodel: "Hu-hu-hu-*hu*." Then eight wand-bearers, dressed like the couriers. Circling the fire many times, they silhouetted their black forms against the glow; then they turned to show their faces; again they made dark shadows; and all the time their chant wailed above the thunderous whizzer. Finally they grouped themselves on the dancing-space and swung into figures like the quadrilles that used to be done on ball-room floors. Beautiful foot-work in this, slim quick feet pounding tracks in the earth, beads rattling, long-waisted bodies turning with angular grace, never missing, never faltering, and wet with sweat in spite of the cold which kept the audience muffled to the eyes in blankets.

Then the Yebetchai. Often this dance is introduced by a visiting team, and it is always done in full regalia and accurately and well. Most unforgettable is that terrific wailing chant, that insistent urgent note which will not let the gods rest, which must rise to the very top of that red globe of light, pulsing into the darkness and into the infinite.

Long waits between. The sky was well covered with a spreading of clouds, which a couple of hours ago had seemed so inadequate. Then the sun show. Many dancers, probably two dozen, some in costume, some in store clothes, all wearing moccasins, and all moving with the steady exalted solemnity of dancers before the gods. One man in kilts of bright red silk and pendant fox-skin, wore on his back a feather-bordered disk, which is the sun symbol. His mate, in similar costume, wore the sign of the moon, smaller and not so gaily colored. Every dancer carried a large reed frame, like the skeleton of a kite, put together with a cat's-cradle of strings and decorated with floating eagle-down. They all chanted as they moved round the fire, making obeisance as they bent their heads and dipped their symbols toward it. The act ended with a quick spirited dance: rapid rhythmic movements, with the beautiful floating plumes tinted pink and rosy red in the firelight.

This dance was repeated several times, as were the others, many teams competing. During one appearance of the feathered kites, snow began to fall; quiet fluffy flakes looking like the down on the reeds, hissing gently in the fire, and misting across the dark branches. A few white people got themselves fussily into cars, which were heard straining on the distributors and finally crashing into gear and roaring off into the silence. Navajos huddled closer into blankets, mothers patted coverings closer about sleeping children. Otherwise they paid no attention to the storm, which, after all, did not last long. It was as though some god had drifted over, dropping a few feathers from his costume to assure his people that the message was getting through.

Several acts of magic came along after midnight. First the dance of the arcs. A chorus came in followed by eight men bearing the arcs: slender wands arching from one hand to the other, which held bunches of piñon needles. They danced round the fire, dipping the arcs toward it, went through a stately dance, and finally produced their magic. The dancers knelt in two facing rows; each dancer held his head very steady while his vis-à-vis placed the arc over it, where it stood without touching, except as the bunches of piñon came close to the ears. All the time they called: "*Thohay, thohay* (Stay, stay)," the magic word which held the arcs. The string which rested on the man's head was quite invisible in the firelight. Then they rose and, holding backs and necks in frozen erectness, they danced slowly out of the circle. This act was well done and it brought approving murmurs from all our Navajo neighbors. It was done again and again, several times by the first group, once by another group, and always without a mishap.

Then came the yucca trick. As the group made their queer twisting entrance, we saw that the leader carried the root of a yucca plant, with its spiny leaves, which stay green all winter. The dance around the fire was short, but the chanting seemed more than usually insistent in its repetitions. Finally the group gathered, kneeling around the leader in such a way as to hide him and the plant completely. That this was to be a good trick was evident from the way the Navajos crowded around the actors, especially young men. The insistent chanting was continuous; the suggestive word "Thohay" was repeated over and over. At last the group parted, leaving a lane through which we could see that the yucca plant had miraculously grown a tall bud in the center of the leaves. Again the group closed, and when it opened for the second time, we saw the great creamy blossom of the yucca, beautiful as when it blooms naturally in July or August. There could be no doubt about it: there stood the blossoming plant, complete. Loud murmurs of approval, and increasing tensity as the men again hid the leader and the plant. Again the circle opened and we saw the fruit, fully matured. This time the audience chortled with delight. The actors rose and shuffled out, whining, serpentining, taking no credit apparently for the completed growth which they left behind them that any doubter might go and assure himself of its reality.

Next came a large group carrying many properties. The whizzer and the rattler led. Then a man in a fur cap carrying a flat ceremonial basket. Then a man with a short flat board, painted, and decorated with feathers. When they had completed the ceremonial circle, saluting the fire, the performers arranged themselves in a crouching group and chanted hard, as the young men pressed them close. Finally they sat back and showed the board standing upright in the basket, which was filled with spruce twigs. The chanting then began in earnest, a steady vibration, gaining constantly in power and intensity. For a long time nothing happened. Then, wabbly but unmistakably, the sun symbol began to rear its curving edge above the twigs in the basket. Very slowly, very uncertainly it rose, the chanting voices creating its power, demanding its success. Slowly, with great difficulty, but without any doubt, it climbed the stick. Once or twice it almost fell, and everyone gasped, even imperturbable Navajos nervous in the face of possible failure. But it made it; unquestionably that little feathered symbol of the sun climbed, without human aid except the voices, to the top of the stick, rested there a moment, and then more easily, but jerkily, climbed down again. This one drew thunders of applause.

More appearances of the Yebetchai dancers, more repetitions of other acts seen before, and then the dancing feather. This time the dancers were accompanied by a small boy, probably not more than ten or twelve years old. He was stripped and painted, he wore feathers on his cropped hair, moccasins on his feet, and around his middle a kirtle of red silk. His little body was lithe and beautiful as he solemnly circled the fire with the men, one of whom carried a flat basket and a long feather. The group clustered to hide their arrangements and then opened out into an ellipse, at one end of which the boy stood above the basket on the ground. Across the basket lay the long eagle-quill. The men began to chant and the boy to dance, his slim feet in perfect time to the singing, his body erect and graceful. Suddenly, without warning, the eagle-feather rose in its basket and stood on the tip of its quill, straight and true for a moment. Then it began to dance. It danced in perfect time with the boy, up and down, turning to the right and to the left, never losing a beat, never showing uncertainty; like a living thing it danced. The crowd drew close; breath was held as everyone watched the astonishing accuracy with which the feather followed that little dancing figure.

Then an outrage occurred. Suddenly a beam of hard white light cut across the fire-lit gloom and showed clearly the several strings which led from the feather to the men in the kneeling group. It was only a moment; it was met with scornful groans, and it was, most unhappily, a flashlight in the hand of a young Navajo. The performers made no sign of distress. Without a flicker of annoyance they kept up the chant, the boy danced, the feather gyrated, the act finished as though no vandalism had occurred.

Another act was rather funny, and we noticed women shaking sleepy children awake to look at it. A basket again, filled with spruce and piñon. As the chanting went on, a tiny animal, probably a weasel, poked his stuffed head out of the greenery, looked from side to side, and ducked in again. This brought delighted squeals from children, who immediately forgot that they had been sleepy.

Two men danced, brilliantly, the Feather-dance. It is a spirited rapid leaping, feet scarcely touching the ground, and snapping away from it almost to the man's buttocks. Face to face they danced, feathers moving up and down in their hands, the chorus chanting sparkling, snapping syllables. Every now and then the dancers flew past each other to exchange positions and dance face to face again. It is a great test of agility, of skill, of endurance; and a good team is known and respected all over the reservation.

### The Fire-dance

The dull terrifying cold of just before dawn. Wind ferreting in through the circle of branches and sneaking down one's neck in spite of all wrappings. The ground colder than ever and more than ever full of unnecessary bumps and hollows. Many small fires burned down to glowing chunks of wood smothered in ashes, and everyone seemed to forget to build them up again. At last many young men came in, dragging great trees for the central fire, which was harried out of its glowing peace into fierce flaring, crackling, roaring heat again. When it was at its hottest, and one suffered under attacks of cold from one side and heat from the other, suddenly the loud burring call of the fire-dancers filled the air.

Their cry is a trilling made with the tongue against the lips, like the fluttering of a quickly burning fire. Heard outside, it was exciting, thrilling, wild. Then into the circle of light dashed the dancers, about fourteen of them, all naked and all painted white, heads as well as bodies. Each man carried a large bundle of shredded cedar bark almost as long as himself. One man brought several. They circled the fire too, but with leaping dash instead of the querulous whining crawl of the other groups. There was no chorus, but the dancers never ceased their trumpeting inhuman call. For a long time they fought the idea of the fire, circling toward it until the terrific heat drove them off, then yelling, turning, and daring each other to approach it again. Finally the leader threw himself flat and poked his faggot along the ground until it ignited from coals at the base of the fire. Then he rose and, sounding a great call, threw the bundle over the fence to the east. Taking other bundles from the man who followed him, he threw one in each direction. Before the last brand started on its whirling arc, he lighted all the others from it, the naked shivering figures gathering close around him and waiting until their brands were flaming well.

Then began the real dance. The men, racing in a circle round the fire, close to the unbearable heat, whooped like demons and beat their own bodies and each other's with the flaming brands. One man beat the bare back in front of him until it slipped away. Then he flared his brand over his own back, showering sparks, he straddled it as he ran, he turned and threw its flames over the man who followed him. They washed each other's backs with flame. They leaped so close to the fire that their bare feet seemed to be treading on live coals. The figures, following each his own devices, together made a painting such as Doré might have done for Dante's *Inferno:* pale inhuman figures, capering in the firelight, bathed in the red glow and the showers of orange sparks, always calling that queer suggestion of flickering flame. It seemed to last a long time; actually until the cedar brands were well burned out. Then each man dropped his smoldering bark and, still trilling loudly, ran out of the corral. Intense, brilliant, savage.

As the dancers left, spectators swarmed in to pick up bits of the burned cedar, sure protection against danger of fire for the year to come.

· ·

By this time the east was showing white, that comfortless early morning light which makes everyone ghastly. Even brown Navajo faces looked gray. White people appeared as at the end of a long illness or a terrific debauch.

HO SHUN I
(Interior of a Medicine Hogan)

[NILS HOGNER]

The fire was burning low again, but nobody built it up. Then the chief medicine-man came in. He had not been seen all night, his task having been to sit in the hogan, chanting. Now he entered, accompanied by his assistants, and chanted while they scattered water on the fire at the four ceremonial points. Then young men tore gaps in the circle of branches, one opening toward each direction. As the medicine-man went back to the hogan, they demolished the whole corral, leaving the branches on the ground.

Day was full by that time, and the circle of prostrate branches was like a stage with all the scenery removed and the curtains rolled up. The only important matter seemed breakfast, especially coffee.

## THE NIGHT CHANT

THE NIGHT CHANT IS SAID TO HAVE COME FROM THE PEOPLE of the " Red Rocks ": that is, those who lived in the Canyon de Chelly. It is probably the most sacred ceremony, for the gods themselves appear; also goddesses, for Navajos have no more use for celibacy on Olympus than on the reservation. The ceremony is sometimes called the Yebetchai after the principal figure, the maternal grandfather of the gods.

Like the Mountain Chant, it is a nine-day sing, and the days are filled with all the elaborate, intricate, exacting detail of preparing properties, making sand paintings, and chanting prayers over the patient. The care required in all the minutiæ of handling the simple things used is amazing, as reported by Dr. Washington Matthews, who spent eight years among the Navajos studying their ceremonies. He learned such things as the order in which yucca withes must be picked up, what feathers precede in the making of prayer-plumes, and why there are just so many thongs of buckskin on a moccasin.

A few items of this mass of information are interesting, even to the casual observer. All the buckskin used ceremonially must be got without the shedding of blood. The deer is tracked, run into a blind, thrown, and smothered with sacred meal stuffed into its nostrils. The skinning must be begun with a stone knife, though nowadays the job is finished with steel. Pollen and meal are used interchangeably in prayer to symbolize life, though pollen is probably considered more sacred. Sometimes it is sanctified by dropping into it a small bird or animal, which is allowed to struggle there, but never to die, as that would make the meal dead too.

Masks are made of the sacred buckskin in lodges specially built for the purpose. They are the property of the medicine-man, who carries them round in a bag. Only the paint needs renewing each time.

The accompaniment is provided by beating on a ceremonial basket with a drumstick made of yucca. At the end they turn up the basket carefully so that the evil, which has come out of the patient and collected under it, may escape without doing harm to anyone.

## THE INITIATION

ONE YEAR WE ARRIVED JUST AS THE CANDIDATES FOR INITIA-
tion were gathering in a sheltered arroyo. It was a sunny
November day, but the air was sharp. Not many spectators
were present — just a few interested elders, as at a school
function. Probably fifty children sat in a semicircle, boys
on one side, girls on the other, with fathers and mothers
standing behind them. All the youngsters crouched under
blankets, which were hooded over their heads to hide their
faces.

Then came Yebetchai, who is also called Hastse-yalti,
and his mate, Hastse-baad. They moved with a quick jogging step and they hooted queerly, the goddess in falsetto.
Both parts are taken by men. Hastse-yalti's mask was a
bag-like hood of soft buckskin, with a fringe of red horsehair from ear to ear, a coronet of eagle-feathers, and a
spruce collar. A fine white buckskin hung from his shoulders over ordinary dress; but they told us that in the old
days his whole costume was white buckskin. He delighted
our eyes, however, with great chunks of turquoise in bracelets, necklaces, and rings. His lady was smaller, and her
mask, very stiff and square at the top, was merely tied over
her face, leaving her long hair flowing down her back. She
wore kirtle, knitted stockings, brown moccasins, and jewelry, and her slim masculine body was covered with white
paint.

As the divinities cantered up, we saw that the little boys
were being stripped behind blankets held to screen them.

When all were ready, each little shivering figure stepped out and looked bravely at the strange creatures who approached, frisking, making unearthly sounds, to administer sacred meal and the strokes of a yucca whip. First the goddess applied the meal, then the god applied the rod, on legs, bodies front and back, and arms. Each boy stood bravely while the strokes fell, not too heavily, and then sat down again and muffled his head in his blanket.

The girls' ordeal was much less severe. As each girl dropped her blanket, showing a tousled black head and bright anxious eyes, the goddess marked lines of meal on the soles of the feet, the palms, the shoulders, and both sides of the head. Then Hastse-yalti approached, armed, not with a whip, but with white and yellow ears of corn, covered with sprays of spruce. He gently touched each child where the meal had been put, turning the corn as he did so.

Then the children, coached by hovering parents, hid their heads again, as though in a game, and the deities took off their masks and called upon the children to look. So the secret was revealed! The terrible supernatural creatures with whom their infant souls had been terrified were not gods at all, but merely men: probably somebody well known, like " Son of Many Mules," an uncle; or a neighbor met every day, nice old " Grandson of the Boy who Made Arrows."

A further thrill was coming. For the unmasked performers passed slowly round the circle, putting a mask on each child's head; so every boy looked upon the world through Hastse-yalti's eye-holes, and every girl gazed through the square sockets of Hastse-baad. This had to be very carefully managed, for unless the actor sees the child's eyes very clearly through the holes in the mask, he will surely go blind. At last the row of beaming children, aware now of all the grown-up secrets, marched proudly by the masks, as they lay on a blanket, and sprinkled meal.

Often adults take part in this ceremony too, for it must be gone through four times before one may personate the gods; and in these degenerate days children are often in schools at the right time, and tribal initiation must be put off until they are grown.

## THE LAST DAY

ALL THE LAST DAY EVERYBODY WAS BUSY GETTING READY for the big night. We knew that the medicine-man and his assistants were conducting final rehearsals in the lodge, for we heard chanting nearly all day. Outside, the crowd gathered. The patient's family was entertaining, of course, but friends helped. Many brought sheep or goats, their skinned legs sticking up stiffly in wagons. Men cleared the dance ground of trees and stumps; they built the " green-room," a roofless shelter for dressing; and all around the camp we heard the steady tattoo of their axes as they brought down the enormous quantity of wood required to keep so many fires burning all night. Another vibration was on the air too: the persistent beat of chanting, off among the trees, where teams of dancers practiced steps and songs for the night's performance. In the great central arbor women moved about the fire, broiling mutton with that terrible woolly greasy smell, and handing ribs and legs of it to hungry callers, with chunks of bread and steaming cups of coffee.

Like all the Navajos, we sat in our spruce and piñon shelter, eating and drinking and chatting with friends as they strolled by. They gave us bits of gossip. "He Hops," the lame trader, and his wife were having trouble. Jeanette had gone to the mission hospital to have a baby, but it hadn't come yet. "Gah," which means "Rabbit," was selling liquor to the boys behind his pop-stand, and the headmen were angry and were going to do something about it. "Gah" is a usual name for white people, because they move and jump round so much; we thought it was going to prove very suitable in this case.

Just before sunset we saw a strange rite. The patient came out of the hogan, wrapped in his blanket and carrying a flat basket of sacred meal. We had not seen him before, and we were struck by his tragic suffering face, as he stood on a buffalo robe, facing the east. With uncanny calls and strangely hesitant steps four masked figures pranced jingling out of the wood. They were the gods of war, and they came brandishing knives and bows and arrows to scare the evil away from the sick man. They did this by moving round him, chanting and cavorting all the time. He stood solemnly, sprinkled them with meal, and watched them perform the same exorcism round the medicine lodge also; for it might have gathered some of the bad medicine. As he turned to go back into the hogan, we could see how very wan the patient looked, weary, no doubt, with the strain of the long ceremony and with the anxious waiting for relief.

### THE NIGHT OF DANCING

BY SEVEN O'CLOCK WE WERE SETTLED COMFORTABLY among blankets, our backs against the medicine hogan. Inside we could hear the steady muffled pound of chanting. Outside, it was cold, and our eyes smarted from the smoke. An irregular ellipse of wagons curved from the hogan to the green-room, about a hundred yards away, vague in the fire-lit dusk. The wagons were covered prairie schooners, with their white canvas tops drawn into arches, and almost every arch framed a woman holding a child. With warm vivid colors in blankets and velvet blouses, dark cheeks, shining eyes, smooth black hair, and splashes of silver, turquoise, and coral jewelry, they were like barbaric Madonnas nursing their babies there. Below the wagons was a dado of tall-hatted men, and below that more women and children squatted on the ground around low cooking-fires.

As the audience settled, men walked out into the cleared space and made speeches. Henry Chee Dodge first. He is a heavy-set, broad-faced man, who commands respect among the whites as well as among his own people. He began quietly, and the crowd was attentive at once. Like all Navajos, Chee Dodge has a resonant, carrying voice, which boomed off into the stillness without apparent effort. He spoke, they told me, of the question of land, assuring his people that Washington would deal fairly with them if they maintained order and good faith on their part. He deprecated the use of whisky, and he called upon every Navajo to refuse to buy it. This brought murmurs of approval from everyone, even from young men who had obviously had some. Dodge walked up and down as he talked, gesticulating.

Then a different type of man spoke: a long, slim medicine-man from a distant part of the reservation. He was buttoned tightly into a black sack-coat, and his thin legs were covered with black trousers. Nevertheless he looked thoroughly Navajo, for his moccasins were fastened with huge turquoise-studded disks, his hair was in a queue, fine bracelets gleamed when he raised his arms, and he wore a scraggy, mandarin mustache. He spoke in sonorous phrases, with harsh undertones, guttural inflections; it is a picturesque language, Navajo. I hoped he was discussing high matters; but no, they said he was advising the People to send their children to school, on the ground that they could not get out of it anyhow, and that young people must understand the ways of the whites " in these days." He said, I was glad to know, that children need not fail to be good Navajos because they learn the ways of the whites. He urged that they be taught the ways of the ancients too.

Presently government policemen and others began to push the crowd back, making sounds and gestures like policemen everywhere, and gradually clearing the dancing-ground. Then there was quiet while more wood was put on to the fires, and a settling movement ran around the circle.

Suddenly " Hu-tu-tu-*tu*, hu-tu-tu-*tu*," the eerie cry of Hastse-yalti, cut the air, and he came out of the medicine lodge, followed by four blanketed figures. They went right through to the green-room, giving the impression that they were not interested in us, that this appearance did not count.

Soon they came back, led by the medicine-man and Hastse-yalti. The four were masked in hoods: blue to symbolize the sky, with a yellow band across the bottom for the evening glow, and black cross-lines to indicate falling rain. They had red or yellow hair like Hastse-yalti's, but instead of his raying feathers they wore only two, rising from a fluff of owl's feathers over the right ear. Their bodies were smeared white, and they wore kirtles of the grandest things they could find. One looked like an old-fashioned lambrequin off of grandmother's mantel, one was red silk edged with a ball fringe, one had a Hopi kirtle, and the last man had adapted an American flag to his uses. Stunning belts with silver disks as big as plates, the ubiquitous dangling fox-skin, knitted blue socks, brown moccasins, and masses of jewelry completed the gods' regalia. Hastse-yalti was duller, but probably warmer on a cold night, in a dark flannel shirt; his buckskin, however, was soft and velvety, and his jewelry gleamed more richly under the firelight than when we saw it by day.

The medicine-man, sprinkling a path of meal for the gods to tread, was a fine stately figure. I knew that he could remember the Bosque Redondo, and I wondered what he thought of today's conquest. No Navajo dance is dominated by white crowds as some of the Pueblos' are, but I saw the priest's fine eyes flash toward a group of noisy white men, who had evidently been drinking. Then he stood impassive, waiting for the patient, who emerged again from the lodge, sprinkled the deities with meal from his basket, and gave each one a sacrificial cigarette. The dancers kept up a gentle jogging during this rite, and during the long prayer which the medicine-man intoned, followed, line by line, by the patient.

The chant seemed interminable, in spite of the richness of the shaman's tone and the psychic effect of these hundreds of people gathered to bring health to their friend. Each thought is repeated four times, but, condensed from Dr. Matthews's translation, it may be given:

In the house made of the dawn,
In the house made of the evening twilight,
In the house made of the dark cloud,

Where the zigzag lightning stands high on top,
Where the he-rain stands high on top —
O, male divinity,

With your moccasins of dark cloud, come to us!
With your leggings of dark cloud, come to us!
With your shirt of dark cloud, come to us!
With your head-dress of dark cloud, come to us!

With the zigzag lightning flung over your head, come to us, soaring!
With the rainbow hanging high over your head, come to us, soaring!
With the zigzag lightning flung out on high on the ends of your wings, come to us, soaring!
With the rainbow hanging high on the ends of your wings, come to us, soaring!

I have made your sacrifice,
I have prepared a smoke for you.
My feet restore for me,
My legs restore for me,
My body restore for me,
My mind restore for me,
My voice restore for me.
Today take out your spell for me,
Today take away your spell from me.
Far off from me it is taken!
Far off, you have done it!
Happily I recover.
Happily my interior becomes cool,
Happily my eyes regain their power,
Happily my head becomes cool,
Happily my legs regain their power,
Happily I hear again!
Happily for me the spell is taken off!
Happily may I walk

In beauty, I walk!
With beauty before me, I walk
With beauty behind me, I walk
With beauty below me, I walk
With beauty above me, I walk
With beauty all around me, I walk.

It ends with the usual peroration:
In beauty it is finished.
In beauty it is finished.
In beauty it is finished.
In beauty it is finished."

Another sprinkling of meal, and the medicine-man and the patient took their places in front of the hogan, facing the line of dancers.

Hastse-yalti rushed to the east, whooped, held up his stiff little bag of skin, while the dancers whirled to the west, shook their rattles with a low sweeping motion from the ground to their heads, and beat the ground vigorously with their right feet.

" Hu-tu-tu-*tu*," yodeled Hastse-yalti, dashing toward the hogan with his queer quick toddle; and they all swooped and rattled the other way.

Then, to the accompaniment of their rattles, the four gods began to dance, stamping with the right foot, spacing, and suddenly bursting into the sharp ejaculatory chant of the Yebetchai, to me the most haunting of all Indian music.

" Ho-ho-ho-*ho*,
    He-he-he-he — "

many meaningless syllables, repeated the mystic four times, and four short verses. Hastse-yalti never dances; he moved rhythmically back and forth, hooting at the end of every verse to indicate that it had been correctly done. When the act ended, with a final rattle and whoop, he led his team off to the green-room. Men who have done this act well are filled with pride, for it represents hours of practice.

The next act lasted all night, repeated many times by every group and danced by many groups. Dr. Matthews says that the original plan was for four teams to dance twelve times each, with half-hour intervals. A ten-hour show. In practice it is very irregular. Often so many teams come that there are no intermissions at all; sometimes one team dances only a couple of times. The grand total, however, is the same: ten hours of the best dancing the reservation can show. After all, if you are going to travel a hundred miles by wagon across the desert, you don't want to be put off with a meager two-hour performance. Six of the dancers were dressed like the preceding group, but with white masks instead of blue. These are the male divinities. They should be accompanied by six goddesses, but only four appeared. They are costumed like Hastsebaad, who does not come out at night. Usually these parts are taken by boys or small men, who sing in falsetto, giving a wailing overtone to the music. Sometimes women dance, costumed in old-fashioned squaw dresses.

They entered single file, in a long line, and to their haunting, oddly aspirated, raucous call, they began to dance, pounding up and down, feet and hands rising and falling in unison, torsos tightened with the strain, masks leering stupidly. The figures are simple. Dancing in a long line. Dancing in two lines. Movements like a Virginia reel, in which each god scoops up his goddess with an angular gesture, prances with her to the other end of the line, drops her, and moves back into his own line. Torsos are slim and hard, diaphragms pump like bellows to make the forced tones of the song, lean sinewy legs work like pistons under short flapping kilts, left arms hang oddly inert. Always the " Ho-ho-ho-*ho*, he-he-he-he " pounds until it becomes the very measure of your pulse-beat. That is all; all night nothing else, no variation, nothing to break the hypnotic effect of constant, insistent, repetition.

The only relief is provided by Tonenili, water-sprinkler, the clown. As among the Pueblos, since rain brings joy, the Rain-maker must cause mirth and laughter. He is masked and costumed like the others, but in poorer clothes.

" Why? " I asked.

" Why should he dress well," said Andy, who sat next to me, " when he might get his clothes wet with rain? "

Tonenili amused himself all round and among the dancers, who paid no attention to him. Some of the clowns were really funny as they imitated Hastse-yalti, mixed among the dancers, forgot to go off at the right time, and then confusedly rushed away; lost, or almost lost, important parts of their clothing, dropped a fox-skin and then could not find it, though it was in plain sight.

At every interval in the dancing, chanting began in the hogan, so the air was always vibrant with prayer. Whenever a new team appeared, the patient and the medicine-man rose to greet it.

Different teams provided interesting contrasts in costume and in skill. By the small hours everyone had become an expert critic of Yebetchai dancing, if he had not gone to sleep. As the coldest hours come, dancers are likely to wear underwear instead of paint. I watched one beautiful young dancer, poised perfectly on the balls of his feet, his body slim and straight like an arrow, wild and fawn-like even under baggy O.D. trousers.

I turned to an Indian Service man sitting near me.

"Why, oh why, does he wear trousers?" I wailed. "His body is so *beautiful!*"

"Young lady," my friend told me sternly, "don't talk like that to me. I've spent the best years of my life trying to get these fellows into pants. . . ."

Dawn is heralded by a more terrible cold.

Why do people always stop putting wood on fires when it is the coldest?

Just before daybreak the last team went off to the green-room, whooping, prancing, rattling just as vigorously as though it were the beginning and not the end of a long winter's night. We moved eastward as the crowd turned that way, and stood watching the forlorn gray light turn everything dull. Soon muffled shapes on the horizon took form as cliffs, dark blue at first, then dull rose-gray; and finally they stood forth in their glory of color as the red-sandstone buttes we knew.

A group of men, unmasked, came out of the green-room, stood to face the point of sunrise, and as the sun broke through the mist, they sang "The Blue-bird Song," reverently reciting again the legend of creation. It is very different from the night's chanting, more melodious than most Indian music, and it floated softly on the air with the puffs of breath which came from the singers' mouths and disappeared into the blue mist of morning.

APACHES                                    [VICTOR HIGGINS]

# VIII: The Apaches

APACHES ARE DEFEATED. PUEBLOS MOVE SMOOTHLY BE-
tween an outward conciliatory conformity to American
ways and an inner adherence to their own customs; Navajos yield nothing of their own integrity as they slowly
adopt certain mechanical aspects of white civilization; but
the Apache seems completely conquered. Even the casual
observer gets the impression that his capitulation is deeper
than any military surrender. His savage spirit is broken.
The first Americans who met him found him shrewd, keen,
even welcoming; later he proved himself the fiercest fighter
in the southwest. His men, and even his women, showed
more iron endurance, and his chiefs more resource at
strategy and skill at parley, than the American Army could
match. It was only by sheer force of numbers that he was
finally conquered and penned up on reservations; and that
was not until 1887. Now he is sullen and uncommunicative,
often drunken and lazy. In some ways the most tractable
of all Indians, in others he is the most hopeless to reach.

Both Spain and Mexico found the Apache too much for
them. They could do nothing except to barricade their
thick-walled adobe houses with heavy gates and shutters

when they heard he was on the war-path. Pueblos were just as terrified of his very name, which is a Zuñi word meaning "enemy." Early American travelers, rushing across the desert at the dizzy speed of ten miles a day toward California and unlimited gold, found the Apache the greatest barrier across their path. From western Texas to California wandered unrelated bands of these naked, painted savages: shooting arrows from behind rocks, hurling spears from the backs of running mustangs, or in close encounter whirling their war-clubs with enough force to spatter out a victim's brains. The Apache was at home on the war-path; he made no settled habitations. He lived on what the country offered: mesquite roots, wild acorns, prairie-dogs, and rattlesnakes, and on the meat of the horse he had stolen and ridden to death. He knew his country, inch by inch: where there was water, where a hidden trail over an apparently impassable rock wall, where an Indian could lie hidden for hours within a few yards of a white man's wagon train. He could read a trail left on rocks or grass and know how many men had passed and when, and how many horses. He could leave a message for others of his tribe by turning a stone or snapping a twig — signs which few white men could read. It was said that white men could travel the Apache country for weeks without seeing a single Indian, and never be themselves unseen. Then, in the one hour when vigilance was relaxed, might come one of those terrifying sudden attacks. Men were killed, women and children carried off into slavery; and the entire band would disappear like mist, and no Apache could ever account for the outrage. Charles F. Lummis, writing of wars against the

Apache, said that the great difficulty of the American Army was not in fighting, but in finding him.

Naturally there was another side to the picture of Apache raids, one which American Army officers were quick to recognize. And that was that for every Indian outrage, there was a white outrage just as terrible. If the Indians could not control their men, neither could the United States. White men, too, captured women and children or shot them down. White men sold arms and liquor to Indians. Many savages, attacking white settlements, were incited by white men's whisky, armed with white men's guns, even encouraged by renegade whites.

Apaches, like Navajos, could not understand why the United States, having fought Mexicans, became the protectors of Mexicans. So they continued to attack Mexican villages, and to talk peace so successfully that treaties were made and broken faster than the Senate could ratify them. Real war started when Cochise, a Chiricahua Apache chief, met American officers for a parley about the theft of a cow and a child belonging to a Mexican woman. Cochise denied all knowledge of the affair. The officers, who did not believe him, broke the safe-conduct and seized and killed the chief's attendants. Cochise himself slit the tent with his knife and got away. It took ten years of warfare to capture him after that.

There were other warriors just as clever and just as vindictive, other officers just as mistaken in their policy. As they had no tribal union, the Apache bands had to be captured one by one in forty bitter years of fighting. One uprising did not differ much from another; the end was inevitable. Major John C. Cremony, who fought Apaches for many years, has left an account of his enemy, which shows that the Major was a student as well as a soldier, and an officer willing to give full credit to his foe.

He was impressed with the fact that to the Apache the white man was always an enemy. He says that he knew of friendships between Apaches and white men, but in his experience they were extremely rare. The American was the arch enemy, and even small children would run screaming with fright from a white man. An outrage against a Mexican was good; one against an American was excellent. The Apaches knew who would defeat them in the end. Boys were encouraged to play games to develop their skill at hiding, at trailing, even at stealing. There is something strongly reminiscent of Sparta in this Apache educational system. A good thief was considered even more of a man than a good fighter. "Deceit," says the Major, "is regarded among them with the same admiration that we bestow upon one of the fine arts. To lull the suspicion of an enemy — and to them all other people are enemies — and then take advantage of his credence, is regarded as a splendid stroke of policy. To rob and not be robbed, to kill and not be killed, to take a captive and not be captured, form the sum of an Apache's education and ambition, and he who can perform these acts with the greatest success is the greatest man in the tribe."

Women could fight if necessary, but one gathers that as a rule they were too busy, for they did everything else except hunt. They built the brush wikiups which were their homes, and when it was necessary to move, they packed and moved. They planted and tended little patches of beans and corn between raids, and they made blankets and baskets. The work was so heavy that most girls preferred marriage with an older man who already had several wives, especially if he were a good thief, and consequently a good provider. So polygamy was general. American Army men reported that Apache women were on the whole more chaste and less accessible than Navajo women; and they probably knew.

Major Cremony concluded that "those who believe that they [the Apaches] can be tamed and rendered peaceable under any circumstances, are wonderfully in error." The error, though, seems to be on the part of the Major; for the Apaches have not only been tamed and rendered peaceable, but they seem to come closest to the professed government ideal of the Indian who gives up his own ways and adopts the dress, speech, manners, and religion of the American.

The taming process began when General Carleton issued his ultimatum of warfare against all unfriendly Indians. In the round-up which followed, many Apaches were conquered, along with the Navajos, and moved with them to the Bosque Redondo. There they fought with the Navajos, and unconquered tribes attacked them. When the government began to establish them on reservations, Apaches came into conflict with white men who protested against giving desirable land to Indians. So the Apaches were moved from place to place, subjected to distress in unaccustomed climates, and extreme irritation due to the vacillating policy of the authorities. Many a band, driven to frenzy by unfair treatment, went on the war-path and killed hundreds of whites before they could be subdued. The best Apache trick was slipping across the border into Mexico, where American troops could not follow; but the two countries stopped that by a treaty permitting troops to follow the savage across the international line. The end followed soon.

In 1885 Geronimo, the last defiant chief, was captured by American troops in Mexico. He and his band were taken to Florida and put at hard labor. They were later moved to Alabama, then to Fort Sill, Oklahoma, and now the last of Geronimo's warriors are on the Mescalero Reservation in New Mexico. The old chief died at Fort Sill, always longing to return to his Arizona mountains. He is quoted as saying just before his death: " The sun rises and shines for a time. Then it goes down, sinks, and is lost. So will it be with the Indian. . . . It will be only a few years when the Indian will be heard of only in books which the white man writes."

Apaches now live on four reservations: the Mescalero and the Jicarilla in New Mexico, and two in the White Mountains of Arizona. There are about five thousand altogether. The men hate and resent farming, and even the Mescaleros, who have fertile land, wander about with their sheep, goats, and a few cattle. What farming they do is simple. A week in the spring to scratch the soil and plant, a couple of weeks at midsummer for weeding, a week for harvesting in the fall, suffice. They succeed better at herding sheep, an occupation which suits their nomadic nature and allows some scope for their gifts of observation and their knowledge of country, of weather, of desert forage.

The Jicarillas are the most successful; they own sixty sheep per capita, more than any other people in the world.

Apaches still make tiswin, the tribal intoxicant, and mescal, and they take readily to American whisky. The problem of drink, for their agents, is exceeded only by the problem of tuberculosis. Among the Jicarillas eighty per cent of their people under thirty have tuberculosis, and schools have been transformed into hospitals.

During the conquest and the captivity, at least a generation lost its arts. Now Apache women are again making blankets and baskets, and interested people are helping them, here and there, to get back to the old designs and patterns.

Of Athabascan stock, the Apache closely resembles the Navajo in many of his ways. The legends are similar. The Apache uses sacred pollen, though his comes from the tule cat-tail rush and not from corn. He has medicine-men, medicine " sings," and much magic. He wore, in his fighting days, a medicine hat or a medicine shirt to protect him from arrows, he knew incantations, he recognized witchcraft and magicians. The tribe is divided into clans, though no organization appears except as the government has brought it about to assist in administration. Nobody of scientific attainment has studied Apache ceremonial life as Matthews studied the Navajos, or Fewkes the Hopis, or Stevenson the Zuñis. Many ceremonies are lost. Generally the Apache has become so sullen and so unapproachable that the white man knows him least of all the southwestern tribes. The old fighter, defeated, holds sternly to his last stronghold, that of silence concerning his own inner life.

# IX: Apache Dances

## THE MESCALERO APACHE FOURTH OF JULY

We REACHED THE APACHE CAMP-GROUND ABOUT TEN
o'clock at night. Driving out from the nearest town, we had
passed many cars, most of them loaded with white people.
In a few we saw Indians, dressed like whites. Our car lights
flashed on feathery mesquite and on the thick leaves of
greasewood, which filled the air with its pungency in spite
of the dust. Then we saw the rough red boles of pines, and
their mountainous odor took the place of the heavy smell
of greasewood. Once we ran along a stream which rippled
coolly on that hot July night.

Twenty miles from town we reached the camp. Lights
streamed up against the tall feathery tops of pines,
and even from the road we saw a few tepees: slim,
tapering cones built of saplings and covered with tarpaulin
or buckskin. Fires inside tinted them like shells. Dark
figures moved against a blare of light at the center
of the encampment, and hundreds of cars were parked
around it.

As we drew up, an Apache came up to us, showing his
policeman's badge.

"That's right," he said; "you park there. You're all right. I'll watch your car. That's all right. And if you need anything, you just ask for Matthew. I'm Matthew."

Matthew somehow broke the illusion, for from his conversation we felt that there was little here that was Indian. The soft flush of fires in the tepees was lost in the flare of gasoline lamps on the frame booths around the arena; and we had to strain our ears to catch even a hint of the Indian chant which was murmurously pounding along under the mechanical stridor of phonographs like a persistent though receding tide.

They were dancing to the chant; men and women, white and red, hand in hand, moving slowly in a large circle and kicking up the dust in a sideways shuffle. It was like the circle dance of the Navajos. Matthew said they call it "Friendship-dance." Among the dancers were men old enough to have ramped and fought with Geronimo; sullen-looking Apache boys in silk shirts; giggling girls, both white and red, in calico or organdie; a few white couples, the men careful to place themselves between their women and the contamination of the Indians; Mexicans looking pale and puny beside the swarthy Apaches. Three white youths, obvious "Easterners" and ostentatiously out to do the right thing by the Indians, danced hand in hand with Apaches, their solemn faces uplifted. One wore beaded headband and moccasins, bright blue against his Boy Scout shirt and shorts; when it began to rain, he added a yellow slicker to his ensemble and gravely went on dancing. We were disappointed to see no Apache skin and bead costumes, no bright color, not even gay shawls, except on an occasional Mexican flapper, heavily rouged and uncomfortably high-heeled.

At the western side of the arena towered the ceremonial tepee, no less than forty feet tall, and feathering out at the top in uncut pine. The lower part was banked with scrub-oak, which also made its entrance, a narrow lane jammed with people. We worked our way through until we stood at the lodge door. The floor was covered with broken golden straw, and in the middle a hole had been dug for the fire, which is not allowed to go out during the entire four-day ceremony. It threw a wavering glow on the faces of two medicine-men who sat there chanting. Each man rested his left hand on a long wand stuck into the ground, and in his right he shook a rattle of animal hoofs, beating time to the low steady recitative. It was much like a Navajo chant, but without the same resonant quality.

These men, we knew, were conducting the ancient puberty ceremony, known delicately by neighboring whites as the "Coming-out Party." The tepee is built at dawn on the first day, with elaborate rites. This chanting and the dancing of the little girls are the main ceremony, and on the last morning the tepee is dismantled, also ceremonially. Matthew said that we should see the maidens dance tomorrow. He, as glib and as uncommunicative as the true white man's Indian, told us that we had missed the Crown-dance, which would be done again tomorrow night. This is unrelated to the puberty ceremony, and their incongruous union is due to the fact that government officials permit only this one annual get-together. Consequently these two ancestral tribal observances must be given on the American

Day of Liberty, and so close to the highway that they are attended by more whites than Indians.

Outside the tepee we came upon the orchestra for the dancing: four men chanting to the notes of a tomtom made by stretching an inner tube over a metal drum, boldly labelled: "Firestone." The circle had broken and couples were dancing as they do in the Navajo Squaw-dance, but without touching. They went back and forth, in a sort of impersonal and divorced one-step, with set impassive faces. This is a pay-to-get-away affair, but the women are less insistent than the Navajos. Matthew said that the boy paid whatever the girl asked; it was bad manners not to.

Hamburgers and hot-dogs sizzled in the booths, Mexican venders ladled ice-cream into cones, tops snapped off of pop-bottles, the gasoline lamps sputtered and flared. Every now and then the hard cracking of fire-crackers or the long zooming of a sky-rocket. White people talking in the "Yes, ma'am, you-all" dialect. It was such a crowd as might be seen at any Fourth of July celebration from eastern New Mexico to Florida. We decided to go back to town, hoping for something more Indian tomorrow.

### The Fourth of July

As we drove out that hot Fourth of July morning, we picked up a youth trudging along the dusty highway. He had lived all his life among the Apaches, and when he learned that we were interested, he agreed to talk.

"I'll tell you what I know," he said, "if you won't use my name. I'd rather keep what little friendship they have

for me than to have my name in a book. It's no honor for
an Apache to be a white man's friend, you know. They hate
us so. I don't blame them for hating us," said Apache
Friend.

He pointed out a frame house such as the government is
trying to substitute for the old tepees. "They use the house
for horses and sleep in the tepee," he said, amused.
"Those people are of Geronimo's band."

Geronimo's son hangs about a trading-post and permits
tourists to photograph him, but most of the Apaches have
no more to do with whites than they must. Even the children
in the schools look sullen. Apache Friend said that many
of them run away, thirty or forty annually, and disappear
into the mountains, or are brought back for whippings and
solitary confinement. The older people carry the typical
Indian reserve to the highest degree. They show none of
the amused tolerance which greets a white visitor in a
pueblo, nor any of the haughty indifference of the People
at a Navajo sing.

I asked an Indian Service man about it. "What is the
matter with these people? They look broken, crushed."

He tried to put me off with official figures as to how much
fine timber there is on the reservation, how many frame
houses, how many peach-trees. But I persisted: I did not
mean material things. I wanted to know what had happened to the spirit of this fiercest, hardiest, nearest invincible of all the tribes. At last he told me.

"After all," he said, "these people have been prisoners
of war for a long time."

I remembered what another Indian Service man had

told me: that these people have rich land, and leisure, and whisky. They have had less to struggle against, in nature, than the Navajos, or even the Pueblos.

. .

When we reached the encampment, dust had been pulverized to a powder which never seemed to settle, but which had whitened the pines many feet above the ground. The American flags on the booths hung limp. Flies buzzed about sticky children. Few people were in sight. We watched an old hag who was working about one of the tepees, her flat bare feet plodding under a dirty calico wrapper belted with a strip of cretonne. She hauled water, chopped wood, butchered a sheep hung under a tree; and between times she lugged two fat babies about, one on her back, the other tagging behind.

We had hoped to see the *débutantes*, and soon they came by, passing from the ceremonial tepee to the family shelter. The old rule requiring them to spend the entire four days in the ceremonial lodge has broken down. They looked about fourteen, though Apache Friend thought they were older, and they were pretty and shy. They wore buckskin dresses, probably old ceremonial gowns, as most families keep these beautiful garments, which they no longer wear. Both dresses were of soft yellow buckskin with fringed skirts and over-blouses and deep fringed yokes falling over the arms. Their high boots had beaded toes, and a few beads decorated the dresses. The dignity and grace of this costume compared with the dress of the other girls were startling. Each girl wore two eagle-feathers tied to her crown and falling down behind, an odd effect over bobbed hair. All Apache women were, traditionally, daughters of war, and the eagle brings luck in war. Pitiful survival among a people too crushed even to fight for their own clothes, their own names, their own religious rites.

It was a long, hot day. Most of the white people and the young Apaches had gone down the road to a baseball game between the Apaches and a team from El Paso. We watched an Apache girl in a spotted dress pick up a white beau. They sat at a hot-dog booth eating, her beautiful smooth brown legs showing above very low socks.

Matthew came by to assure us that we were all right. Then he turned to another policeman and spoke low.

"Yeah," he said, "they got a Mexican girl and an Apache boy, over there behind the camp. They took 'em both to the hoosegow."

Six tall Navajos stalked by, a blessed relief to the spirit, for here was real, unashamed, unreconciled Indian. These men felt no compulsion to imitate the white people they saw. They had the drabness of shirts and trousers well subordinated to a barbaric lavishness of silver and turquoise. They all wore large hats, and one had a folded blanket hanging over his shoulder. They walked about like people of the castle watching the doings of the peasantry.

Late in the afternoon Matthew came round to say that Kiowa visitors from the Kiowa reservation were going to dance; so we found seats on the wood-pile and sat teetering on a log which upheld a couple of Apache women on the other end. They were part of a group dominated by a large dame, conspicuous in a bright pink blanket and gold-rimmed spectacles. She sat in a rocking-chair. The others, in calico, organdie, and black satin, made the best of up-turned boxes and the logs. They chatted. I could not hear the words, but the voices were curiously like those of white women. None of the low chuckling of Navajo women, or the lilting murmur of Pueblos or Hopis. These Apaches sounded like the typical small-town American women who were attending their show: the same inflections, maybe the same ideas. It just happened that their skins were velvety brown instead of red and shining.

Apaches gathered in the arena. Navajos condescended to show some interest. White people made wise-cracks. Then the Kiowas appeared; four men for the orchestra and four dancers.

Two of the dancers were in nondescript clothing, one in bright blue underwear; and a small boy had set off his yellow union-suit with beaded vest and moccasins and por-cupine head-dress. The blue man, a lithe young fellow, was decorated all over with mirrors, each surrounded with ray-ing eagle-feathers tipped with red puffs of down. He wore a porcupine roach, also fluffy with down, and from his head to his heels flowed long streamers of feathers and bells.

All danced together, but the blue dancer completely outshone the others. He danced with quick sure steps, his feet lightly patting the earth to the jingling *obbligato* of his bells. Crouching, he whirled and pivoted, and sometimes he bent his limber body so far back that his roach almost swept the ground. The two colorless men patiently made a background for him, and the little yellow boy did his best.

Then the six Navajos danced a Yebetchai. They wore no masks or costumes, but a medicine-man led them with scattered meal, and they were grave and dignified. Something hard and strong came across that stifling dusty place with their vigorous caterwauling: something of the uncompromising desert where the spirit of the Navajo still lives, unconquered.

Hot vicious puffs of wind had been raising clouds of dust all afternoon, but about sunset the thunderous heat suddenly precipitated itself into rain. For half an hour hard, spattering drops came down briskly, while the setting sun cast long, golden bars between the clouds and made vivid the red of the pine boles and the green of the needles. It was a most refreshing rain; it cleared the air, washed the trees, and drove most of the white people away. Also it made us feel cold in our dampened clothes, so we went into the cook-shelter, where a large fire was burning. Many Apaches had gathered there, and old crones stooped and mumbled about the embers where they were baking ceremonial bread for the dancers: the bread of mesquite beans, which was the ancient desert fare.

The sun went down. The moon came up. Little cook-fires popped up everywhere; and the place took on a look of enchantment, with red light shining through canvas, and the lofty dignity of the ceremonial tepee rising lordly above the eating-shacks. Shortly after sunset the crown-dancers came. Apaches call them this because of the head-dress; whites usually miscall the dance the Devil-dance. Captain

John G. Bourke of the American Army, who wrote an account of the ceremony in 1887, says that the performers represent gods, so he called it the Spirit-dance. Bourke also says that it was given " only upon the most solemn occasions, such as the setting out of a war party, the appearance of an epidemic, or something else of like portent." I wondered, as I watched, whether the present predicament of the tribe looks to the medicine-men more like a war or an epidemic.

As the figures approached the fire, they appeared thoroughly savage, with their blackened torsos, hidden faces, and towering crowns. Their bodies were covered with stripes, spots, and zigzags of red, yellow, and white, and their legs were hidden under long, fringed buckskin skirts and high boots with upturned toes. The only modern touches were Scotch plaid shawls around their waists and bandannas around their necks. The personality of the man was hidden under an unwrinkled hood of black buckskin, so smooth that it molded to the features; and the personality of the god appeared in the skeleton-like superstructure of yucca withes which topped it. The crowns varied in detail according to the clan of the dancer; but every one was wider than the man's shoulders, not less than two feet tall, and so intricate and beautiful in detail as to suggest snow crystals. They were yellow and painted with symbols in which sun and moon and lightning seemed to predominate. Each dancer carried two swords of yucca, whittled thin and decorated with lightning marks.

They first stopped before the medicine-man, who sprinkled pollen. Then each man approached him, with a

straddling, hopping step, knees bent, swords held outward
from flexed elbows, body and huge delicate head-dress
turning with startled suddenness from side to side. He
chasséd back and forth several times, and finally brought
his swords together behind the medicine-man's neck and
gave place to the next man. All the time they gave the weird
clarion call of the hoot-owl, a sacred bird to the Apaches,
a devil to other tribes.

When all had made this salutation, they began to dance
round the fire, silhouetted like great goblins against the
blaze. The dance is as angular as though the men were
animated wooden figures on strings. Broad, heavily mus-
cled backs turned, swinging the head-dresses jerkily from
side to side; wooden swords moved as though attached to
wooden arms, long skirts swished softly, and the raucous
calling persisted until the air was filled with it. What it
meant did not appear, but it had an element of obscenity
not usual in Indian ceremonies: they were like ribald demons from a savage hell, devils rather than spirits, as they
danced under the crowns of the gods.

. .

This dance was repeated all night, with occasional intervals for the Friendship-dance or the Squaw-dance. Whatever went on outside, there was a never-ceasing murmur
from the tepee where the medicine-men carried on their unrelated ceremony for the virgins. It was so dark in there
that I could scarcely see until my eyes grew accustomed
to the blackness, which was relieved only by the dull

reflection from the fire-hole. Opposite the entrance two deer-skins had been laid on the ground, and there the little girls knelt: quiet in their heavy dresses, pale brown faces bent, hands upheld with the palms outward in a gesture suggestively Japanese. At certain points in the chanting a crooked old witch of a woman bent over to pound a prayer-stick into the ground around the hole. Apache Friend said there was one for each song, and that by morning the circle would be complete. Now and then a passing car threw a beam of white light through the leaves, and I saw clearly the tired faces of the men, the wizened old women, the demurely drooping maidens.

The girls danced one at a time: a gentle shimmying step from one end to the other of the buckskin on which she stood. Hands up, eyes down, the buckskin dress softly whispering as they danced, they moved like hypnotized victims, impersonal, without volition. At intervals one of the old women wailed: a long-drawn, shuddering plaint, as though for all the sorrows of all the women of the world. Were they lamenting, I wondered, for these young things facing the sufferings of womanhood, or for the departed savage glories of their tribe? Whatever it was, their animal-like lamentations filled the very air with woe.

This continued all night. Men chanting. Old women marking the end of each song with a prayer-stick. Enchanted maidens kneeling helpless, or rising to dance within the narrow radius allowed them; still under a spell, quietly acquiescent before a world to which they were introduced by that mournful old-woman wail.

Apache Friend said that at dawn the girls would run a

race, pursued by the youths — a race which used to be the last dash of virginity, resulting in marriage. Now, said Apache Friend, it is merely a friendly game for boys and girls to get acquainted.

Maybe.

### THE JICARILLA APACHE FIESTA

MID-SEPTEMBER IN NEW MEXICO. ELECTRIC SUNSHINE: A vivifying warmth that stimulates and relaxes. The rainy season is over, and the sky is so clear that one can see right through it to infinity. Large white clouds turn silver flanks to the sun and drag lazy shadows across the mesas. Along the streams and ditches where Mexicans and Indians have planted little orchards, ripe fruit drops over broken adobe walls. Gathered corn waits in multi-colored piles to be braided and hung away in store-rooms. Every flat adobe house flames with long strings of aromatic chili. Women have peeled melons and stuck them up like bare skulls on sticks to dry, and laid trays of peaches and apples in the sun. On the mountain sides aspens have turned yellow, and frost is beginning to touch the tree-tops in the valleys.

Pueblo people are ready to trade their crops for Navajo blankets and silver and for Apache baskets. And a good place to trade is where the Jicarilla Apaches hold their *fiesta* at Horse Lake on September fifteenth. White visitors find it a long journey from Santa Fe, more than a hundred and fifty miles of mountain and desert road; but Indians come even farther than that, arriving in time for several days' barter before the feast. The feast itself seems unimportant; it is probably an affair arranged by the government and of no tribal significance to the Apaches. There are foot- and horse-races, baseball games, tugs of war — all sorts of contests between the Jicarillas of the mountains and those of the plain. But the people! The real show is the people.

One year I watched them all day long.

I sat on the running-board of a weary car, caked with hard mud, dusty and scratched from the bumping journey up the Chama River, past dreaming Mexican towns which have not changed their ways in a hundred years, and across rolling uplands covered with piñon and cedar trees. Here we were in an amphitheater of the mountains. Pines and smaller evergreens came tentatively down from the hills and hesitated, leaving miles of tawny grass, speckled with gray sage. In the middle lay the lake, a low marshy pond, unbeautiful in itself, but reflecting great beauty of shining clouds and pointed, wavering pines against incredible blue. Everywhere were tepees: white, ivory, and dull soft tan; hundreds of tepees, and around them hundreds of Apaches gathered from all parts of the reservation. Here and there Navajos and Pueblos had made brush shelters beside their wagons.

Friends from all the Indian country stopped to greet us. Tall, slender San Ildefonso was there with his gentle wife. Her Oriental beauty was swathed in scarfs of cerise and magenta, flowing from her shining hair to her small buckskin boots. They had a load of black jars to sell, fruit to trade or to eat, a couple of babies to help enjoy the fun.

Isleta came by. More stolid, these people. The man's heavy shoulders were outlined in crochet lace over red flannel, and his flat-topped hat rested on his hair in a queue. His wife was broad and comfortable. She ducked out from under the flat basket of grapes on her head and laid aside her fringed shawl. It was hot, and she was glad to stretch her heavy buckskin legs in the shade of our car. They reported good trading as we munched winy grapes. They had exchanged a wagon-load of grapes and peaches for baskets, bracelets, and a fine war-bonnet. Feathered war-bonnets used to be worn only by plains Indians, but Indian shows are bringing them into more general use.

As we talked, I watched the shifting crowd: a kaleidoscope changing so rapidly that it was hard to catch detail. Unlike the Mescaleros, these Apaches have plenty of gorgeousness. Almost every man had a beaded band on his hat, and many wore moccasins heavily incrusted with beads. Young blades swaggered in red or green silk shirts and beaded vests, assessed by a trader as worth from eighty to a hundred and fifty dollars. The old custom of plucking the eyebrows and lashes has died out, but nearly all had strong red or yellow lines across the cheeks.

The women also were painted, but they ran to red spots on high cheek-bones. Their costumes reflected their lives, both past and present. I saw many stunning wild creatures in beaded buckskin dresses, high boots, long braids falling over their shoulders, and beaded bands around their heads. Full calico skirts of one color banded with another showed the influence of lady teachers of the nineties. Bright silk handkerchiefs over the shoulders — any woman's love of finery. Heavy metal-studded belts such as cowboys wear on bucking horses — she has not lost her tribal art of horsemanship. In every belt a huge, vicious-looking knife. Is she as subdued as we believe? We watched those knives all day. They chopped wood, butchered sheep, dug holes for tepee poles and trenches for drainage, cut bread; and each woman wielded her knife with a careless adroitness fascinating to see.

In the course of the morning a Franciscan monk arrived from the nearest town. He unhitched his horses and, assisted by a Mexican boy, made an altar in the back of his buckboard. They spread a lace-edged altar-cloth, placed the pyx and the chalice and the missal. The priest adjusted the chasuble and alb over his rough Franciscan gown, and the boy donned a white surplice. A few people gathered. Mexican women turned up the French heels of badly fitting shoes and bent flowered hats as they knelt. Mexican men got stiffly down on one knee and fingered rosaries in gnarled hands. Several children followed the doings of their elders. I watched to see the Apache congregation gather. A few stood awkwardly near, but most of the Apaches were engaged in trading, in racing, in multifarious Indian affairs. A dozen people, perhaps, were aware of the mass. The acolyte served, moving the missal from side to side of the altar, and genuflecting as he crossed behind the priest, who stood in the dust reverently raising the Host in his hands as he murmured the sonorous Latin phrases.

After the mass the priest came to call on us and to share our thermos of ice-water. " It's a slow job," he said, " Christianizing these people. They do not understand. . . ."

A relay race was announced, but we were too lazy to move, too comfortable in the sun, which soaked us through and through. It was more fun, and easier, to watch the crowd from where we sat. The runners passed us, going to the ends of the course: nice-looking boys, slim and brown, with bright silk tied around their heads, and their feet in moccasins, except one modern youth in running-shoes. The crowd gathered along the runway, shouting, and we got occasional glimpses of the race.

As the hours passed, the shouting grew wilder, and more and more Indians came along reeling. Mescal and whisky are powerful in the Jicarilla. Some walked two by two, heads bobbing loosely. Some could not stand up very well in twos, so they went in threes. A couple dashed by, spurring a small horse. The man wavered in the saddle and would have fallen a hundred times if it had not been for his spouse sitting behind him, almost as uncertain, but holding on to her man with all the steadiness she could command.

An Indian Service man asks me to say that I saw these things several years ago; the Jicarillas are much more sober now.

Navajos had brought copper bracelets to trade. Two men and a woman stopped to talk with us and share our cigarettes. The woman would not smoke. She sat, tucking her skirts around her feet, and refreshed herself with a bunch of purple grapes. The men wished to sell us a blanket or a ring, very new and white. The fine old piece one of them wore was not for sale. They had no English, and our six Navajo words were soon exhausted, but it was clear that only the car would be a fair trade for that necklace. Much laughter. Then they wandered on, taking their copper bracelets among the Apaches, who still prefer it to silver.

A Hopi from Sichomovi, visiting friends in San Juan, had sold many sashes and kirtles. He showed us the turquoise he was taking home.

A Zuñi Priest of the Bow, who had come over the old trail by way of Acoma and Jemez, had turquoise too. He needed feathers, as Zuñis always do.

" You come Shalako? " he asked. " You come my house, I like blue feathers."

Jemez joined us. Three young men had come with a trader. A Ford truck was their hotel and their shop, as well as their conveyance. They rode on the seat and slept in the body, where blankets were piled on top of their stock in trade. A small barrel on the running-board gave tepid water through a rubber hose in response to the most primitive method of siphoning. Jemez was swapping canned goods and fruits for *jícaras,* the baskets which Apache women make and which all other Indians find so useful.

Jemez did not think much of the Apache dancing which was going on steadily in two long facing rows. Jemez offered to dance for us, privately. So they produced a tomtom, and one drummed and chanted while the others danced. One dance followed another, all calling for the skill of trained dancers; sure foot-work, swift transformations of rhythm and tempo, gay prancing, vivid appreciation of their own masterly performance. Taos strolled up. Taos watched the virtuosity of Jemez with something less than full approval. Taos, wrapped in a heavy robe of red and blue English broadcloth, was beautiful, but dissatisfied.

" I got some Taos boys here," he said. " We could dance for you, only we don' got a drum."

Jemez was a bit dubious about sharing the applause, but we managed to negotiate a diplomatic loan, and Taos danced too: the Hoop-dance, which is Taos's favorite for white people. A slim bent body slips in and out of a hoop, never losing a step, crossing his feet as he dances, now in and out of the hoop, which is the merest plaything and never in the way.

Then they sang. Laguna, hearing, came up. Laguna was very American, as befitted a young man from the most modern of all the pueblos. He was dressed like a white man, and he had come on business. A sheepman, he had been discussing the price of wool in the Boston market with Jimmy No-Tongue, an Apache wool-grower. Jimmy owns a thousand head of sheep, which represents an income of three thousand dollars a year. But Jimmy and Mrs. No-Tongue are not proud; they dress as the other Jicarillas do, and Mrs. No-Tongue is using her wealthy leisure to make fine baskets. They would not stay, but Laguna liked our canned peaches. When his throat was well refreshed, we persuaded him to sing.

" Sing a Laguna love-song," I asked, " the one I heard at the First American."

That brought the Indian out through the white man.

" That's for white people, not Indians. Indians don't sing about anything as silly as love. When we sing, we sing about things that matter: rain and sun and corn."

So Laguna sang his own songs about the things that are important: rain and sun and corn.

The long afternoon slipped down into evening. The little lake mirrored bright clouds, and then a whole flaming surface of color. The pines were purple and then black. A wind brought the sharp odor of the sage. Women wielded their knives on firewood; every tepee was illumined by a crackling blaze, and cooking-smells tempted people away from the games. Movement never ceased, and all around we heard the beat of tomtoms, the rise and fall of voices, singing.

As night came on, the pines withdrew to become a part of the mountains, and the fires made spots of light under a skyful of stars. Suddenly I knew how alien I was in that Indian world. It is a separate world. The white man sees it, he touches it, some even have the temerity to try to break into it, to change it. But they cannot. For this is a world apart, a brown world of brown people. They come out of their world sometimes to speak to us, for they understand our langauge; but when they withdraw into their world, we cannot follow. They live close to the earth. The mass for a pale god who died on a cross did not reach these people. They do not understand. A religion of an idea, of an ideal, is foreign to them. Their religion is of earth and the things of earth. I thought of all these brown people whom I had seen dancing their prayers, pounding them with their feet into the earth, which is their mother. Her ways are close to them, even when they are hurt. They understand the earth, they dance their prayers into the earth; and they pray for real things for sun and rain and corn. For growth. For life.

# Index

i